Contents

Unit 1 Consonants

Theme: My Favorite Things

Unit 2 Short Vowels

Theme: Amazing Animals

Long Vowels

Theme: Let's Play

UNIT 4

Consonant Blends, Y as a Vowel

Theme: Everybody Eats

Endings, Digraphs, Contractions

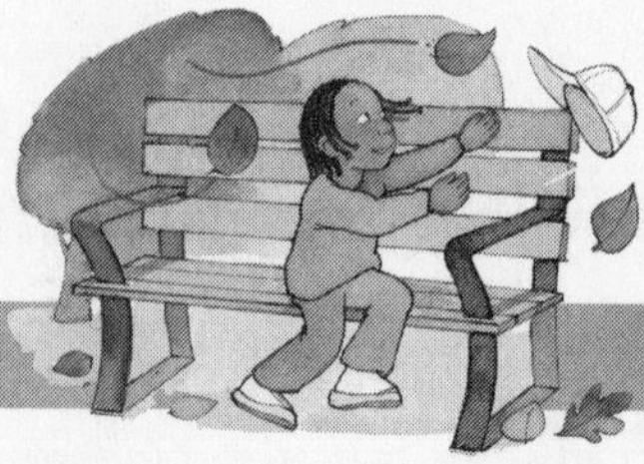

Theme: Whatever the Weather

Tree House

by Shel Silverstein

A tree house, a free house,
A secret you and me house,
A high up in the leafy branches
Cozy as can be house.

A street house, a neat house,
Be sure and wipe your feet house
Is not my kind of house at all—
Let's go live in a tree house.

What is your favorite place to be?

Dear Family,

In this unit about "My Favorite Things," your child will be learning about consonants and the sounds they make. Many of your child's favorite things begin with consonants, such as home, pets, music, fun, and books. As your child becomes familiar with consonant sounds, you might try these activities together.

- Help your child make a Letter Book. Your child can print a letter on each page, then tape or glue on pictures that begin with that letter.
- Read the poem on page 5 aloud. Help your child to identify the consonants at the beginning of words such as house and secret.
- Your child might enjoy reading these books with you. Look for them in your local library.

The Very Hungry Caterpillar
by Eric Carle

A Pocket for Corduroy
by Don Freeman

Sincerely,

____

Estimada familia:

En esta unidad, titulada "Mis cosas favoritas" ("My Favorite Things"), su hijo/a estudiará las consonantes y sus sonidos. Muchas de las cosas favoritas de su hijo/a comienzan con consonantes, como home (juegos), pets (mascotas), music (música), fun (diversión) y books (libros). A medida que su hijo/a se vaya familiarizando con los sonidos de las consonantes, pueden hacer las siguientes actividades juntos.

- Ayuden a su hijo/a a hacer un Libro de letras. Su hijo/a puede escribir una letra en cada página y después unir con cinta adhesiva o pegamento dibujos que comiencen con esa letra.
- Lean en voz alta el poema en la página 5. Ayuden a su hijo/a a identificar las consonantes al principio de palabras como house (casa) y secret (secreto).
- Ustedes y su hijo/a disfrutarán leyendo estos libros juntos. Búsquenlos en su biblioteca local.

The Very Hungry Caterpillar de Eric Carle

A Pocket for Corduroy de Don Freeman

Sinceramente,

____

Name ________________________________

B
b

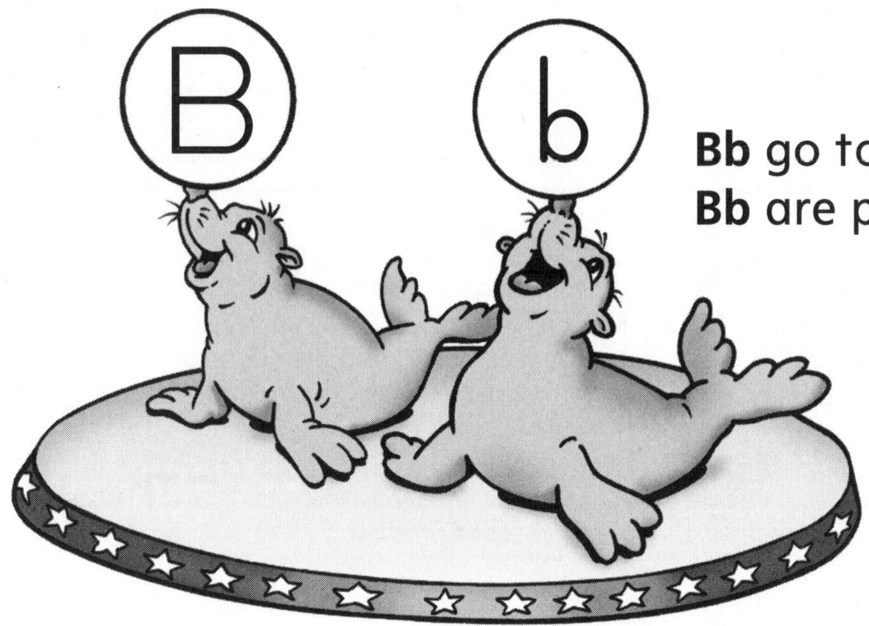

Bb go together.
Bb are partner letters.

▶ Color **each ball that has partner letters on it.**

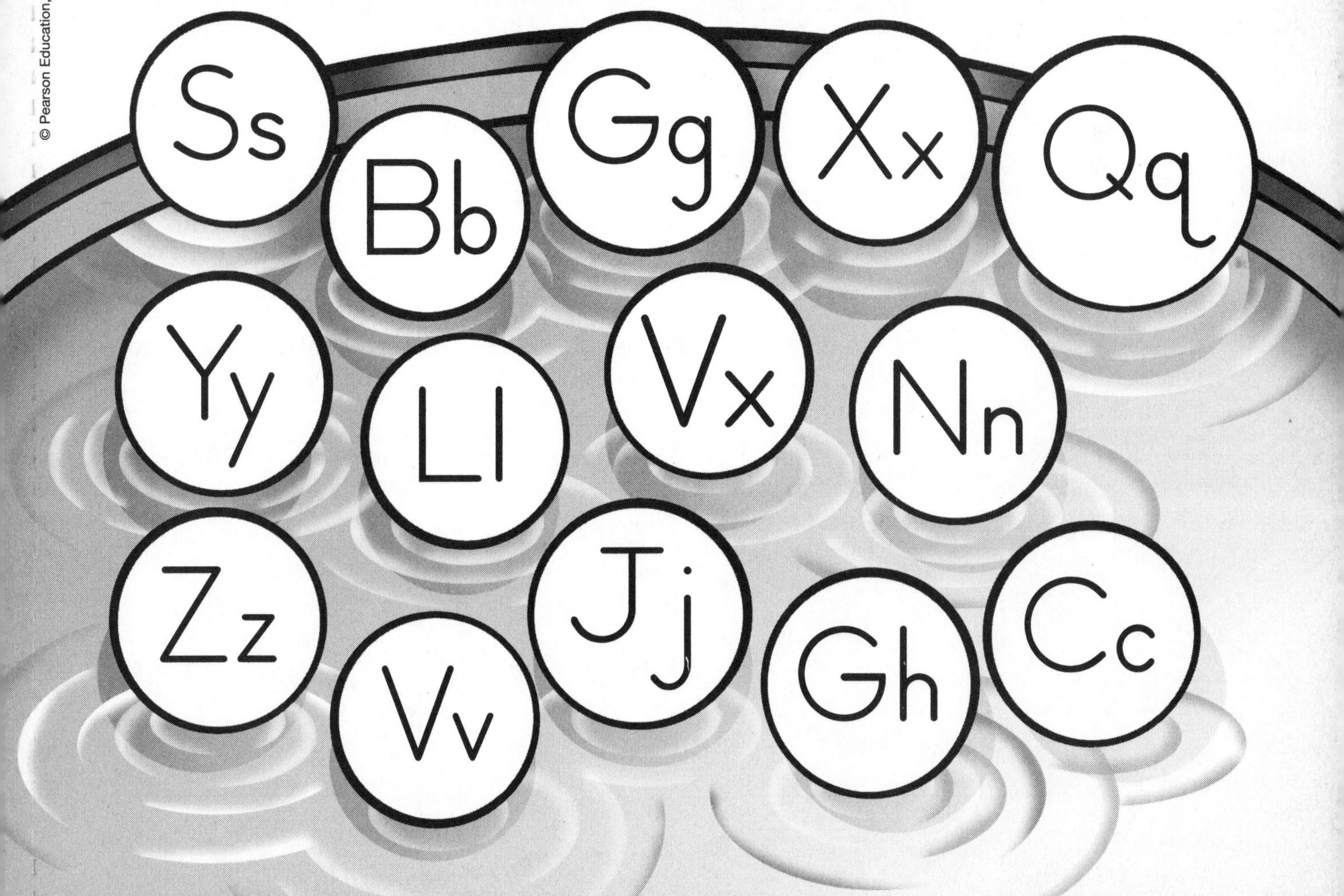
Ss
Bb
Gg
Xx
Qq
Yy
Ll
Vx
Nn
Zz
Vv
Jj
Gh
Cc

Look at the letter above each picture. Circle each word that begins with its partner letter.

1. F
   - fox
   - card
   - fan
   - meat
   - fish

2. d
   - Dave
   - Sam
   - Don
   - Dina
   - Mary

3. H
   - home
   - boat
   - hill
   - king
   - hook

4. k
   - Ken
   - Kyle
   - Tara
   - Kurt
   - Matt

5. M
   - nose
   - monkey
   - hand
   - milk
   - mask

6. t
   - Tom
   - Tyler
   - Tina
   - Mia
   - Jake

7. P
   - dish
   - pig
   - peel
   - top
   - pen

8. r
   - Rosa
   - Ryan
   - Bobby
   - Katie
   - Ross

9. w
   - Wendy
   - Helen
   - Will
   - Wyatt
   - Sarah

Ask your child to write his or her name, then write partner letters for each consonant.

Name ________________________________

Suzy sat on the sand.
Suzy sat by the sea.
Suzy sat in the sun.
Suzy sat with me.

Sand begins with the sound of s. Circle each picture whose name begins with the sound of s.

1.

2. 

3. 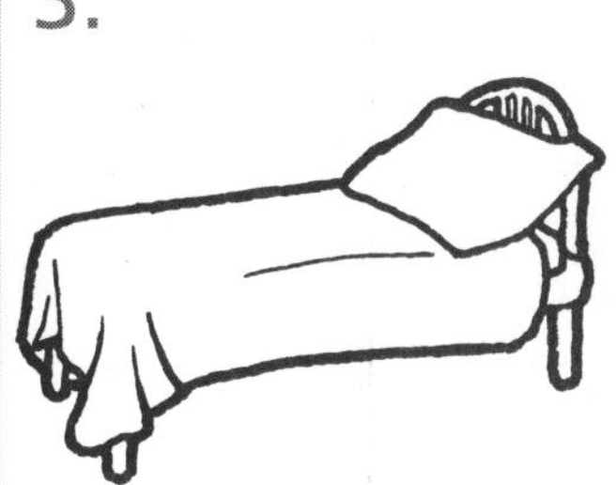

4. 

5. 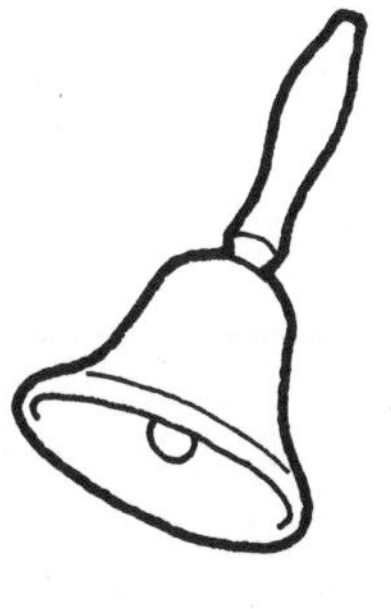

6. 

7. 

8. 

9. 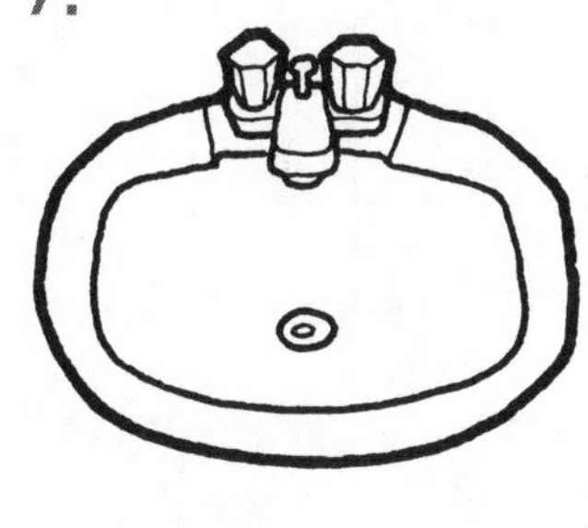

10. 

11. 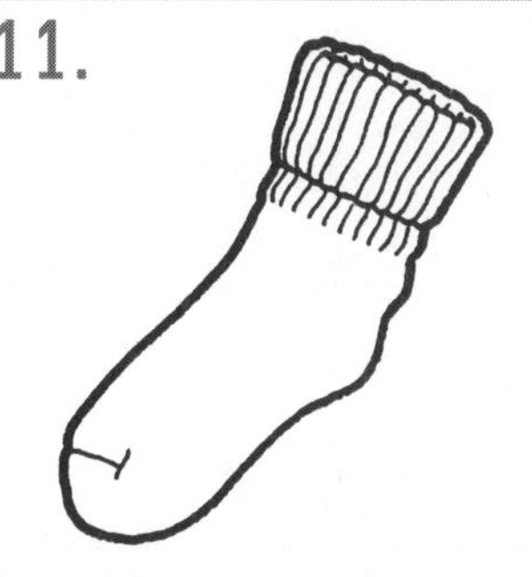

12. 

Say the name of each picture. If it begins with the sound of s, print s on the line. Then trace the whole word.

1. ___aw	2. ___ent	3. ___un
4. ___ix	5. ___oll	6. ___ock
7. ___uit	8. ___at	9. ___ail
10. ___orse	11. ___ink	12. ___eat

Say, "Sister Sue sells ____." Ask your child to finish the sentence with words that begin with *s*.

Name ______________________________

Ten toy tigers
Sat down for tea.
Ten tails tipped the table—
Oh, dear me!

Tea begins with the sound of t. Circle each picture whose name begins with the sound of t.

1.	2.	3.	4.
5.	6.	7.	8.
9.	10.	11.	12.

Say the name of each picture. If it begins with the sound of t, print t on the line. Then trace the whole word.

1. op
2. ire
3. aw
4. ent
5. ape
6. ed
7. en
8. ack
9. ub
10. ose
11. oys
12. un

Ask your child to name three objects in your home that begin with the sound of *t*.

Name ______________________________

Let's bounce the ball high,
Let's bounce the ball low.
Let's bounce the ball fast,
Let's bounce the ball slow.

Ball begins with the sound of b. Circle each picture whose name begins with the sound of b.

1.	2.	3.	4.
5.	6.	7.	8.
9.	10.	11.	12.

Say the name of each picture. If it begins with the sound of b, print b on the line. Then trace the whole word.

1. ag
2. oat
3. all
4. elt
5. ock
6. ox
7. at
8. un
9. us
10. ed
11. oys
12. ug

Say "Buddy bought a ___." Ask your child to add a word that begins with the sound of *b*.

Name ______________________________

Say the name of each picture. If the name **begins** with the sound of the letter in the box, **print** it on the first line. If it **ends** with that sound, **print** it on the second line.

1. b
2. t
3. s
4. b
5. t
6. b
7. s
8. b
9. b
10. s
11. t
12. s

Say each picture name. Draw a line through the pictures in a row that begin with the same letter sound. Write the letter that wins in each game.

1.

2.

6 10

3.

7

Ask your child to name each picture, then say the beginning consonant for the picture name.

Name ______________________________

My hamster has been running
On his wheel since half past five.
He's gone a hundred miles by now,
So when will he arrive?

Hamster begins with the sound of h. Say the name of each picture. Circle the beginning letter of the picture name. Then circle each picture whose name begins with the sound of h.

1.	2.	3.
S	T	B
T	B	H
B	H	S
H 	S	T

4.	5.	6.
S	B	T
H	T	H
T	H	S
B	S	B

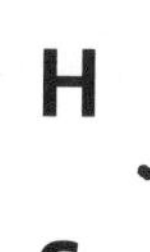

Say the name of each picture. If it begins with the sound of h, print h on the line. Then trace the whole word.

1. ___at

2. ___an

3. ___eart

4. ___ot

5. ___am

6. ___op

7. ___and

8. ___ill

9. ___ose

10. ___ey

11. ___eel

12. ___en

Point to the picture of the hen. Ask your child to think of other animals whose names begin with *h*.

Name ________________________________

Mom gave me a muffin for lunch.
Mom gave me a muffin to munch.
The muffin I munched was yummy.
The muffin is in my tummy.

Mom begins with the sound of m. Circle each picture whose name begins with the sound of m.

1.	2.	3.	4.
5.	6.	7.	8.
9.	10.	11.	12.

Say the name of each picture. If it begins with the sound of m, print m on the line. Then trace the whole word.

1. ___oon	2. ___op	3. ___ask
4. ___all	5. ___ix	6. ___an
7. ___ouse	8. ___ap	9. ___ilk
10. ___op	11. ___eart	12. ___eat

Point to a picture. Have your child say its name and then think of a word that begins with the same sound.

Name ______________________________

Kite begins with the sound of k. Say the name of each picture. Circle the beginning letter of the picture name. Then circle each picture whose name begins with the sound of k.

1.
H
M
K
T

2.
M
K
T
H

3.
K
T
H
M

4.
T
K
M
H

5.
H
M
K
T

6.
T
H
M
K

Say the name of each picture. If it begins with the sound of k, print k on the line. Then trace the whole word.

1. ey
2. ike
3. ing
4. ook
5. ite
6. ork
7. ilk
8. itten
9. itchen
10. etchup

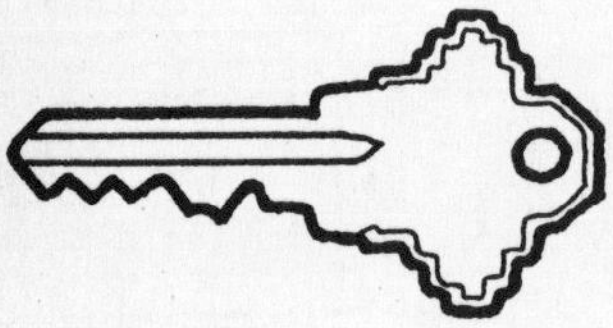

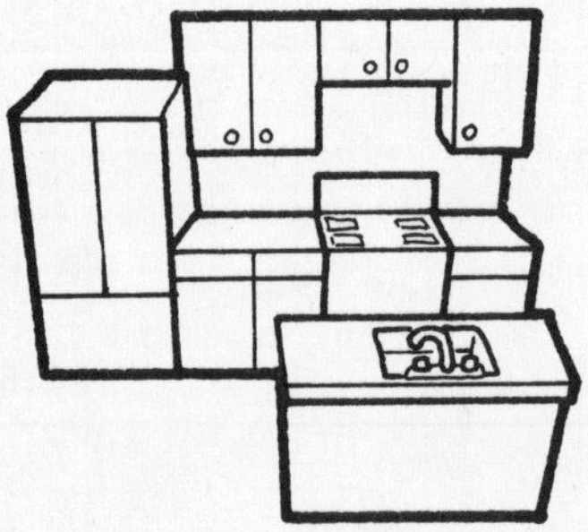

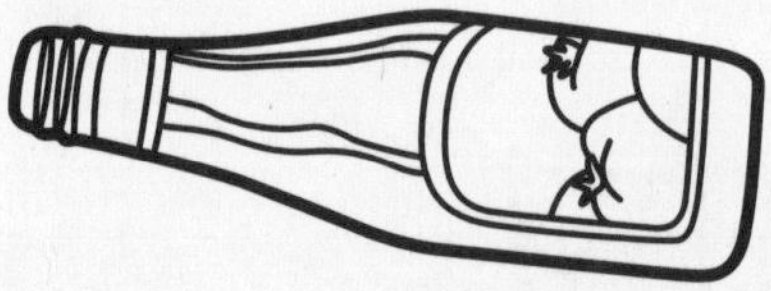

HOME Taking turns with your child, think of more words that begin with the sound of *k*, such as *keep* and *kind*.

Name ______________________________

Say the name of each picture. Find the beginning letter of each picture name. Circle that letter.

1. 	2. 	3. 
H M K	**M K H**	**K H M**
4. 	5. 	6. 
H M K	**K M H**	**M H K**
7. 	8. 	9. 
H K M	**K M H**	**M H K**
10. 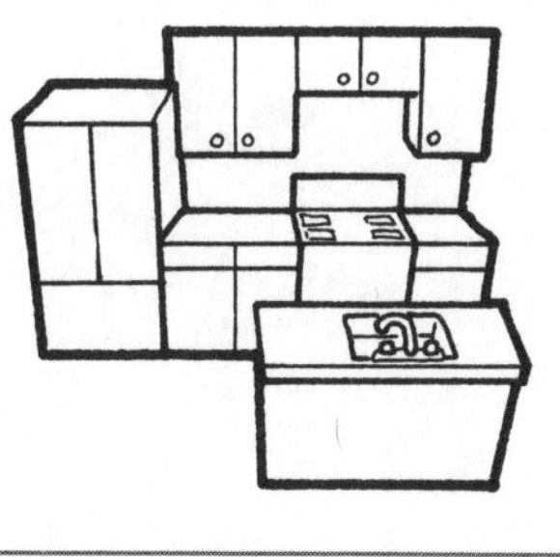	11. 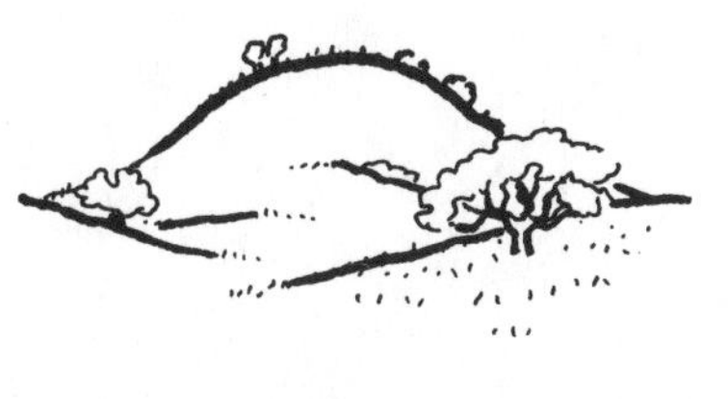	12. 
H K M	**K M H**	**M H K**

Say the name of each picture. If the name **begins** with the sound of the letter in the box, **print** it on the first line. If it **ends** with that sound, **print** it on the second line.

1. k

   k

2. h

3. m

4. m

5. k

6. m

7. k

8. h

9. h

10. k

11. m

12. k

Ask your child to name two pictures that begin with the same sound and two that end with the same sound.

Name ________________________________

Joy can pick a prize.
It will be hers to keep.
Will she take the jacks or the jet,
The jump rope or the jeep?

Jeep begins with the sound of j. Circle each picture whose name begins with the sound of j.

1.	2.	3.

4.	**5.**	**6.**

7.	**8.**	**9.**

Say the name of each picture. If it begins with the sound of j, print j on the line. Then trace the whole word.

1. ___eep
2. ___eaf
3. ___ug
4. ___ent
5. ___eel
6. ___ump
7. ___et
8. ___ouse
9. ___un
10. ___ug
11. ___ack
12. ___ar

Help your child think of sentences using words that begin with *j*, such as *Joe juggled the jacks.*

Name ______________________________

Five furry foxes
Fanning in the heat.
They all run away
On furry fox feet.

Five begins with the sound of f. Circle each picture whose name begins with the sound of f.

1. 	2. 	3. 	4. 
5. 	6. 	7. 	8. 
9. 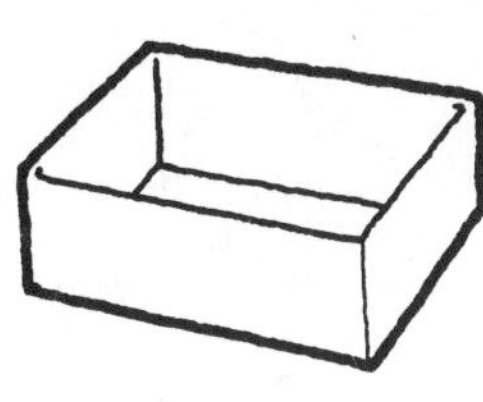	10. 	11. 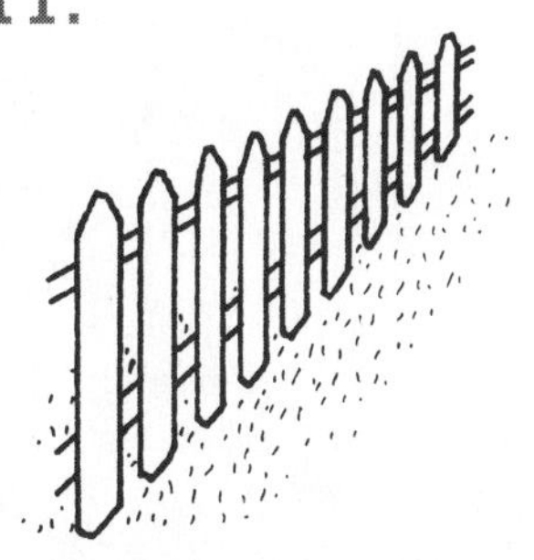	12. 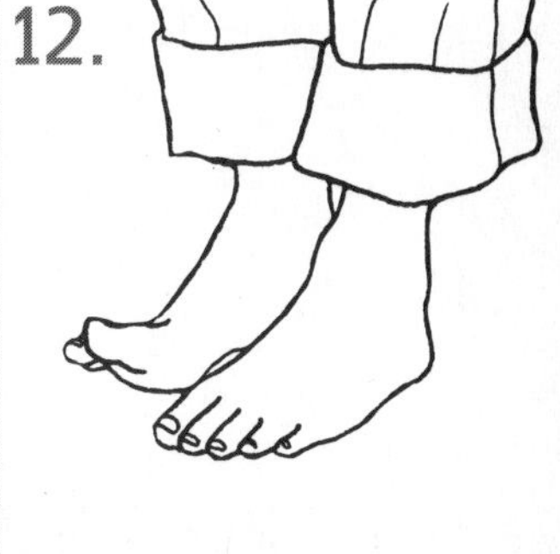

Say the name of each picture. If it begins with the sound of f, print f on the line. Then trace the whole word.

1. ish
2. eaf
3. our
4. eet
5. ive
6. an
7. ail
8. ork
9. ence
10. amp
11. ox
12. ire

Make up riddles for your child to answer with words from the page, such as *What rhymes with box?* (*fox*)

Name ______________________________

Get the gifts.
Do not be late.
Run to the garden,
And open the gate.

Garden begins with the sound of g. Circle each picture whose name begins with the sound of g.

1. 	2. 	3. 
4. 	5. 	6. 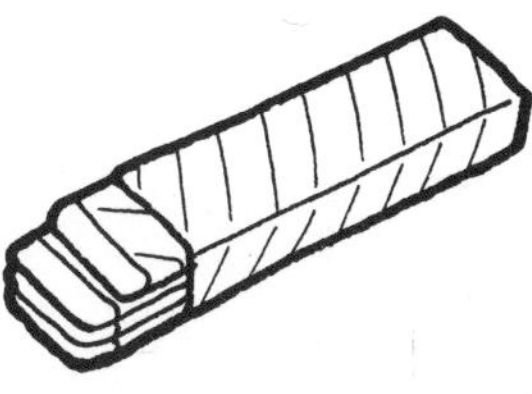
7. 	8. 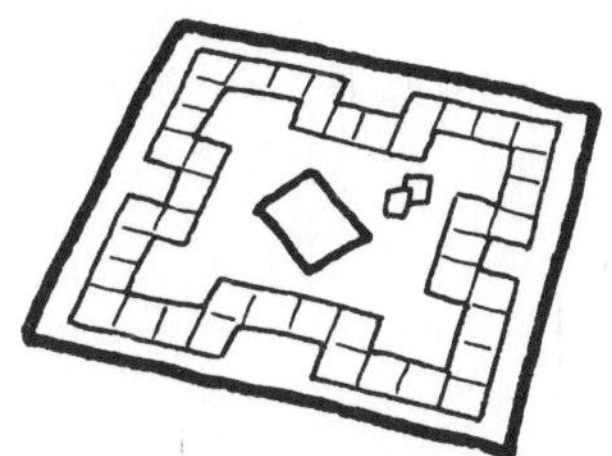	9. 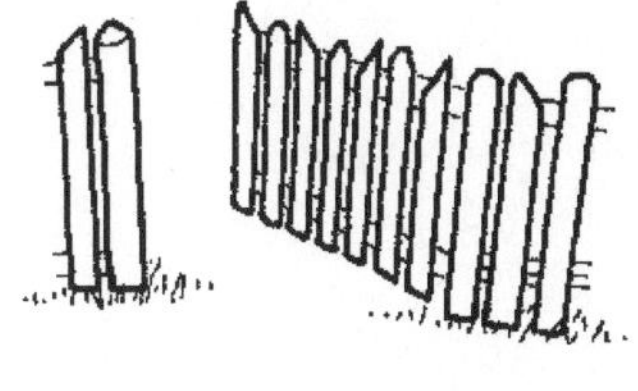

Say the name of each picture. If it begins with the sound of g, print g on the line. Then trace the whole word.

1. ___um
2. ___irl
3. ___ive
4. ___old
5. ___ame
6. ___og
7. ___ate
8. ___ift
9. ___oat
10. ___ag
11. ___ig
12. ___oose

Invite your child to think of more words that begin with g such as *go, get, good, give.*

Name ______________________________

Say the name of each picture. If the name **begins** with the sound of the letter in the box, **print** it on the first line. If it **ends** with that sound, **print** it on the second line.

1. f — f ___
2. j
3. g
4. f
5. g
6. f
7. f
8. j
9. g
10. j
11. g
12. f

Say the name of each toy. Print a letter to finish the word on each sign. Then trace the word.

1.  et

2.  ish

3.  oat

4.  bu

5.  do

6.  ame

7.  eep

8.  arm

HOME

Ask your child to finish sentences using words from the page, such as *Cows and ducks live on a ____. (farm)*

Name ______________________________

Look, look, Lizzy!
Quick, come and see.
A lovely little ladybug
Just landed on me.

Ladybug begins with the sound of l. Circle each picture whose name begins with the sound of l.

1. 	2. 	3. 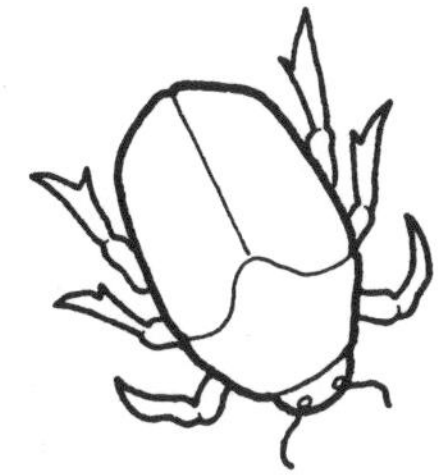	4. 
5. 	6. 	7. 	8. 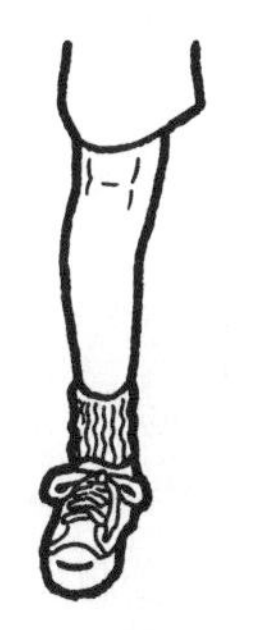
9. 	10. 	11. 	12. 

Say the name of each picture. If it begins with the sound of l, print l on the line. Then trace the whole word.

1. ___og
2. ___ell
3. ___ock
4. ___ill
5. ___ips
6. ___eaf
7. ___amp
8. ___oll
9. ___ake
10. ___all
11. ___id
12. ___etter

Ask your child to use two of the *l* words in a sentence, such as *I saw a log in the lake.*

Name ___________________________

Denny does the dishes.
Dori does them, too.
Dad feeds the dog,
And soon they are through.

Dishes begins with the sound of d. Circle each picture whose name begins with the sound of d.

1. 	2. 	3. 	4. 
5. 	6. 	7. 	8. 
9. 	10. 	11. 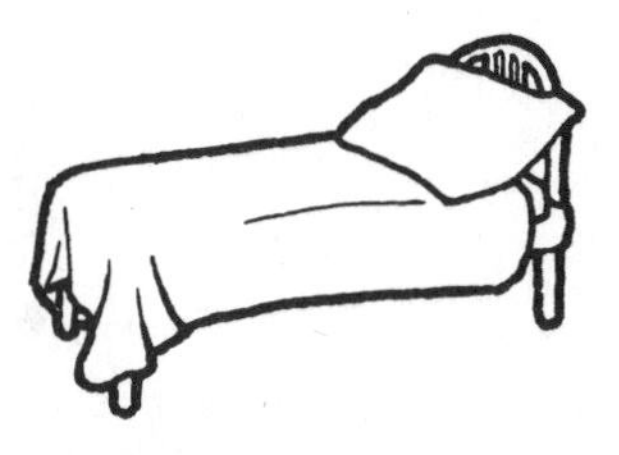	12. 

Say the name of each picture. If it begins with the sound of d, print d on the line. Then trace the whole word.

1. __oll	2. __oot	3. __oor
4. __id	5. __ey	6. __uck
7. __ive	8. __eer	9. __og
10. __esk	11. __ishes	12. __arn

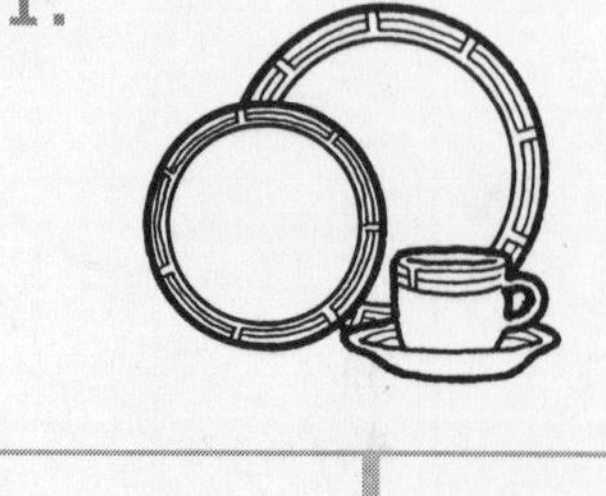

Ask your child to name three objects in your home that begin with the *d* sound.

Name ______________________________

No, no, Nellie.
No, no, Ned.
Do not jump up
On my nice neat bed.

No begins with the sound of n. Circle each picture whose name begins with the sound of n.

1.	2.	3.	4.
5.	6.	7.	8.
9.	10.	11.	12.

Say the name of each picture. If it begins with the sound of **n**, **print n** on the line. Then **trace** the whole word.

1. est
2. en
3. ose
4. ut
5. us
6. ine
7. aby
8. an
9. urse
10. op
11. et
12. ail

With your child, take turns naming as many words that begin with *n* as you can.

Name ______________________

Say the name of each picture. If the name **begins** with the sound of the letter in the box, **print** it on the first line. If it **ends** with that sound, **print** it on the second line.

1. n — n
2. l
3. d
4. n
5. d
6. l
7. n
8. d
9. n
10. l
11. d
12. l

Say the names of the pictures in the boxes. Look for these pictures in the big picture. Circle each one. Write the letter of each beginning sound.

1.  d

2.

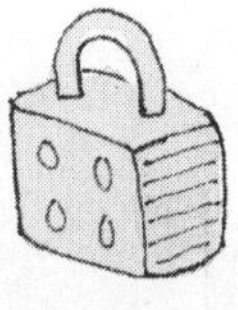

3.

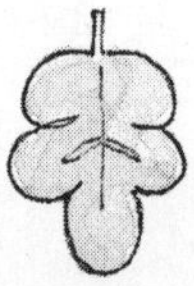

4.

5.

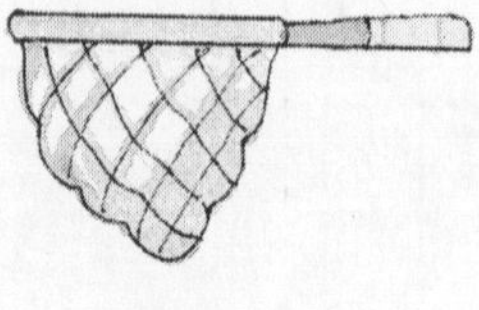

6.

Make up riddles for your child to solve using picture names, such as *I have four legs and I bark.* (dog)

Name ______________________________

We watch from the window
As winter winds blow.
We watch from the window,
And wish it would snow.

Window begins with the sound of w. Circle each picture whose name begins with the sound of w.

1.	2.	3.

4.	5.	6.

7.	8.	9.
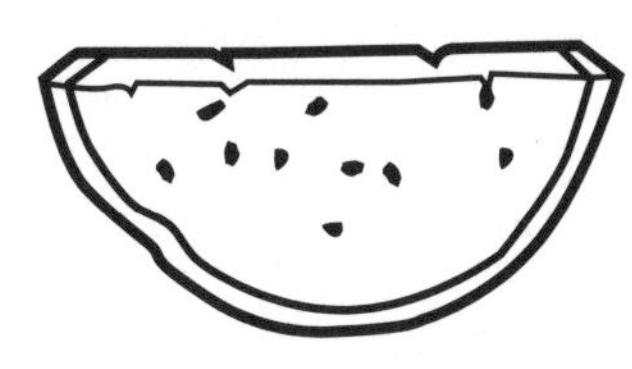		

Say the name of each picture. If it begins with the sound of w, print w on the line. Then trace the whole word.

1. ___agon
2. ___eel
3. ___ing
4. ___atch
5. ___ave
6. ___og
7. ___ey
8. ___allet
9. ___eb

Ask your child to choose two pictures whose names begin with the sound of *w* and use the words in a sentence.

Name ______________________________

Carla has a cape.
She's carrying a cane.
Cory has her dad's coat
To play a dress-up game.

Cape begins with the sound of c. Circle each picture whose name begins with the sound of c.

1.

2.

3.

4.

5.

6.

7.

8.

9.

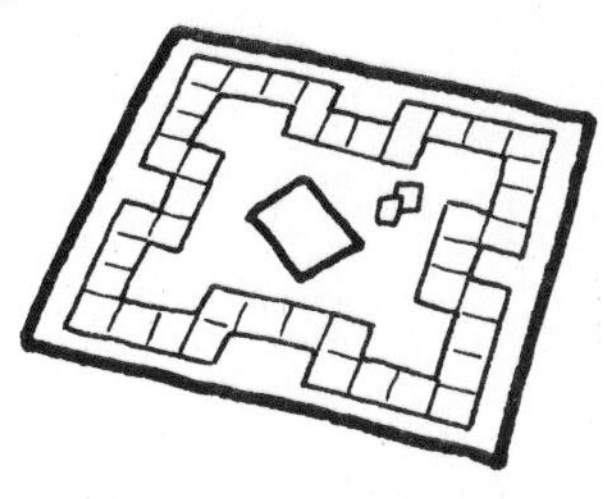

Say the name of each picture. If it begins with the sound of c, print c on the line. Then trace the whole word.

1. ___an

2. ___ap

3. 
___atch

4. 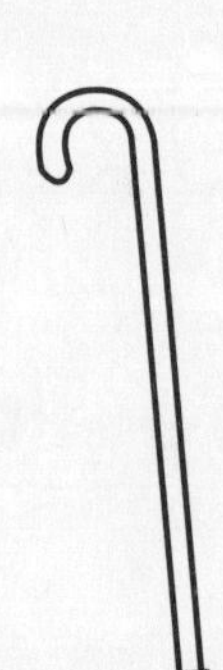
___ane

5. 
___og

6. 
___ake

7. 
___ow

8. ___ar

9. ___up

10. 
___age

11. 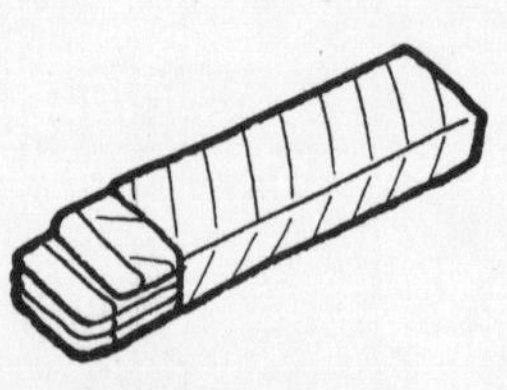
___um

12. 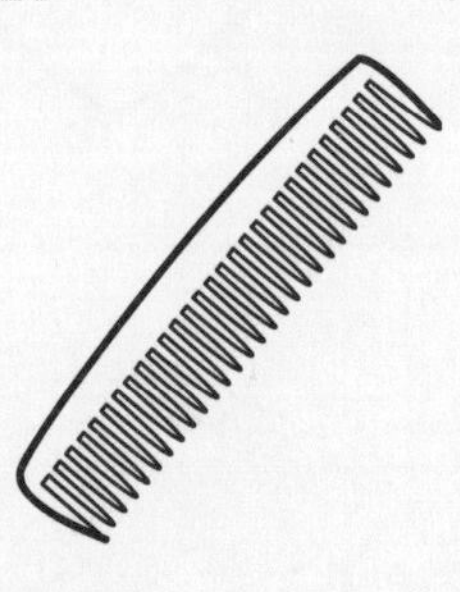
___omb

Ask your child to pick three words from the page that begin with c, then draw a picture showing them.

Name ______________________________

The roses are red.
The ribbon is, too.
I ran over to bring
These red roses to you.

▶ Roses begins with the sound of r. Circle each picture whose name begins with the sound of r.

1. 	2. 	3. 
4. 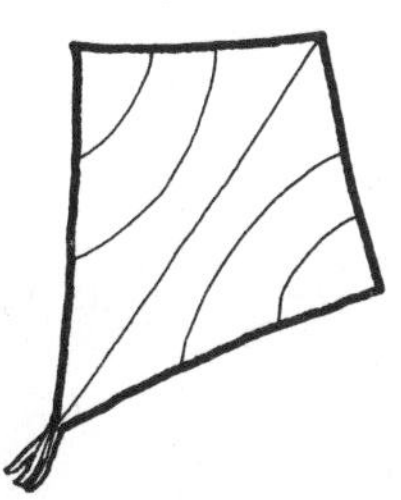	5. 	6. 
7. 	8. 	9. 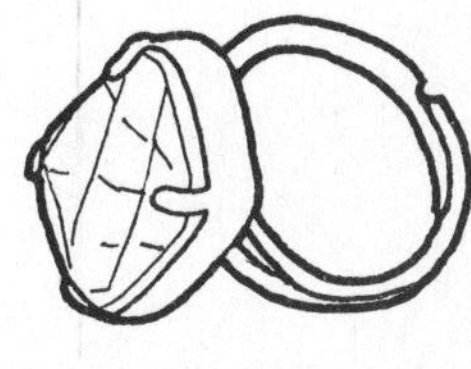

Say the name of each picture. If it begins with the sound of r, print r on the line. Then trace the whole word.

1. ing
2. ake
3. ip
4. at
5. at
6. en
7. adio
8. ips
9. ain
10. ug
11. ake
12. eb

Point to the ring picture and ask your child, *What rhymes with king?* Repeat with rhymes for *rip*, *rat*, and *rug*.

Name ______________________________

Penny passed the peach pie,
Peach pie, peach pie.
Penny passed the peach pie,
Till not a piece was left.

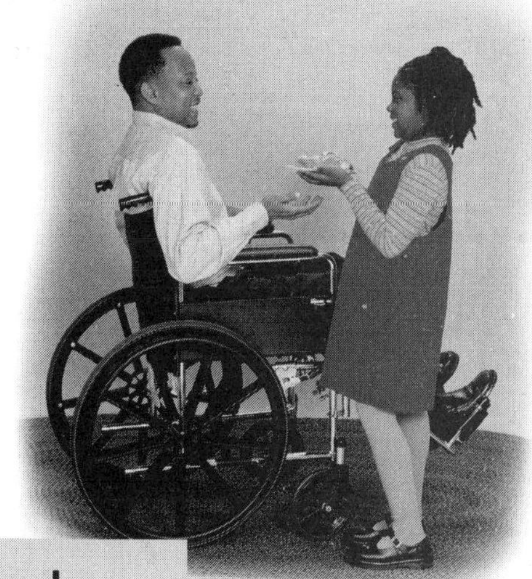

Peach begins with the sound of p. Circle each picture whose name begins with the sound of p.

1.

2.

3.

4.

5.

6.
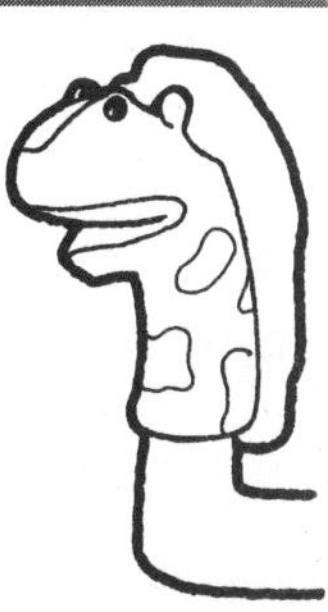

7.

8.
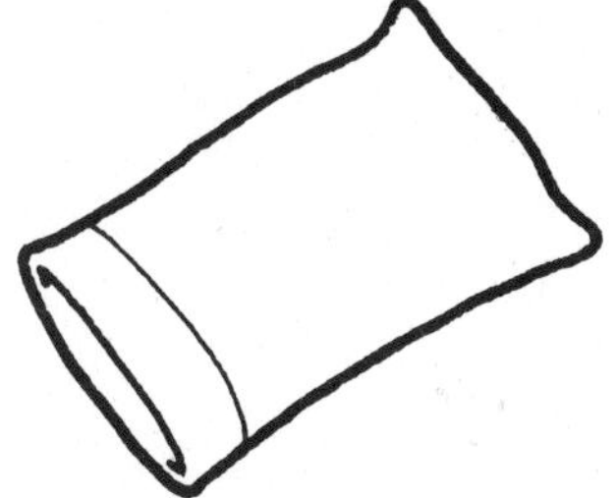

9.
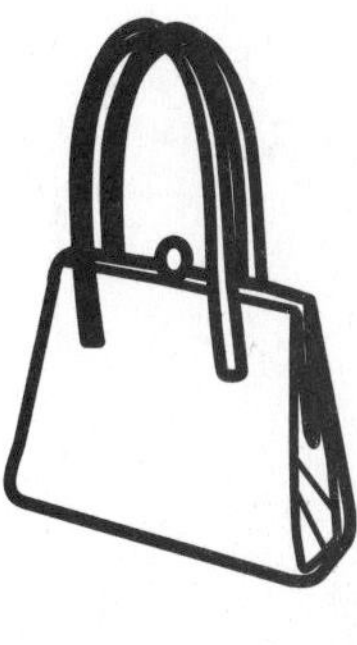

Say the name of each picture. If it begins with the sound of p, print p on the line. Then trace the whole word.

1.	2.	3.	4.
ot	up	ig	ine
5.	**6.**	**7.**	**8.**
oap	en	urse	in
9.	**10.**	**11.**	**12.**
eas	ap	at	ie

With your child, make up a silly sentence using three words from the page that begin with *p*.

Name ________________________________

Quinn's toy duck said,
"Quack, quack, quack!"
"Quiet!" said Quincy.
But the duck quacked back!

Quack begins with the sound of **qu**. Say the name of each picture. If it begins with the sound of **qu**, print **qu** on the line.

1. qu

2. ______

3. ______

4. ______

5. ______

6. ______

7. ______

8. ______

Viv has a valentine.
Val has one, too.
Vic makes a valentine
To give to you.

▶ **Valentine begins with the sound of v. Say the name of each picture. If it begins with the sound of v, print Vv on the line.**

1. Vv	2.	3.	4.
5.	6.	7.	8.
9.	10.	11.	12.

With your child, make up a story using some of the words from the page that begin with *v*.

Name ______________________________

Say the name of each picture. Print the letter for its beginning sound on the first line. Then print the letter for its ending sound on the second line.

1. r n
2.
3.
4.
5.
6.
7.
8.
9.
10.
11.
12.

Say each picture name. Write the word that names each picture. What is the secret message?

1. h o ___
2. ___ a ___
3. ___ a n
4. ___ e b
5. f i ___ e
6. ___ u e e n
7. n e ___

Ask your child what the secret message is.

Name ______________________________

Will Foxie Fox and Oxie Ox
Fit inside our big toy box?
Mix things up and push and pull.
Fox and Ox make the toy box full!

Box ends with the sound of x. Say the name of each picture. If it ends with the sound of x, print Xx on the line.

1. 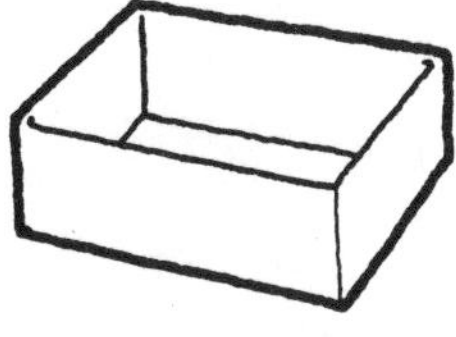

Xx

2. 

3. 

4. 

5. 

6. 

7. 

8. 

9. 

Yesterday I went shopping
With my Grandma Lin.
I got a yellow yo-yo.
You can watch it spin.

Yo-yo begins with the sound of y. Say the name of each picture. If it begins with the sound of y, print Yy on the line.

1. Yy
2.
3.
4.
5.
6.

Say, "In my yard, I have a ____." Ask your child to finish the sentence with words that begin with *y*.

Name ________________________________

Zelda and Zena
Went to the zoo.
There they saw zebras
And lions, too.

Zoo begins with the sound of **z**. Say the name of each picture. If it begins with the sound of **z**, print **Zz** on the line.

1.

Zz

2.

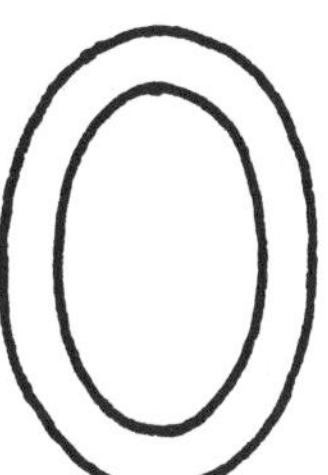

3.

4.

5.

6.

Say the name of each picture. If the name begins with the sound of the letter in the box, print it on the first line. If it ends with that sound, print it on the second line.

1. y

y

2. x

3. z

4. y

5. x

6. y

7. z

8. z

9. x

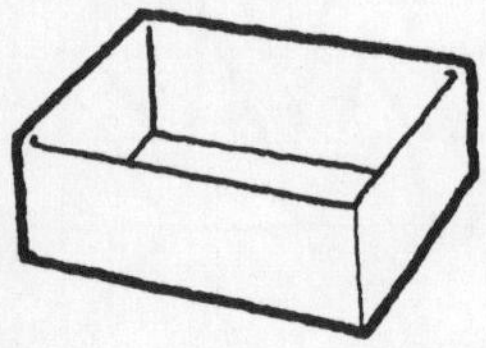

10. z

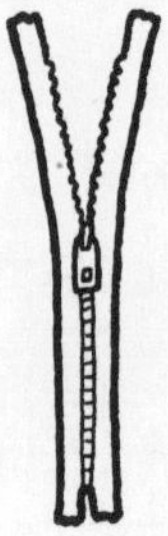

11. x

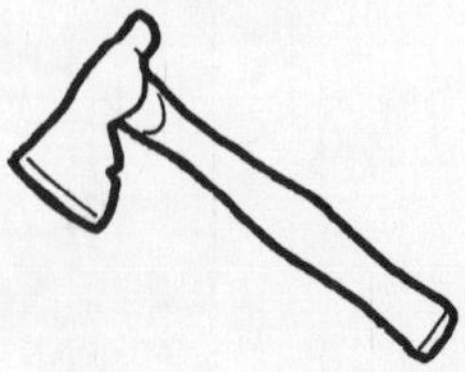

12. y

Help your child to think of more words that begin or end with *x*, *y*, or *z*, such as *x-ray*, *play*, and *zip*.

Name ____________________

Say the name of each picture. Print the letter for its middle sound on the line.

1. t

2.

3.

4.

5.

6.

7.

8.

9.

10. 

11. 

12. 

Say the name of each picture. Print the letter for its middle sound on the line. Trace the whole word.

1. ba__y
2. po__y
3. ra__io
4. wa__on
5. ru__er
6. le__on
7. se__en
8. ro__ot
9. ti__er

Say each middle sound and ask your child to tell you which picture name or names have that sound.

Name ____________________________

Say the name of each picture. **Print** the letter for its beginning sound. Then **print** the letter for its ending sound. The words in the box may help you.

bed	cat	fox	ham	jar	beak
pig	queen	tub	van	web	yard

1.  a

2.  i

3.  o

4. 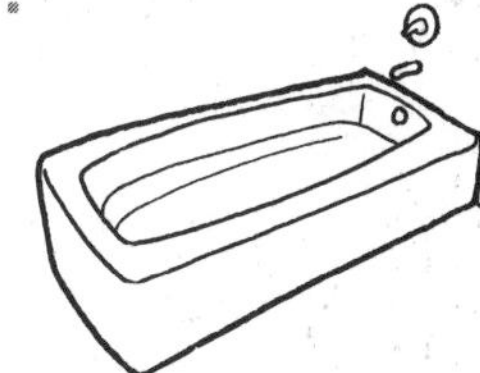 u

5. 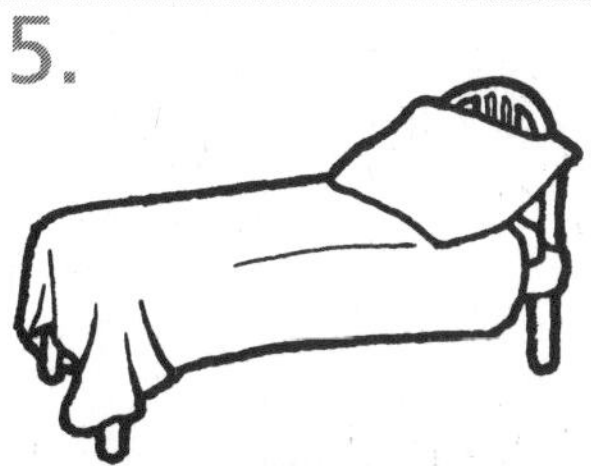 e

6.  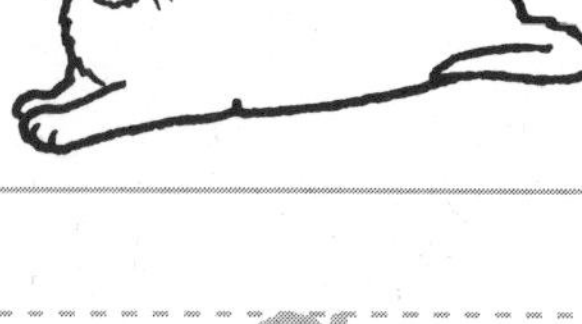 a

7.   a

8.   e

9. 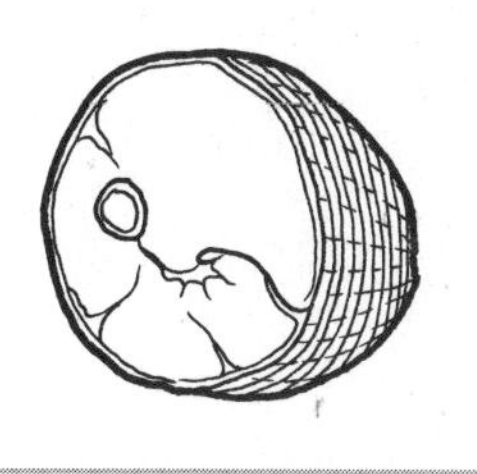 a

10.  ea

11.   ar

12.  uee

Draw a picture of yourself with your friends. **Write** a sentence about the picture.

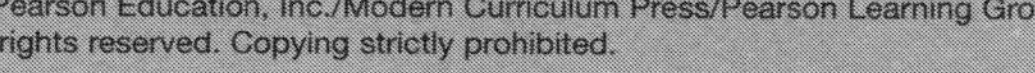

A dog can camp in a tent, too!

4

FOLD

Name ____________________

Camping Fun

It is fun to camp in a tent.

1

A tent can go in the woods
or in a yard.

2

FOLD

A tent can be big or little.

3

Name ________________________________

Say the name of each picture. **Print** the letter for the missing sound to finish each word. **Trace** the whole word.

1. _arn	2. bu_	3. _ase
4. ha_	5. _ire	6. _eart
7. _ug	8. _ebra	9. pe_
10. _ueen	11. _agon	12. tu_

Say the name of each picture. Fill in the bubble next to the letter or letters that stand for the beginning sound.

1.	2.	3.
○ y ○ d ○ m	○ k ○ r ○ w	○ l ○ p ○ t

4.	5.	6.
○ c ○ n ○ z	○ f ○ t ○ qu	○ v ○ w ○ k

Say the name of each picture. Fill in the bubble next to the letter that stands for the ending sound.

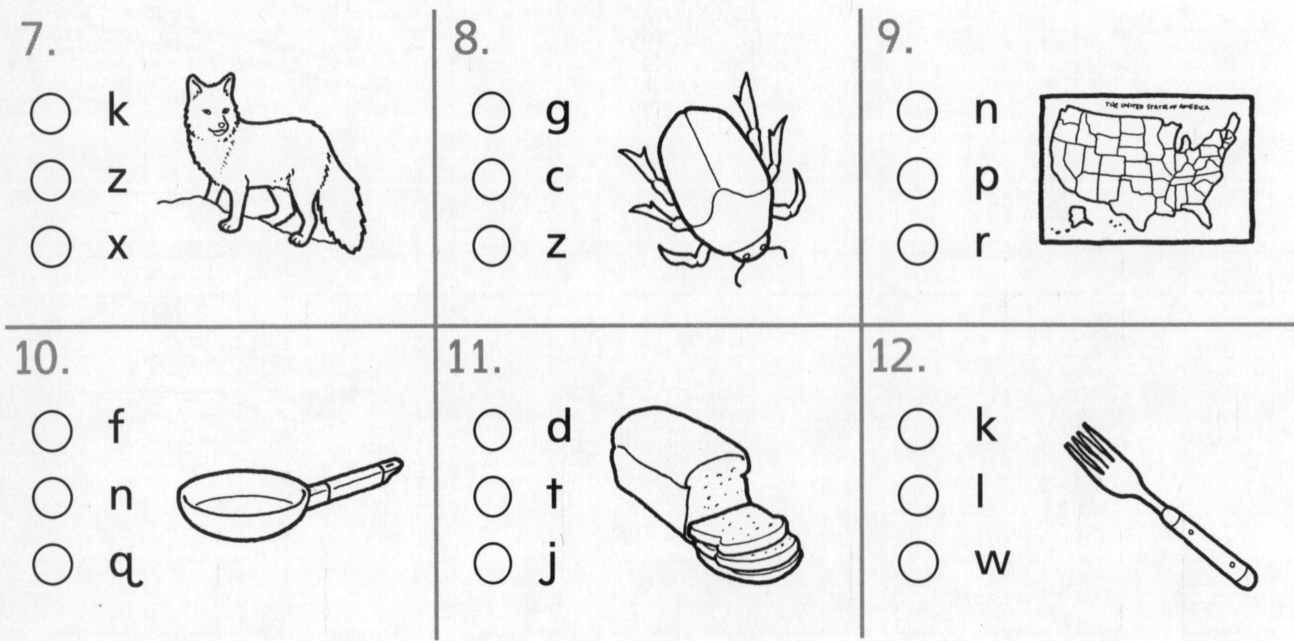

7.	8.	9.
○ k ○ z ○ x	○ g ○ c ○ z	○ n ○ p ○ r

10.	11.	12.
○ f ○ n ○ q	○ d ○ t ○ j	○ k ○ l ○ w

Read Aloud

Frogs Call

Little frogs call.
They sing a song.
Soon the rain will fall.
Tree frogs like wet places.
They hop and jump.
Some tree frogs are green.
Some are red.
Others are blue or yellow.
You can not touch some
tree frogs.
The wet skin can make you sick!

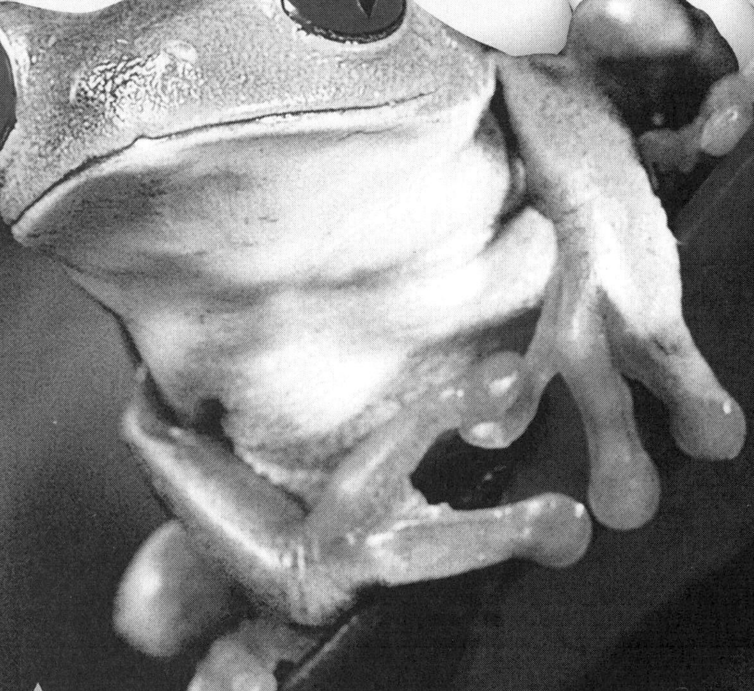

TALK About It What can tree frogs do?

Dear Family,

In this unit about "Amazing Animals," your child will learn about the vowels **a, e, i, o,** and **u** and the sounds they make. Many animal names contain short vowels such as cat, hen, pig, fox, and duck. As your child becomes familiar with short vowel sounds, you might try these activities together.

- Make a collage of animals whose names have the same short vowel sound. With your child, draw pictures or cut pictures from magazines and glue them on paper, one sheet for each vowel.

- Your child might enjoy reading these books with you. Look for them in your local library.

Pet of a Pet by Marsha Hayles

How Chipmunk Got His Stripes by Joseph Bruchac

Sincerely,

___

Estimada familia:

En esta unidad, que trata de "Animales asombrosos," su hijo/a aprenderá las vocales **a, e, i, o, u** y los sonidos que éstas hacen. Los nombres de muchos animales contienen vocales con sonidos breves, como por ejemplo, cat (gato), hen (gallina), pig (cerdo), fox (zorro), y duck (pato). A medida que su hijo/a se vaya familiarizando con las vocales de sonidos breves, podrían hacer las siguientes actividades juntos.

- Hagan un collage de fotos o dibujos de animales cuyos nombres contienen vocales con sonidos breves. Junto con su hijo/a dibujen o recorten fotos de revistas y péguenlos en hojas de papel—una hoja por vocal.

- Quizás a su hijo/a le gustaría leer con ustedes los siguientes libros que podrían buscar en su biblioteca local.

Pet of a Pet de Marsha Hayles

How Chipmunk Got His Stripes de Joseph Bruchac

Sinceramente,

___

Name ______________________________

An ant can dance.
An ant can sing.
An ant can do most anything.

Can you dance?
Can you sing?
Can you do most anything?

Ant has the short sound of **a.** Circle each picture whose name has the short sound of **a.**

1.	2.	3.	4.
	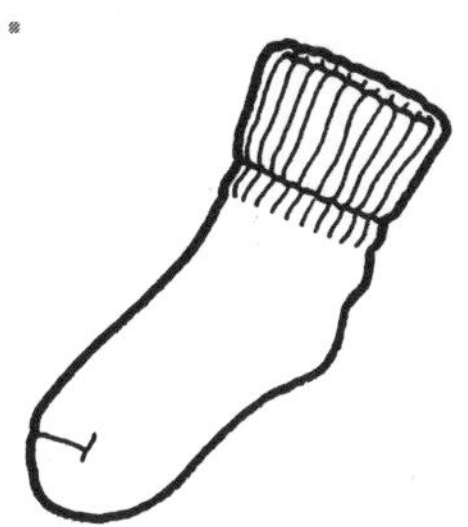	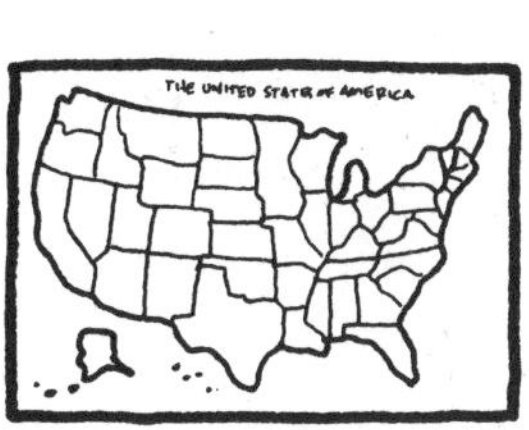	
5.	6.	7.	8.
			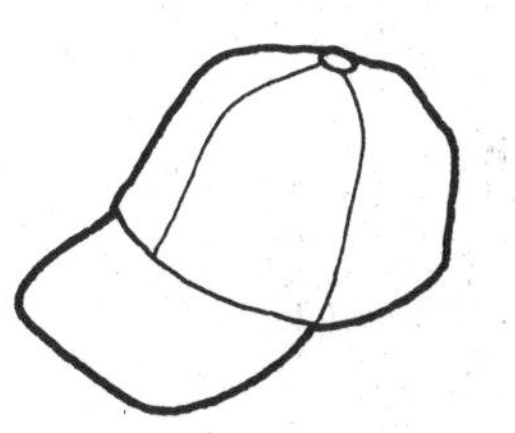
9.	10.	11.	12.
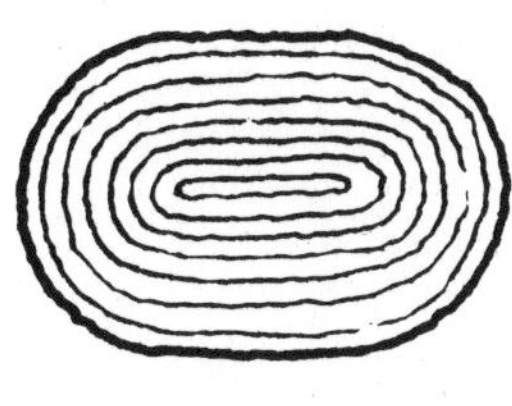			

Say the names of the pictures in each row.
Color the pictures whose names rhyme.

1.

  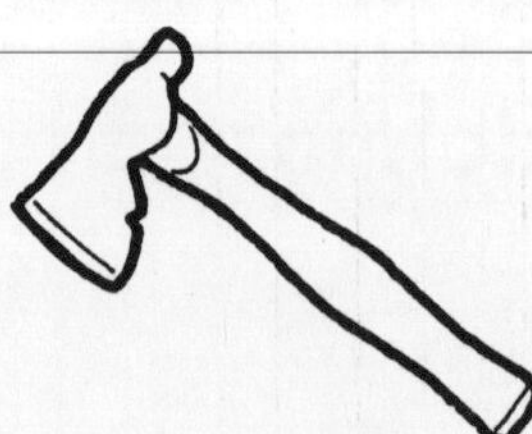 

2.

3.

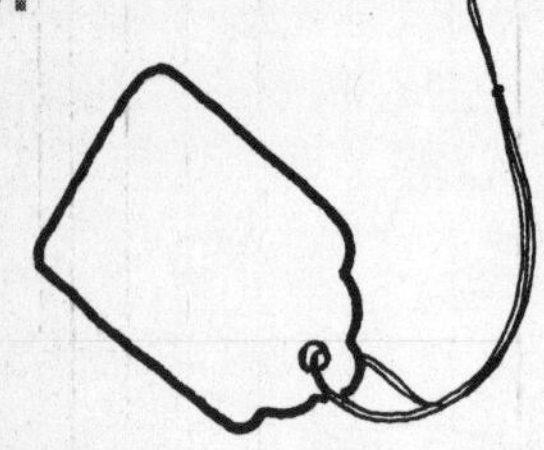  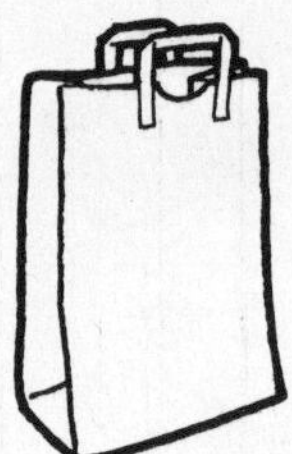 

4.

  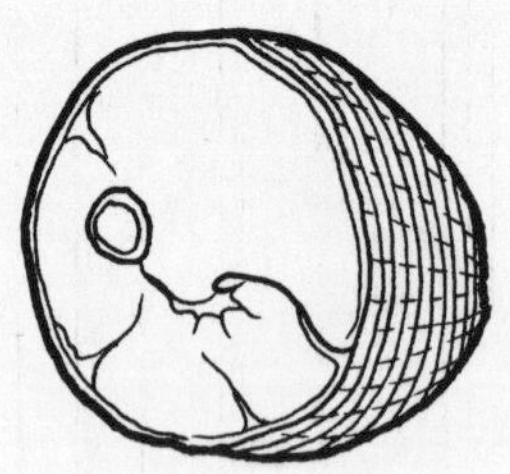 

5.

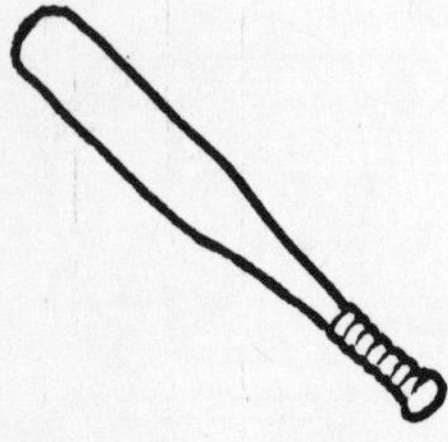 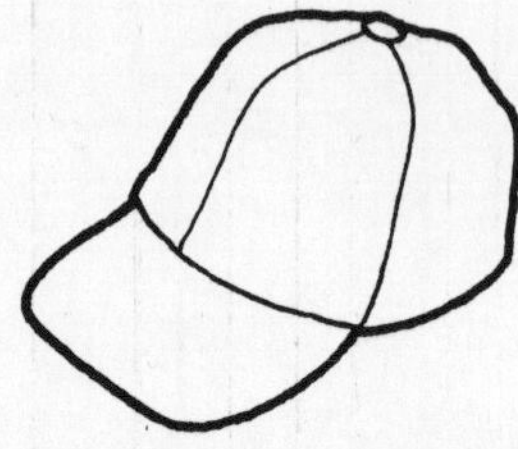 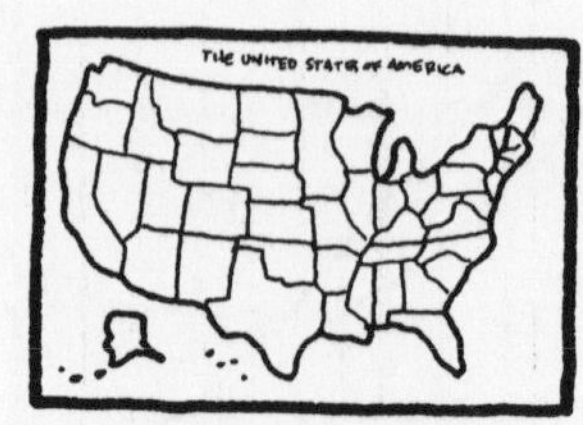 

Help your child use rhyming words from the page to make up silly sentences such as *The rat chased the cat*.

Name ______________________________

Say the name of each picture. Circle its name.

1. 

bat bad bag

2. 

ant wax ax

3. 

nap can cat

4. 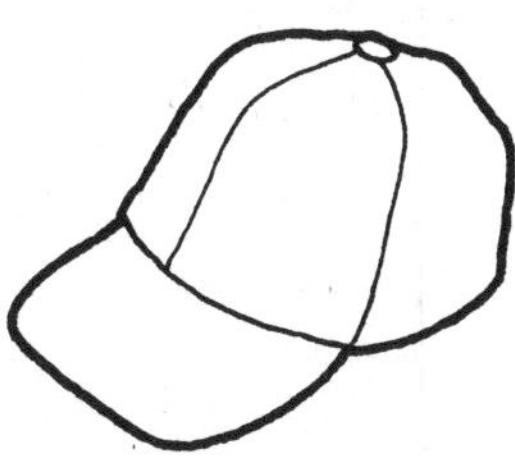

cab cap nap

5. 

man bag band

6. 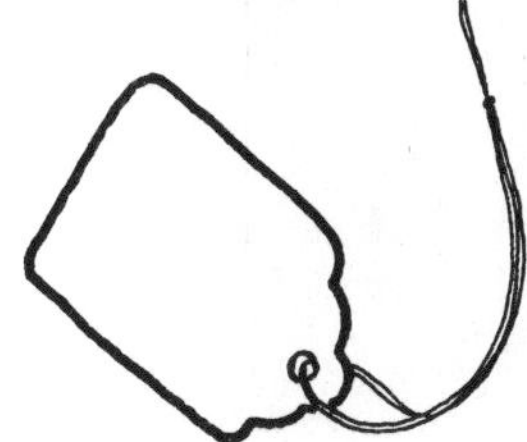

tag rag tap

7. 

fat fan tan

8. 

had hand land

9. 

tap lap lamp

10. 

van had ran

11. 

bad cab dad

12. 

pat pan ran

Read the words in the blue box. Print a word in the puzzle to name each picture.

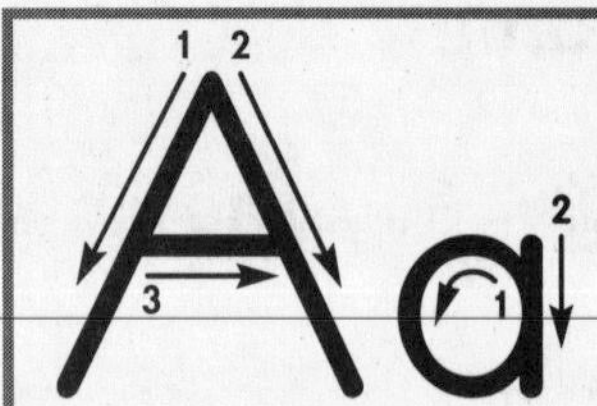

Across →

2. 

5. 

6. 

Down ↓

1.

3. 

4.

bag	cat	hand	hat	map	pan

Use some of the words from the box to write a sentence.

Make up riddles using some of the words from the box. Ask your child to guess each word.

Name ______________________________

Blend the letter sounds together as you say each word. Then color the picture it names.

1.

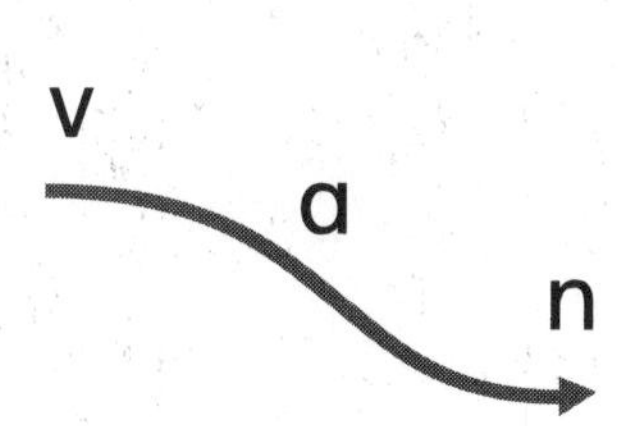

2.

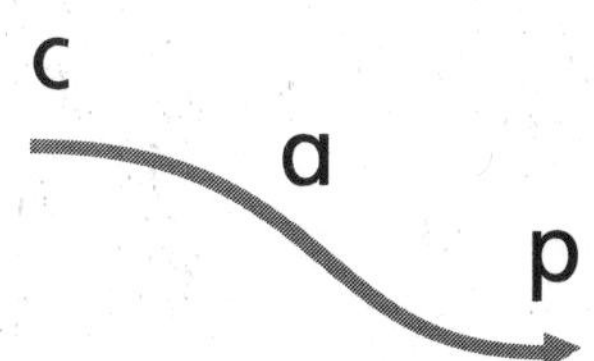

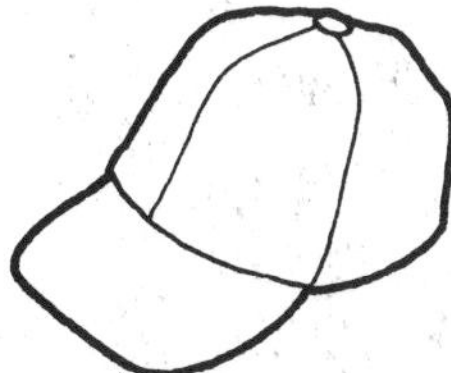

3.

h
a
m

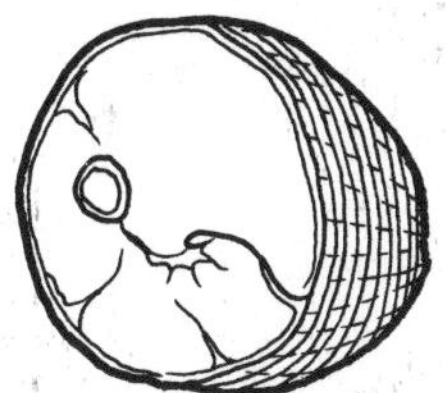

4.

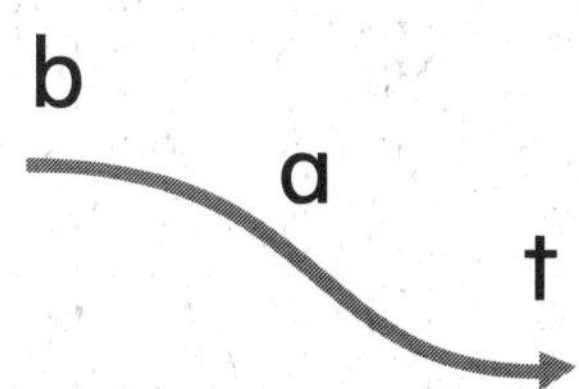

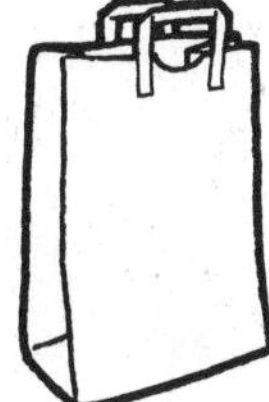

5.

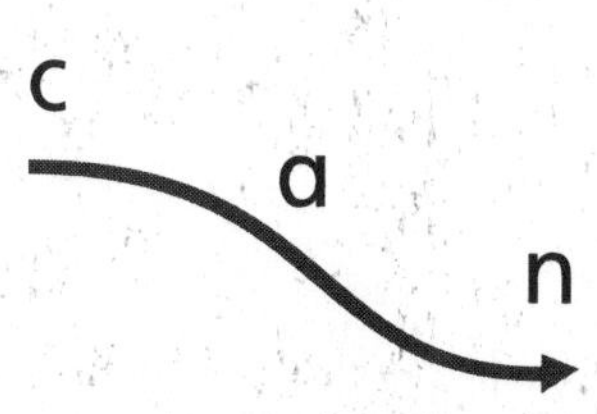

Blend the letter sounds together as you say each word. Print the word on the line. Draw a line to the picture whose name rhymes.

1. m ap — map

2. r at

3. h am

4. t ag

5. r an

6. s ad

HOME Invite your child to say a picture name and think of as many rhyming words as possible.

Name ______________________

Say the name of each picture. Print the letter for its beginning sound. Then print the letter for its ending sound.

1. 
cat

2. 
a

3. 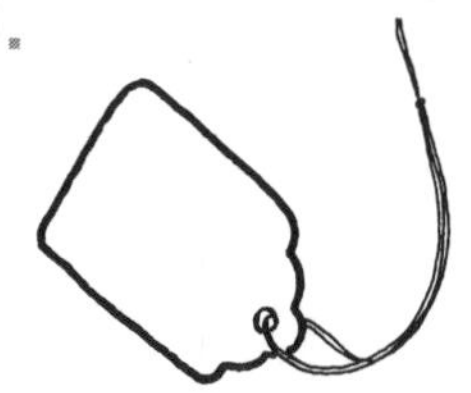
a

4. 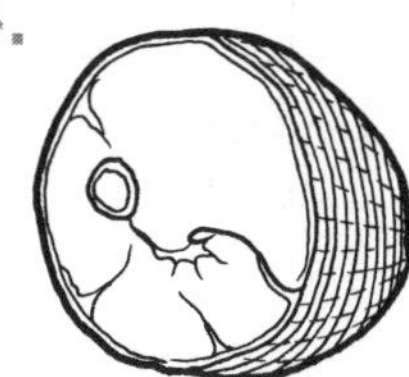
a

5. 

a

6. 
a

7. 
a

8. 
a

9. 
a

10. 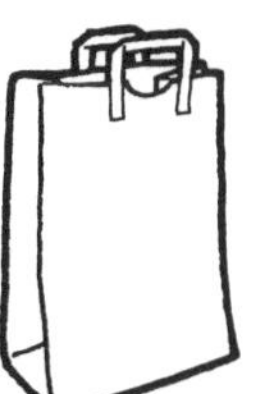
a

11. 

a

12. 
a

13. 
a

14. 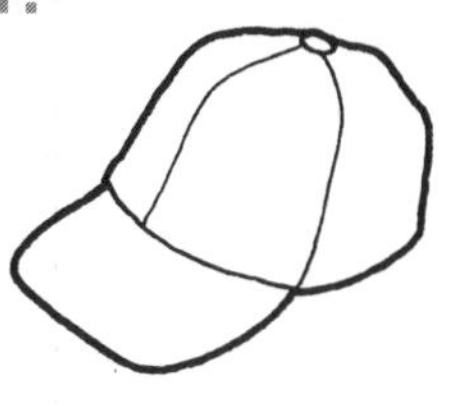
a

15. 
a

16. 
a

Look at the picture. Circle the word that will finish the sentence. Print it on the line.

1. Max is my __________. cat / sat / can

2. He licks my __________. land / hand / ham

3. Max sits on my __________. pad / rap / lap

4. He likes my __________. sad / dad / bad

5. He plays with a __________. bat / rag / bag

6. Max takes a __________. nap / cap / cab

Why does the girl like Max?

Help your child think of sentences using words from the page to continue the story.

Name ___________________________

Say the name of each picture. Print the name on the line. In the last box, draw a picture of a short **a** word. Print the word.

1. 

fan

2. 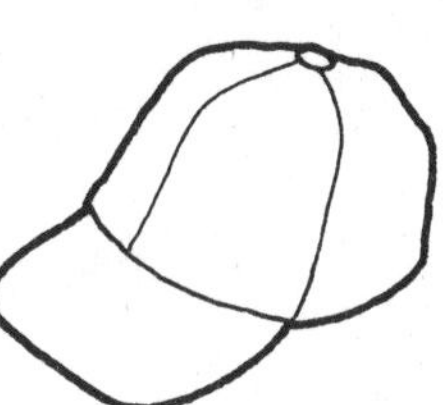

3. 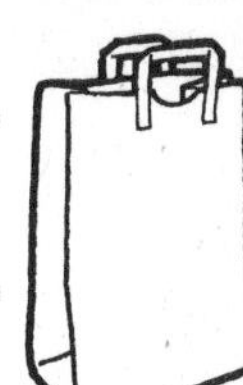

4. 

5. 

6. 

7. 

8. 

9. 

10. 

11. 

12.

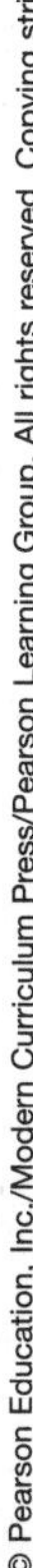

Read the sentences. Circle the word that will finish each sentence. Print it on the line.

1. Jan got in the ______________. — can / van / cat

2. It was time to go to ______________. — cap / lamp / camp

3. In the van, Jan had a ______________. — tap / nap / sat

4. At camp, Jan made a name ______________. — tag / rag / tan

5. Jan made a mask with a ______________. — wag / bad / bag

6. Jan played in the ______________. — band / can / hand

Do you think Jan had fun at camp? Why?

Ask your child questions that can be answered with words on the page, such as *Jan was sleepy so she took a ____.* (nap)

Name ______________________________

Read the story. Use short a words to finish the sentences.

Go, Ant!

The cat takes a nap.
The ant runs fast.
The ant is on the cat.
The cat is up!

The cat taps the ant.
Go, ant, go!
The cat can not get the ant.

1. The ______________ runs fast.
2. The ant is on the ______________.
3. The cat ______________ the ant.

Why does the cat want to catch the ant?

Use one of the letters to make a word with an or ap. Write each real word on the lines.

r y c m p

an

1. __________

2. __________

3. __________

4. __________

c l b n t

ap

5. __________

6. __________

7. __________

8. __________

Write a sentence using one of the words you made.

____

____

HOME

Invite your child to think of more words that end with *an* or *ap* such as *fan, tan, gap, map, rap, zap.*

A bat can go fast.

4

FOLD

Name ____________________

BATS

Written by
Jennifer Jacobson

Photographs by
Dr. Merlin Tuttle

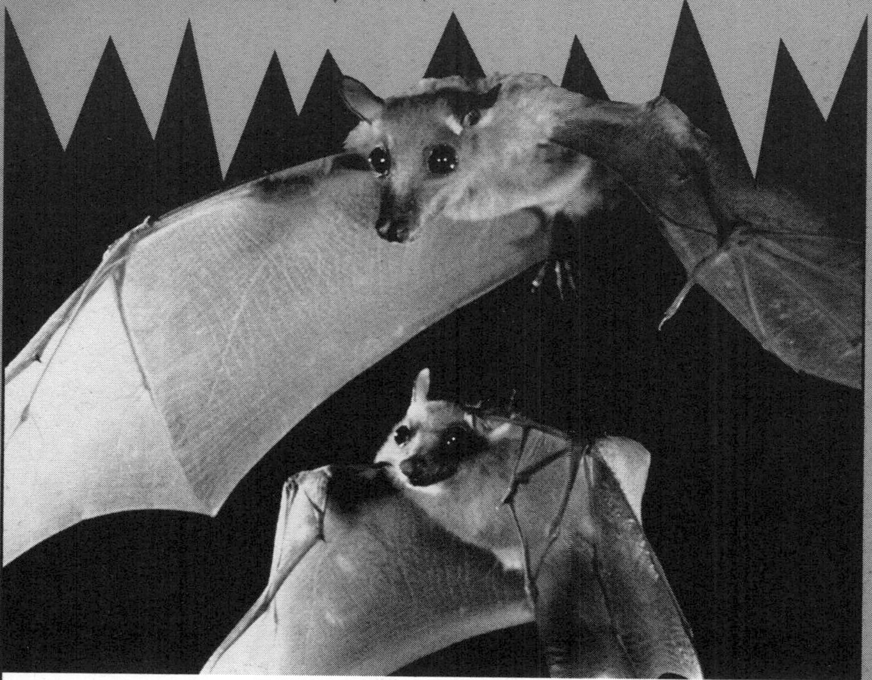

A bat has fur.

1

2

This bat has a bug.

FOLD

3

A bat can go far.

Name ____________________

Read the words in the box. Write a word to finish each sentence.

I	the
My	with
here	said

1. Pal got __________ ball.

2. "Run," __________ Dan to Pal.

3. Pal ran __________ the ball.

4. "Now run __________, Pal," said Dan.

5. "__________ dog runs fast," Dan said.

6. "__________ like to play with my dog."

Unscramble the letters to write a word from the box. The word shapes will help you print the words.

here	my
said	with
the	

1. asdi
2. eth
3. hree
4. hwit
5. ym

Put a ✓ next to each word you can read.

☐ with ☐ said ☐ my ☐ here ☐ the ☐ I

HOME Using any two words on the page, help your child make up a sentence, then draw a picture to go with it.

Name ______________________________

A big pink pig
Ate a big fig,
Put on a big wig,
And did a jig.

Pig has the short sound of **i**. **Circle** each picture whose name has the short sound of **i**.

1.

2.

3.

4.

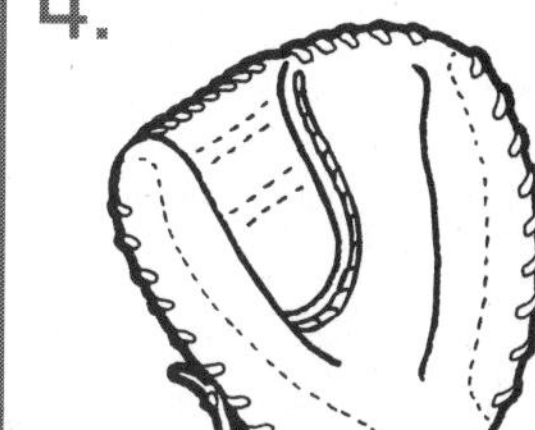

5.

6.

7.

8.

9.

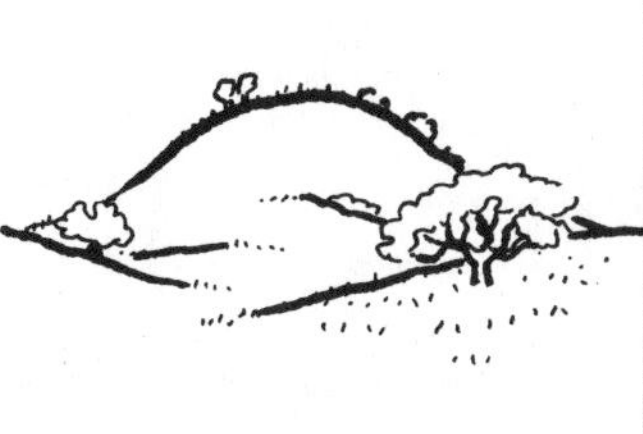

10.

11.

12.

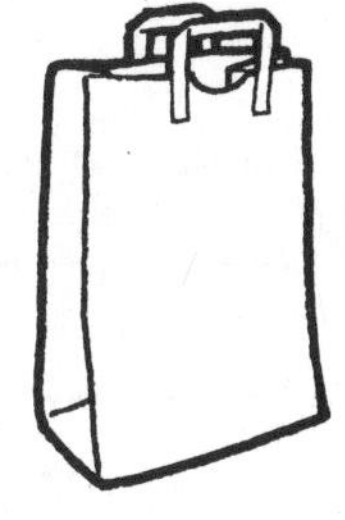

Say the names of the pictures in each row.
Color the pictures whose names rhyme.

1.

  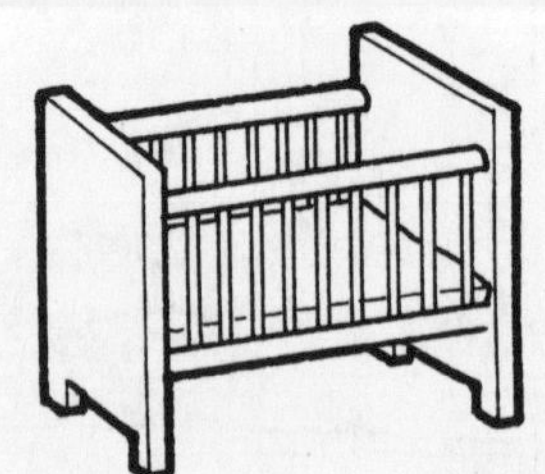 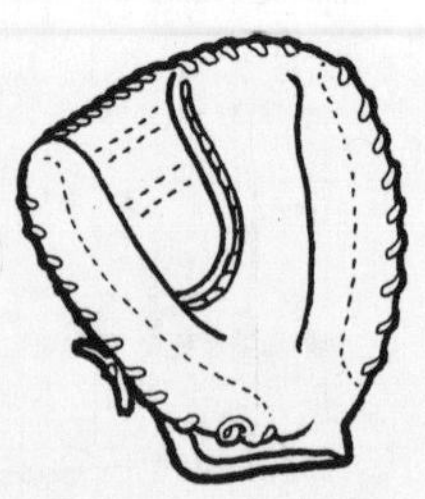

2.

 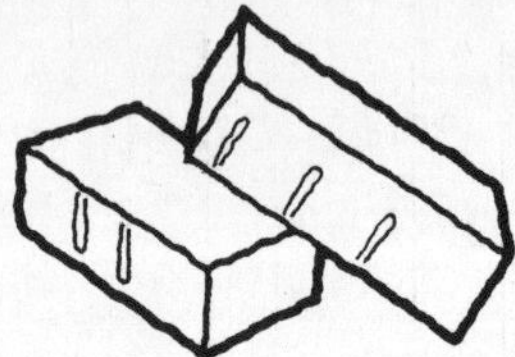  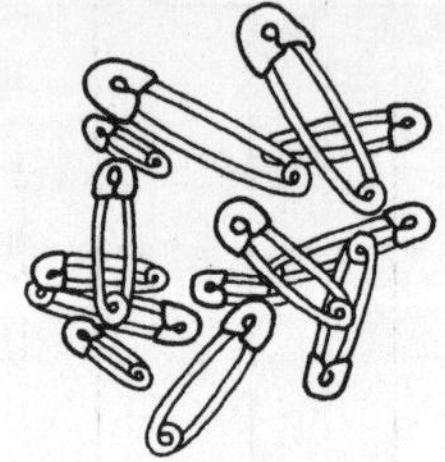

3.

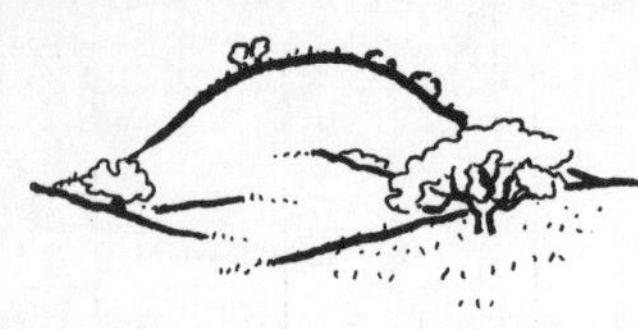 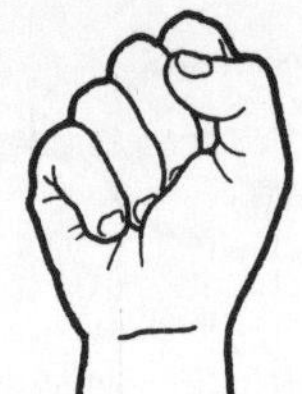  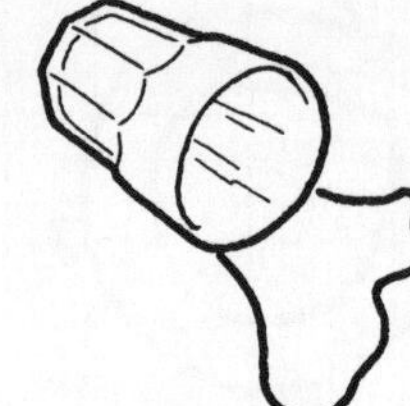

4.

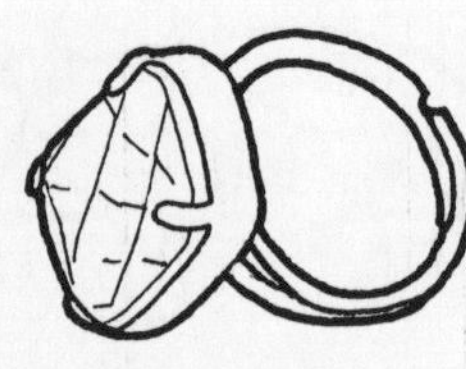   

5.

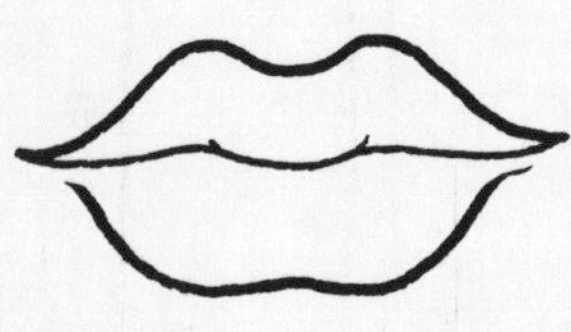  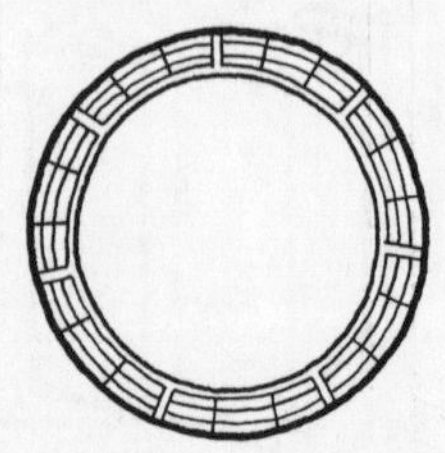 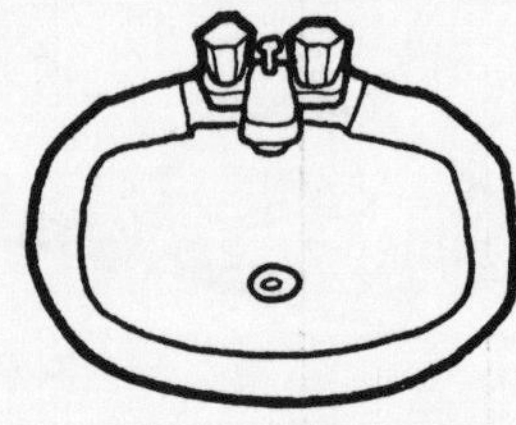

With your child, make up silly sentences using the rhyming words from each row.

Name ____________________________________

Say the name of each picture. Circle its name.

1.

pin wig pig

2.

six ax mix

3.

hid lid did

4.

bib bit bad

5.
fin pin pan

6.
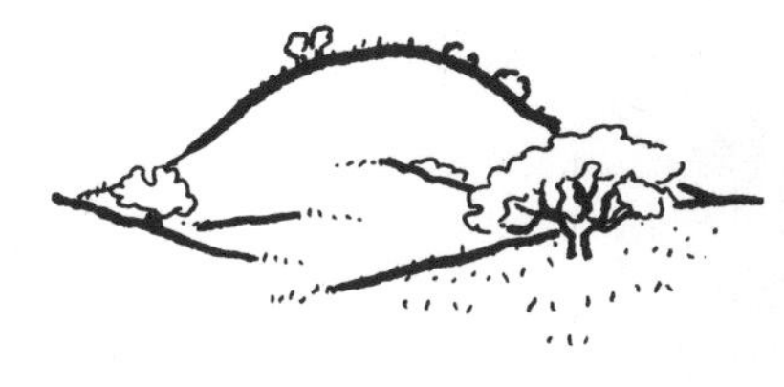
fill hill bill

7.

mix mat mitt

8.
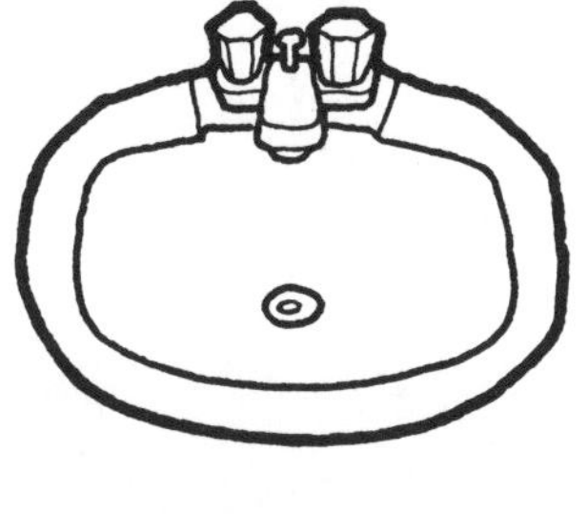
sing sank sink

9.

will milk mitt

10.
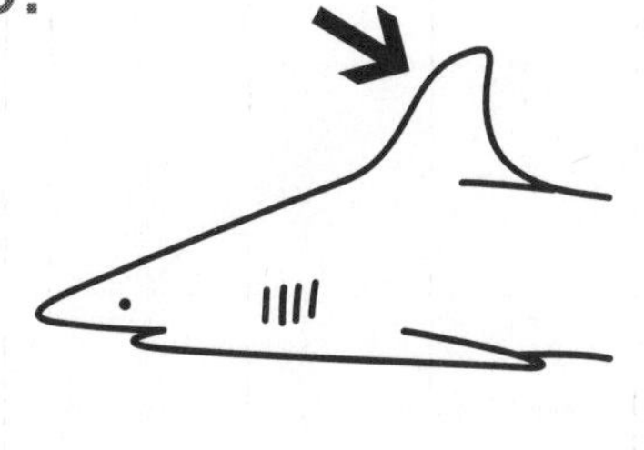
win fin fan

11.

fist fish fast

12.
win wing ring

Farmer Jill's pigs have short **i** words on them. Help Farmer Jill catch her pigs. Circle the short **i** words.

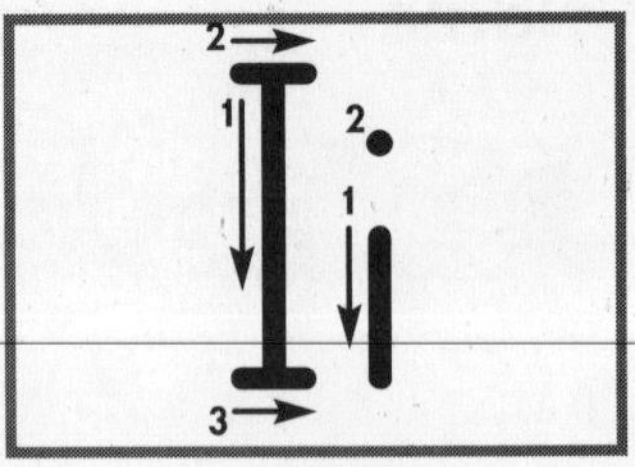

Ii

pin

cat

hill

sink

tag

fan

lid

big

Use some of the short **i** words on the pigs to write a sentence.

With your child, take turns making up poems and rhymes for each short *i* word.

Name ________________________________

Blend the letter sounds together as you say each word. Then, **color** the picture it names.

1.
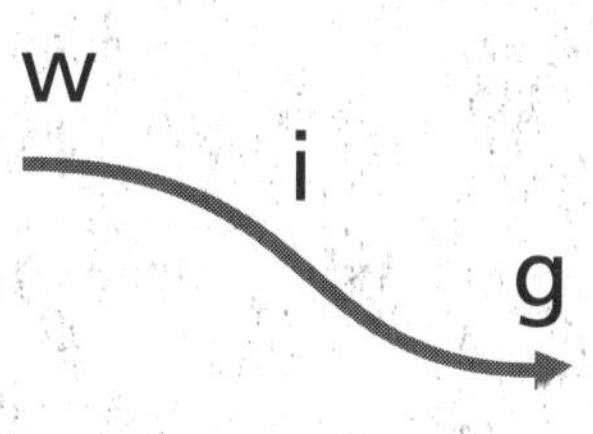

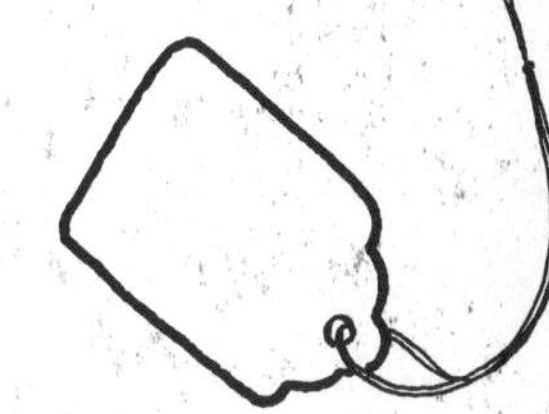

2.
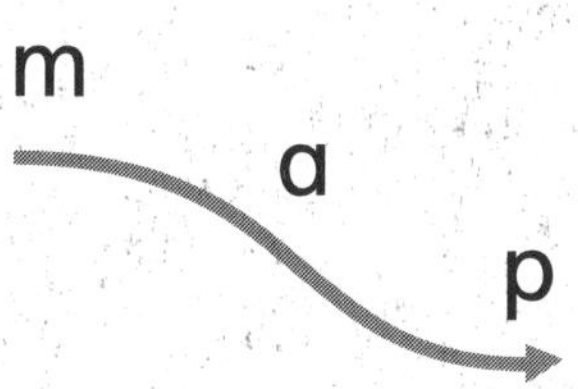

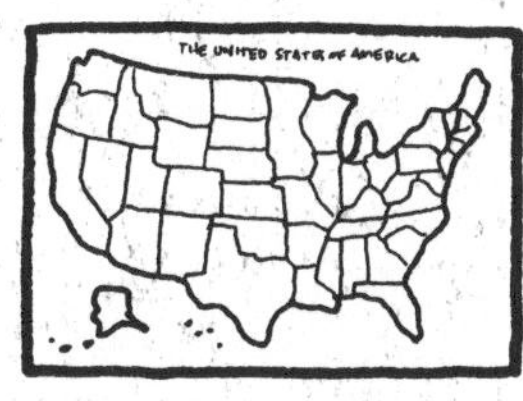
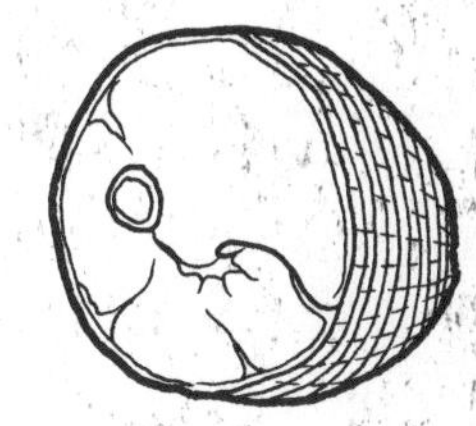

3.

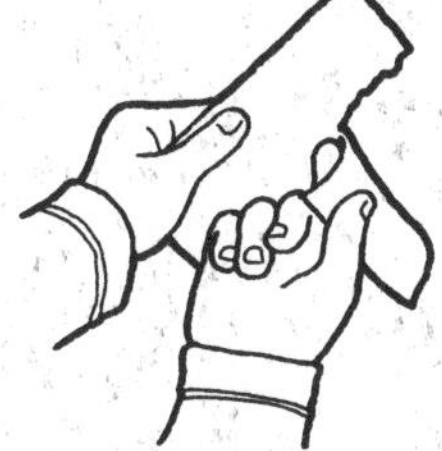
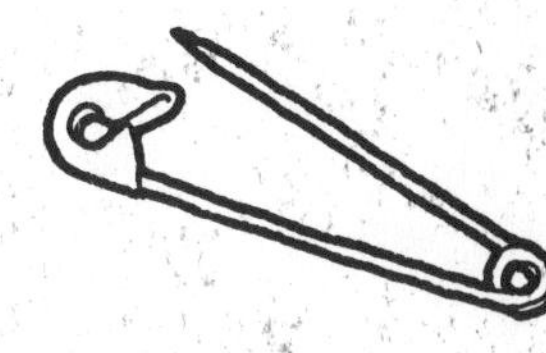

4.
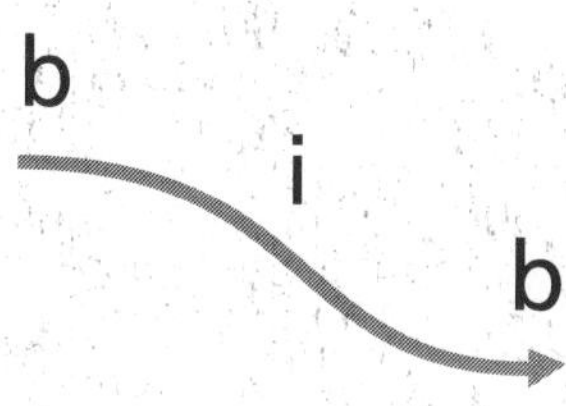

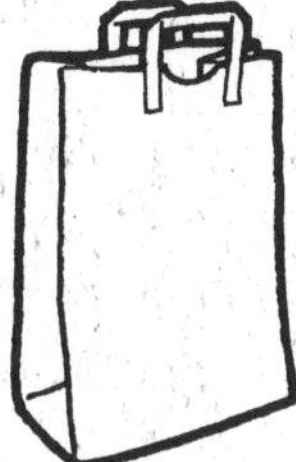

5.
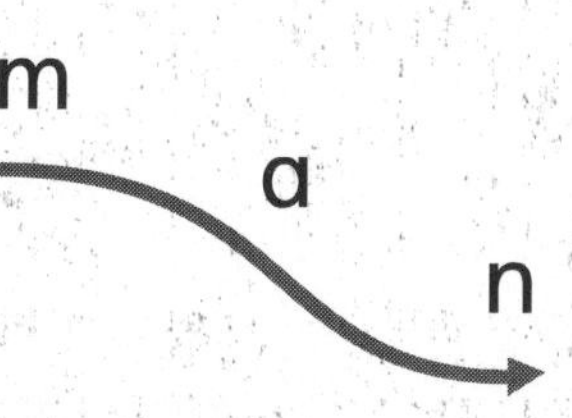

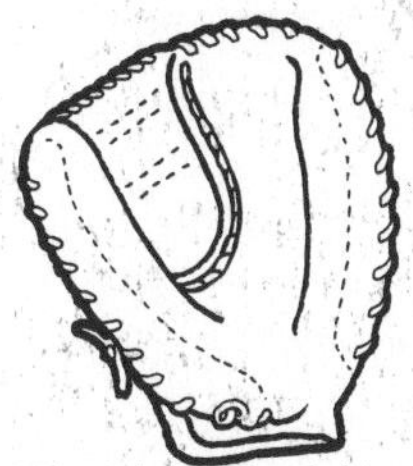

Blend the letter sounds together as you say each word.
Print the word on the line. **Draw** a line to the picture it names.

1. p ig

2. p an

3. s ix

4. c ap

5. r at

6. r ip

Ask your child to think of a rhyming word for three of the picture names.

Name ______________________

Say the name of each picture. Print the letters for its beginning and ending sounds. Trace the whole word.

1.  wig	2.  i	3.  i	4.  i
5. 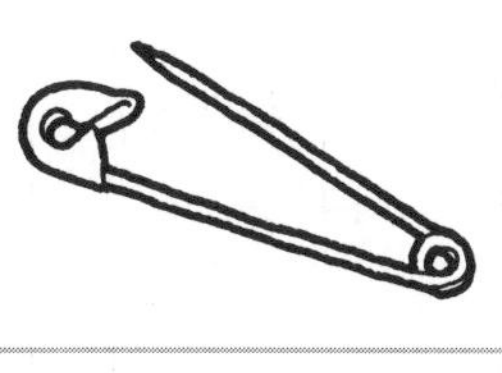 i	6.  i	7.  i	8.  if
9. 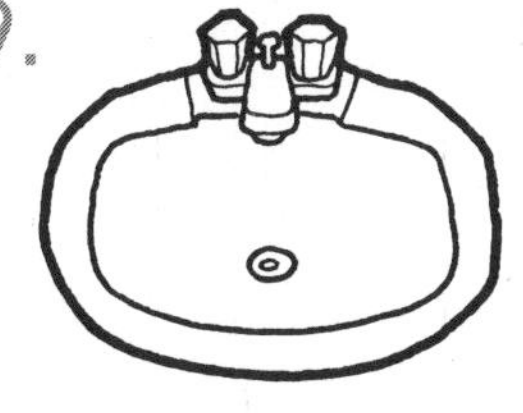 in	10.  il	11.  ip	12. 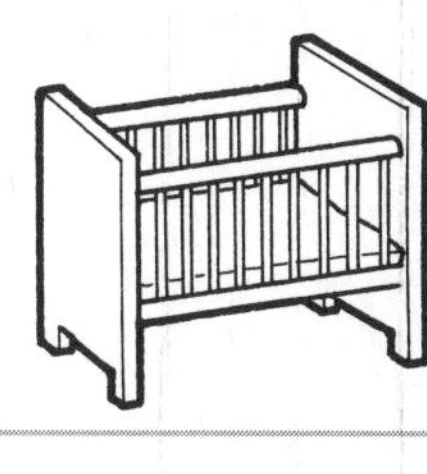 ri
13. 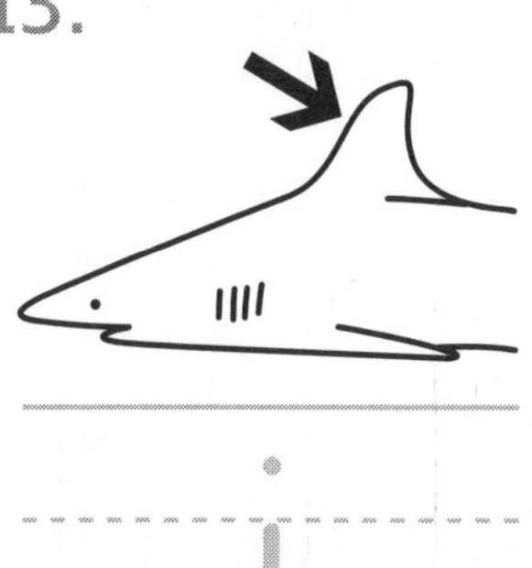 i	14.  i	15. 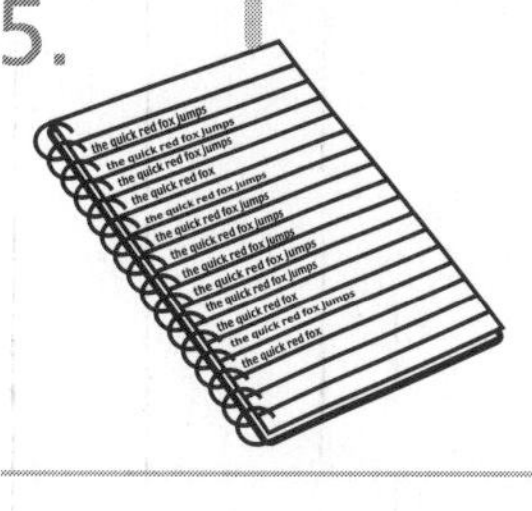 is	16.  is

Look at the picture. Circle the word that will finish the sentence. Print it on the line.

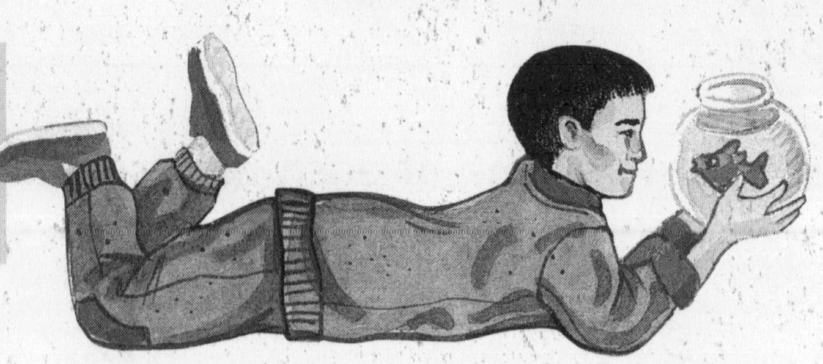

1. I got a ______________. gap gift gum

2. Is it a ______________? milk mitt tip

3. Does it drink ______________? milk mitt mat

4. Will it fit in a ______________? damp dig dish

5. Can it swim in the ______________? sick sink sank

6. It is a ______________! fist fast fish

Did you ever get a pet as a gift? Tell about it.

With your child, pick a word on the page and take turns changing the first letter to make new words, such as *dish—fish*.

Name ______________________________

Say the name of each picture. Print the name on the line. In the last box, draw a picture of a short i word. Print the word.

1.

lid

2.

3.

4.

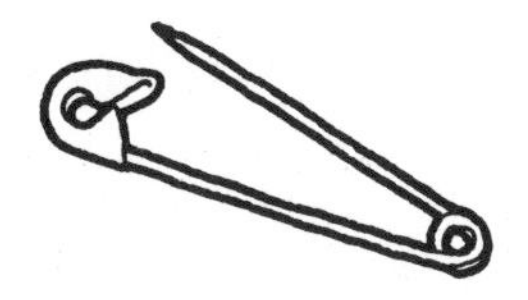

5.

6.

7.

8.

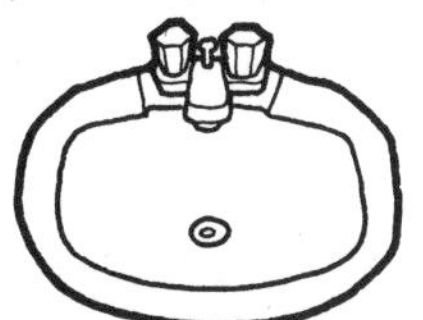

9.

10.

11.

12.

Read the sentences. Circle the word that will finish each sentence. Print it on the line.

1. Jim and Linda were going to ______. dog / dig / pig
2. They went to the top of the ______. bill / hit / hill
3. Jim saw a rock that was ______. rig / big / bag
4. He could just see the ______. tip / tap / rip
5. Linda's truck moved ______. at / it / if
6. She was glad to help ______. him / her / rim

What other things can be used to dig?

With your child, make up sentences with short *i* words such as "With a shovel, I can ___."

Name ______________________

Read the story. Print short i words to finish the sentences.

Fish Tale

The big fish has little fins.
The little fish has big fins.
The big fish likes to sing.
The little fish likes to swim.
The big fish sings to his friend.
The little fish waves a fin.

1. The ______________ fish has little fins.

2. The big fish likes to ______________.

3. The little fish waves a ______________.

Why might the big and little fish be friends?

Use one of the letters to make a word with ig or ing. Write each real word on a line.

b c p f d

ig

1. ______
2. ______
3. ______
4. ______

r s n k w

ing

5. ______
6. ______
7. ______
8. ______

Write a sentence using one of the words you made.

______

______

Ask your child to guess these words as you say them aloud, stretching out the sounds: *j-ig, r-ig, w-ig, th-ing,* and *br-ing*.

The race ends.
The pig in pink wins.

4

FOLD

Name ______________________________

Fast Pig

This pig can run.

1

The race has started.
The pig in pink is fast.

2

FOLD

The pigs zip around the ring.
These pigs can not catch the pig
in pink.

3

Name ______________________________

Read the words in the box. Write a word to finish each sentence.

you	for
like	down
are	do

1. Min and Tim ______________ playing in the sand.

2. Min says, "What did I ______________ with my ring?"

3. "I will help look ______________ it," Tim says.

4. Min and Tim look ______________ in the sand.

5. "This looks ______________ the ring," says Tim.

6. "Tim, ______________ are my friend," says Min.

Write the letter to finish each word. Then print the words on the lines.

down are for do like you

1. d _ w n (down)
2. d _ (across)
3. a r _
4. l i k _
5. y _ u
6. f _ r

1. ______ 2. ______

3. ______ 4. ______

5. ______ 6. ______

Put a ✓ next to each word you can read.

☐ like ☐ down ☐ you ☐ are ☐ for ☐ do

HOME Help your child make up sentences using the words on this page.

Name ___________________________________

Rub-a-dub-dub.
The cub is in the tub.
Rub-a-dub-dub.
The cub likes to scrub.

Cub has the short sound of u. Circle each picture whose name has the short sound of u.

1.	2.	3.	4.
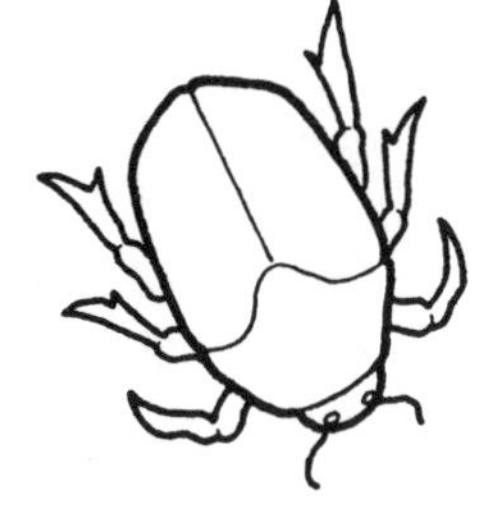	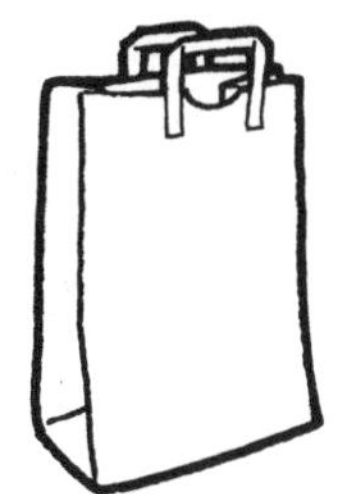		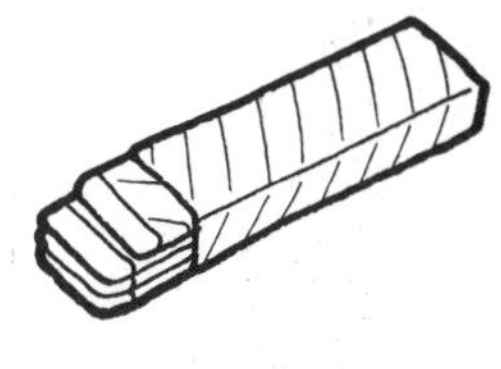
5.	6.	7.	8.
	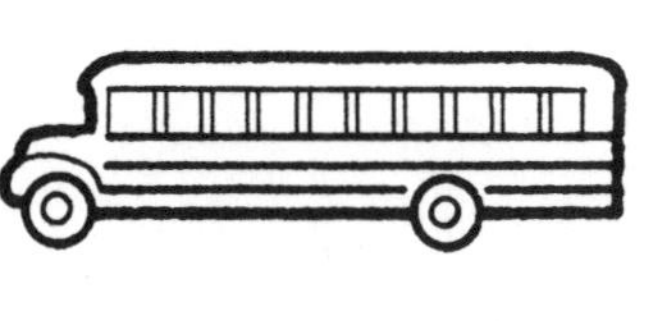	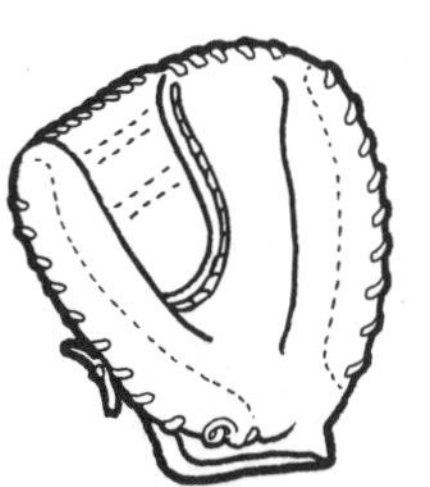	
9.	10.	11.	12.
	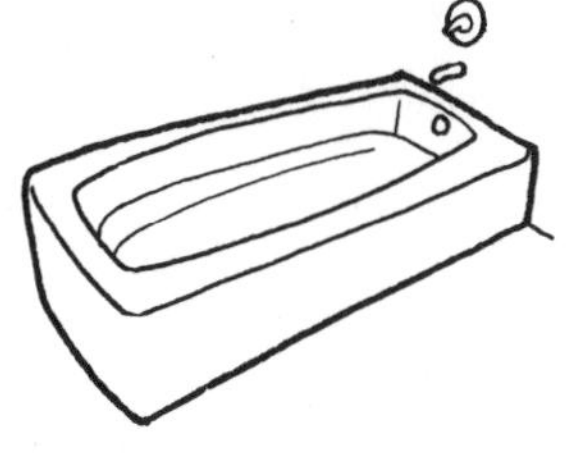		

Say the names of the pictures in each row. Color the pictures whose names rhyme.

1.

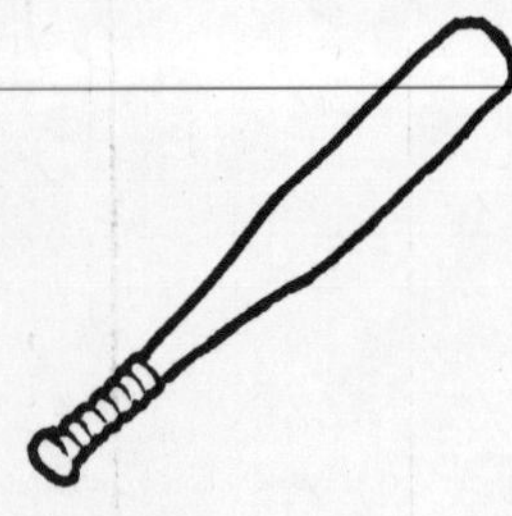

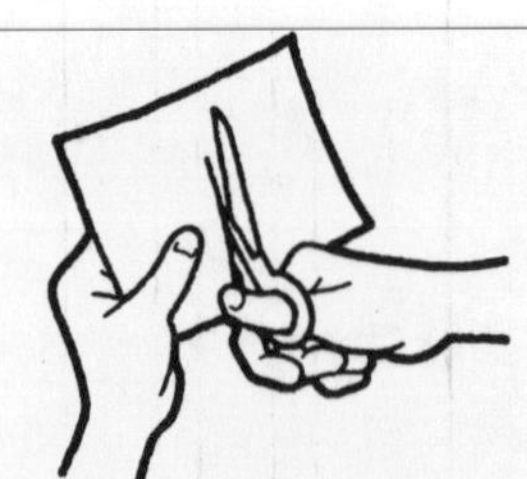

2.

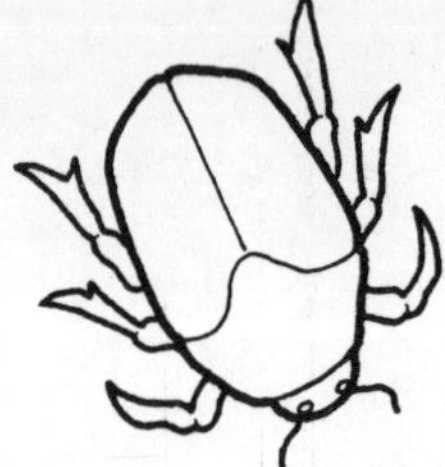

3.

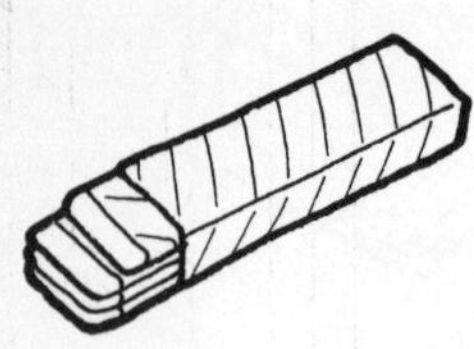

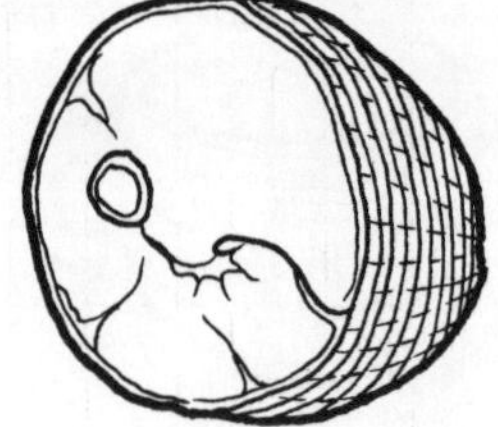

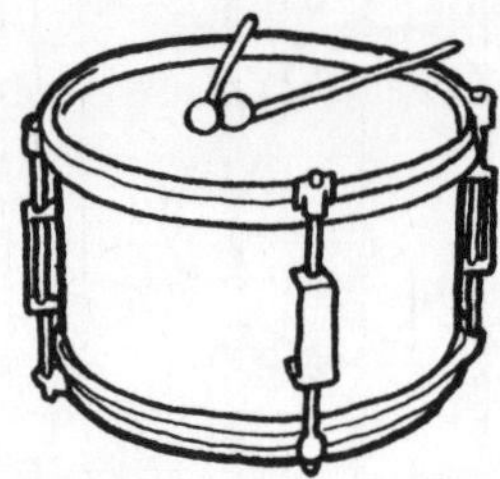

4.

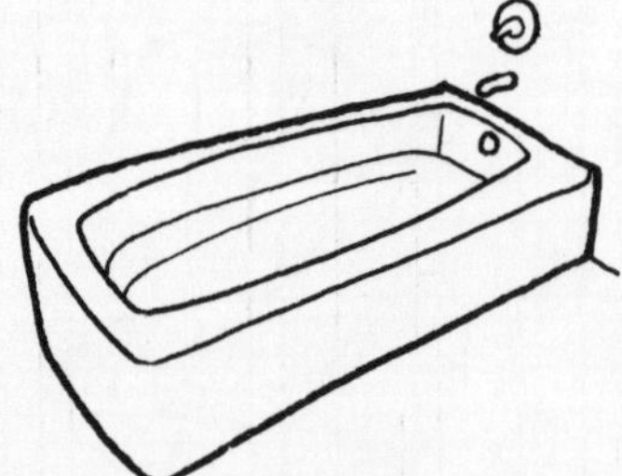

5.

Help your child think of more words that rhyme with the ones on this page.

Name ______________________________

Say the name of each picture. Circle its name.

1.

suds sand sun

2.
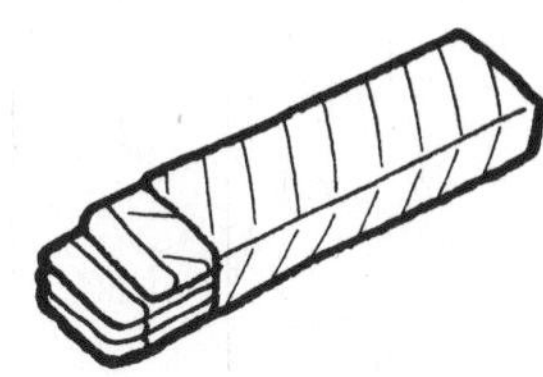
gum mug gust

3.

cut cap cup

4.
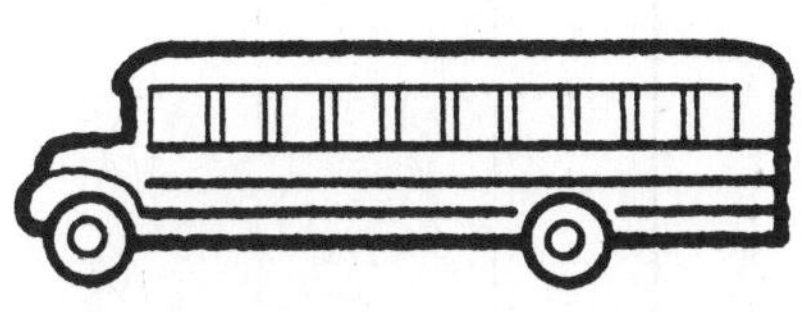
bun bus sun

5.

bag bug big

6.
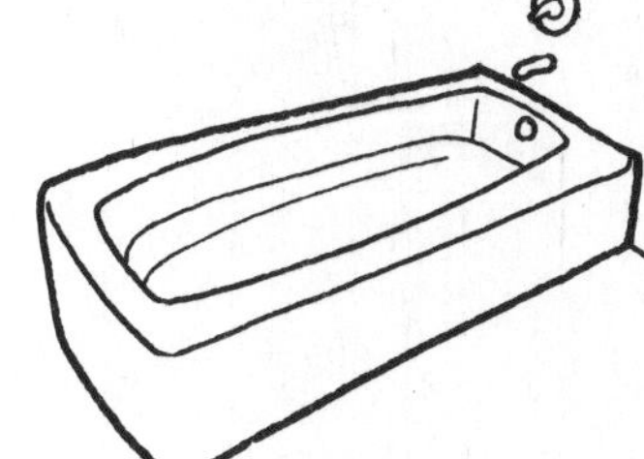
but tab tub

7.
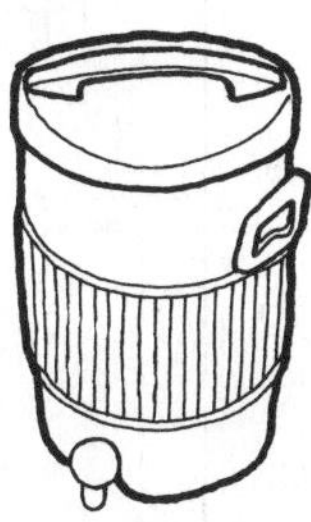
jug jack gum

8.

huts mugs nuts

9.

tuck duck luck

10.
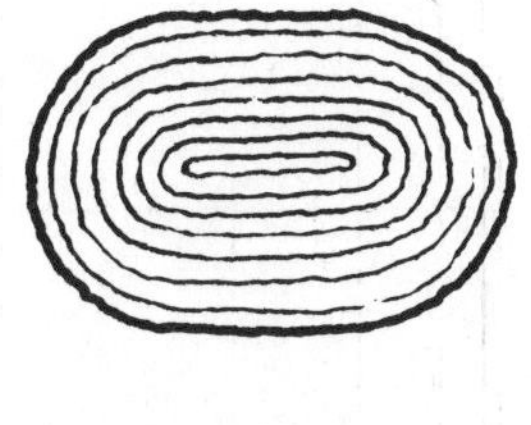
mug rug rag

11.
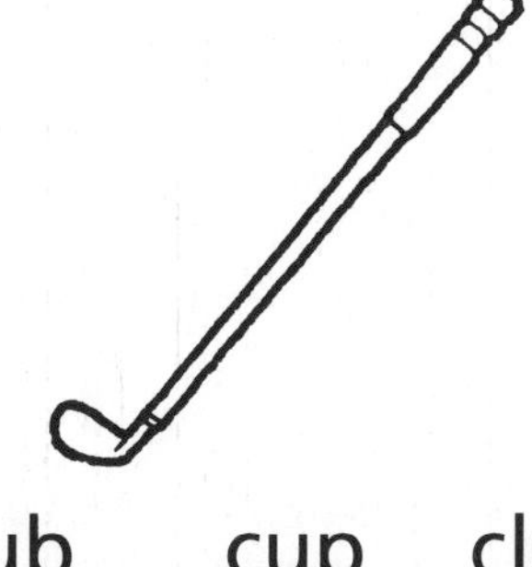
cub cup club

12.
drum dip mad

Help the cub get home. Draw a line from the cub to the first word with the short u sound. Draw a line to each short u word.

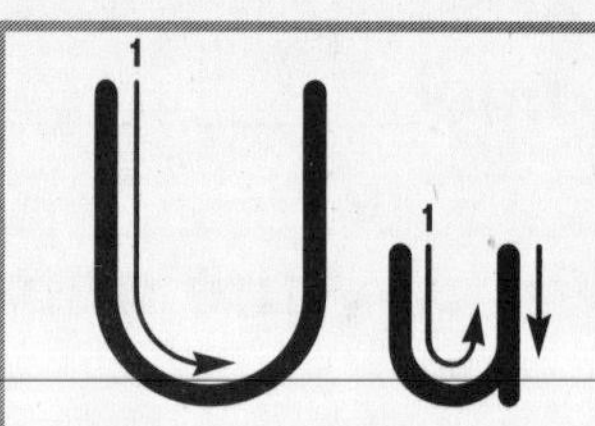

fun

dog

jug

bug

cat

jam

nut

fox

bed

tub

rug

Use some of the short u words from the puzzle to write a sentence.

With your child, take turns naming short *u* words.

Name ______________________________

Blend the letter sounds together as you say each word. Then, color the picture it names.

1. b u g

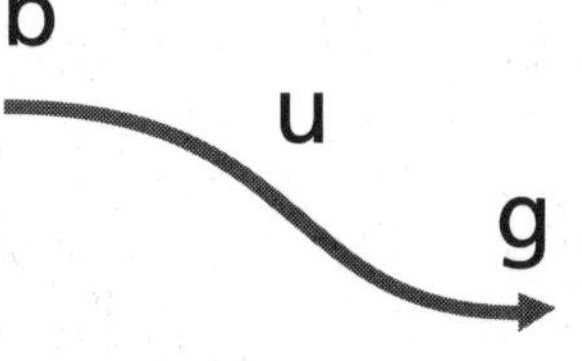

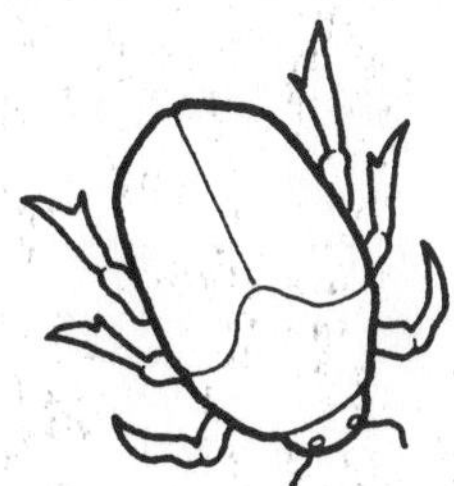

2. c a n

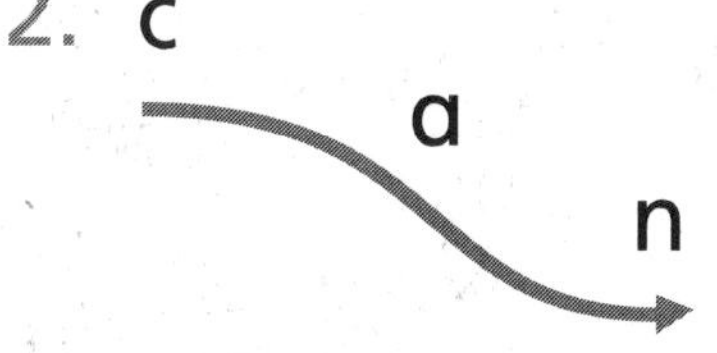

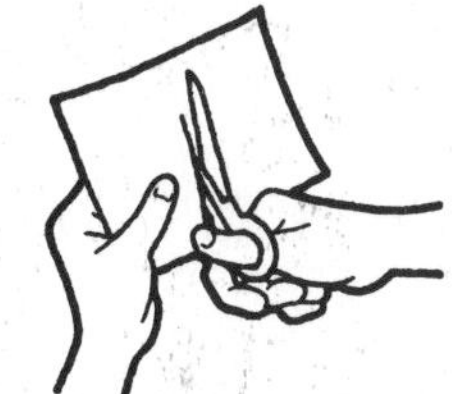

3. p i n

4. t u b

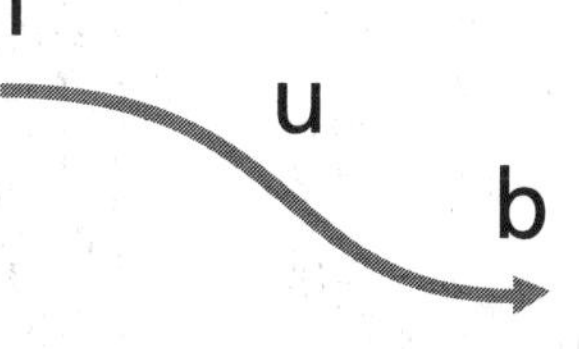

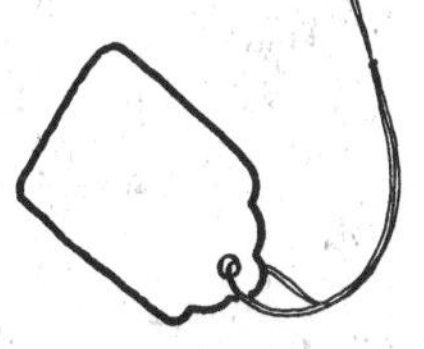

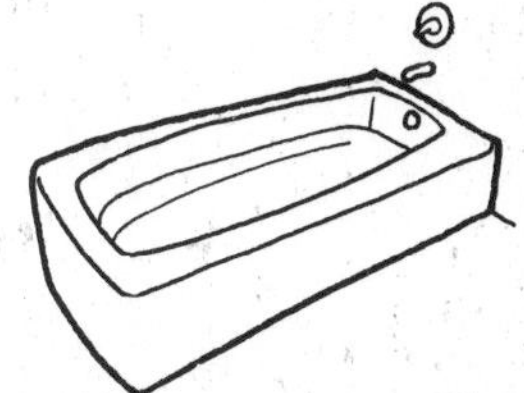

5. r a t

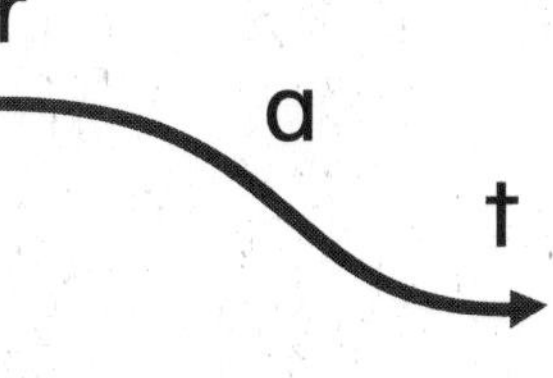

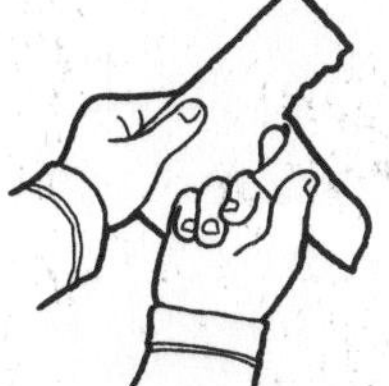

6. w i g

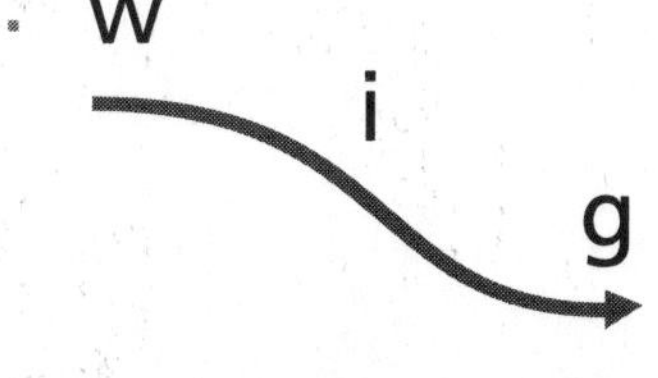

Blend the letter sounds together as you say each word. Print the word on the line. Draw a line to the picture it names.

1. b
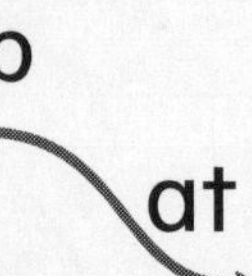
at

2. s
ix

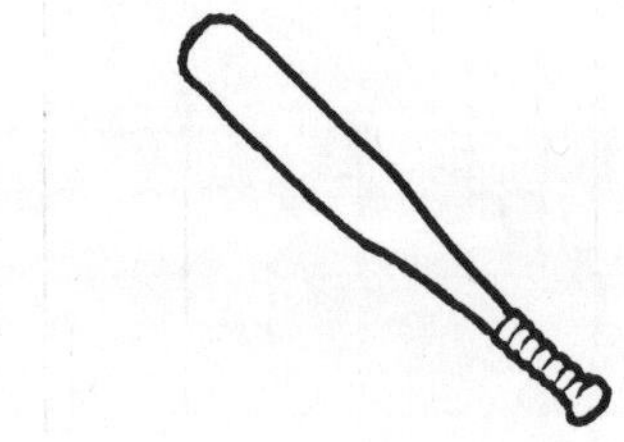

3. r
ug

4. p
ig

5. p
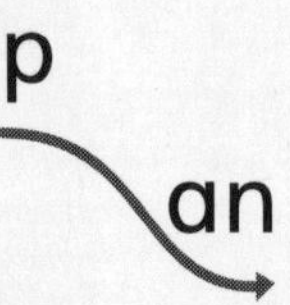
an

6. c
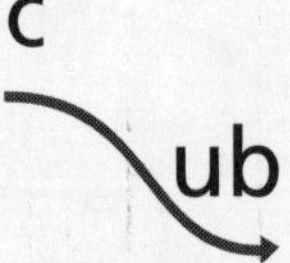
ub

HOME Help your child make up silly rhymes for these picture names, such as *a cub in a tub*.

Name ________________________________

Say the name of each picture. **Print** the letter for its beginning and ending sounds. In the last box, **draw** a picture of a short u word.

1. 
cup

2. 
u

3. 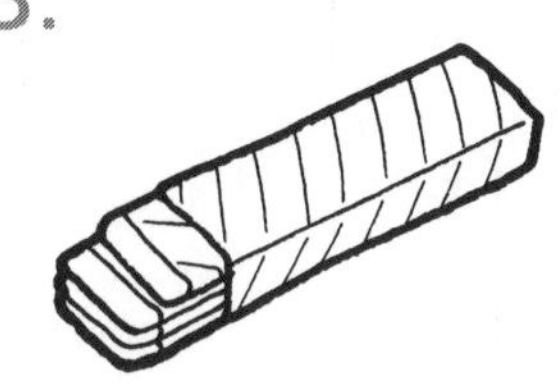
u

4. 
u

5. 
u

6. 
u

7. 
u

8. 
u

9. 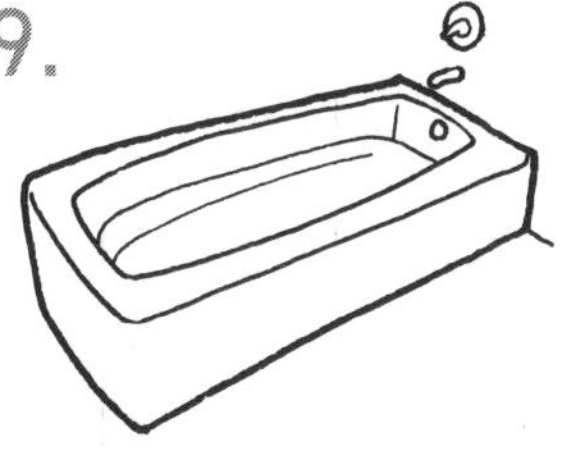
u

10. 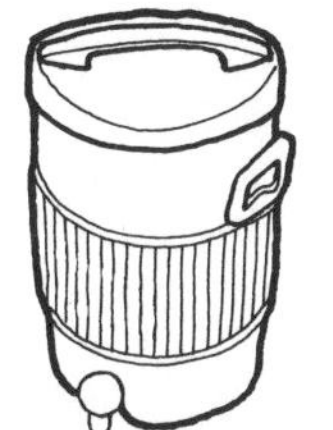
u

11. 
u

12. 
u

13. 
u

14. 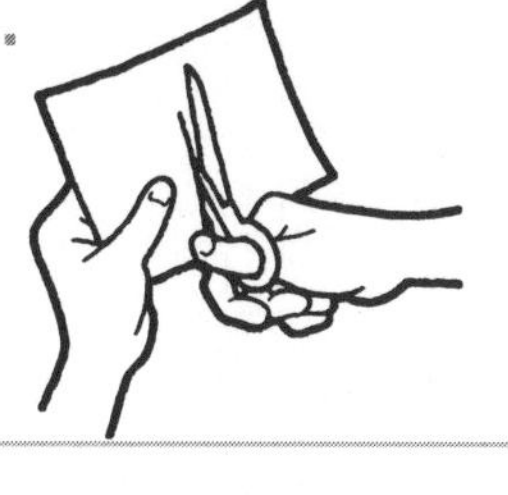
u

15. 
u

16.
u

Look at the picture. Circle the word that will finish the sentence. Print it on the line.

1. Gus sits on the ________. rub rug jug

2. He plays with his ________. pup up cup

3. Soon Gus sees the ________. bud bug bus

4. He jumps ________. hug up cup

5. Gus has to ________. rub fun run

6. The bus is stuck in the ________! mud mug hum

What do you think will happen next?

Ask your child to raise a hand for the short *u* words as you say, *But the bus was just stuck in the mud for an hour.*

Name ______________________________

Say the name of each picture. Print the picture name on the line. In the last box, draw a picture of a short u word. Print the word.

1. 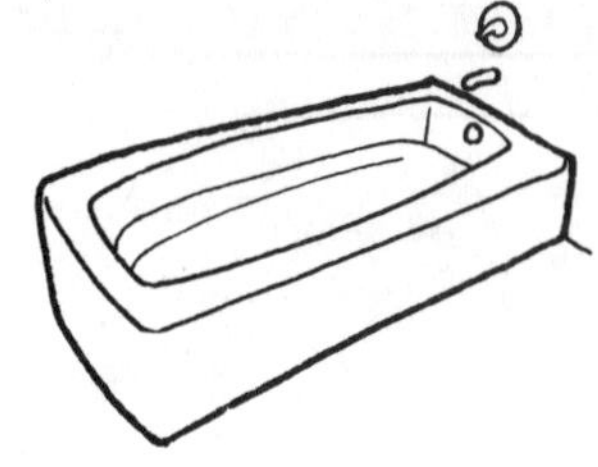
tub

2. 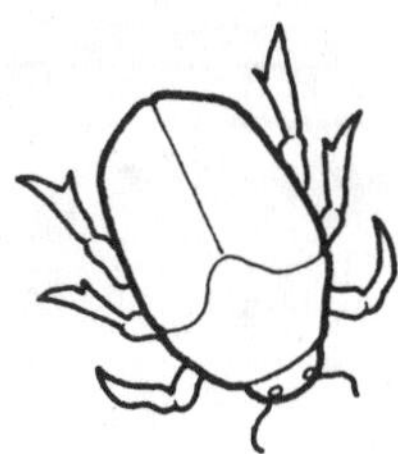

3. 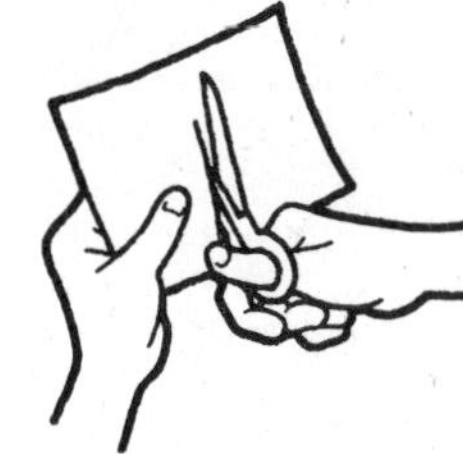

4. 

5. 

6. 

7. 

8. 

9. 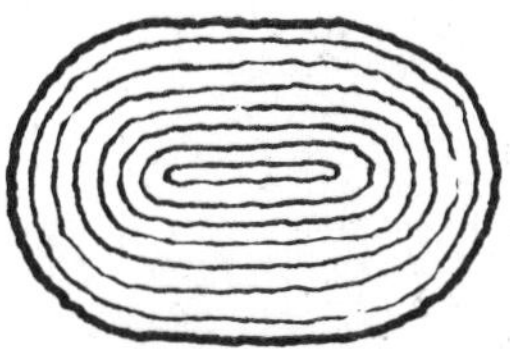

10. 

11. 

12.

Read the sentences. Circle the word that will finish each sentence. Print it on the line.

1. Our farm is ________________. fan / fin / fun

2. I look under trees for ________________. nuts / rugs / suns

3. Bugs buzz and ________________. hut / hand / hum

4. The pigs dig in the ________________. must / mud / mug

5. My dog jumps and ________________. runs / rings / cuts

6. He likes the warm ________________. gum / sun / hum

What are some things you might do at a farm?

Help your child to make up a sentence using the words *fun* and *sun*, then draw a picture to go with it.

Name ______________________________

Read the story. Use short **u** words to finish the sentences.

A Fuss in a Bus

The bug jumps in the bus.
The pup hums in the bus.
The cub runs in the bus.
"Sit down!" says the driver.
"Do not make such a fuss!"
The bug sits.
The cub sits.
The pup does not hum.
No more fuss in the bus!
Now it can go.

1. The __________ jumps in the bus.

2. The pup hums in the __________.

3. The __________ runs in the bus.

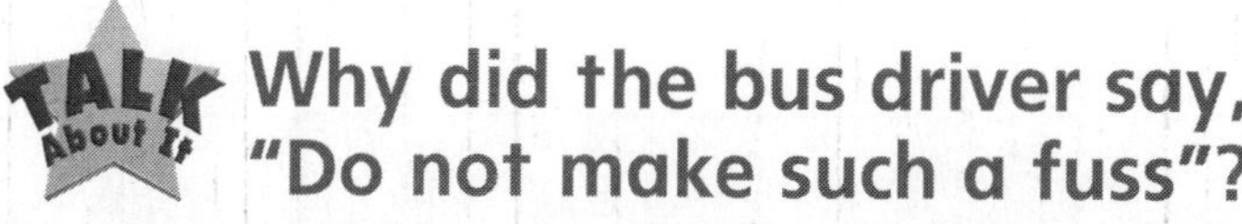

Why did the bus driver say, "Do not make such a fuss"?

Use one of the letters to make a word with un or ug. Write each real word on a line.

b r f s l

un

1. ______

2. ______

3. ______

4. ______

m b k j t

ug

5. ______

6. ______

7. ______

8. ______

Write a sentence using one of the words you made.

______

______

HOME

Help your child think of other *un* and *ug* words.

Put nuts and seeds in the jug.
Watch the fun.

4

Name ______________________

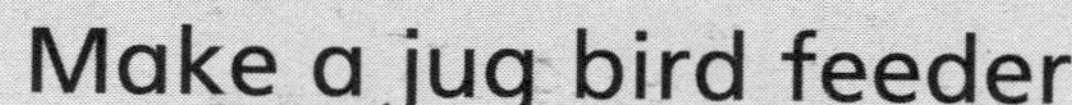

Make a jug bird feeder.

1

Scrub a milk jug.
Cut a hole in the jug.

2

FOLD

Put a string on the jug.
Hang the jug up.

3

Name ______________________________

My dog has lots of spots.
My dog's spots look like dots.
My dog's spots are on his hair.
My dog's spots are everywhere!

Spot has the short sound of o. Circle each picture whose name has the short sound of o.

1. 	2. 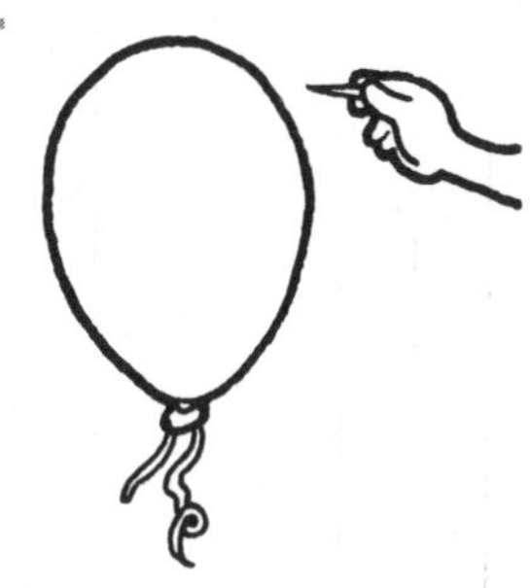	3. 	4. 
5. 	6. 	7. 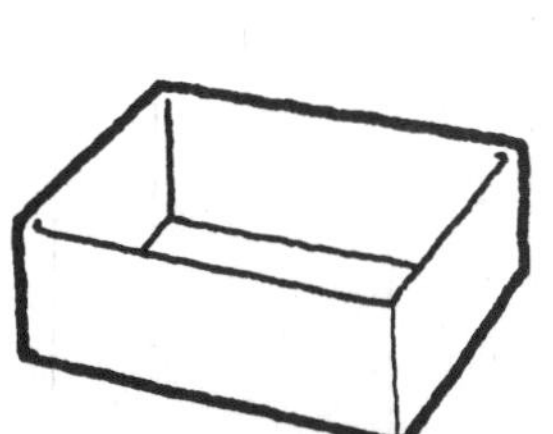	8. 
9. 	10. 	11. 	12. 

**Say the names of the pictures in each row.
Color the pictures whose names rhyme.**

1.

  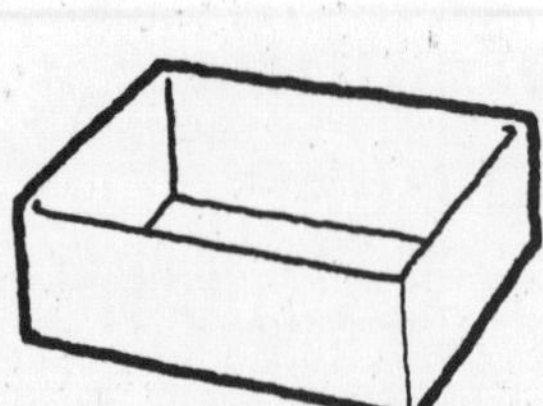 

2.

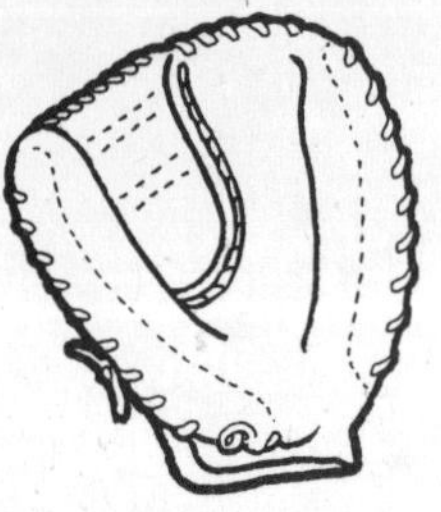   

3.

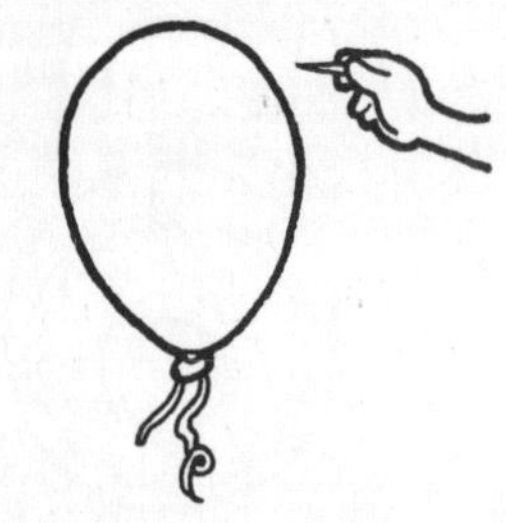   

4.

 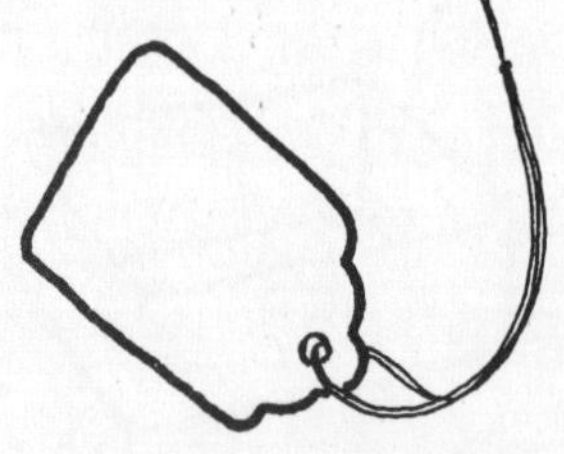 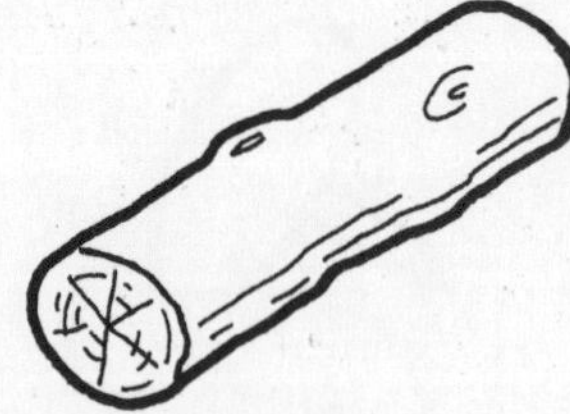 

5.

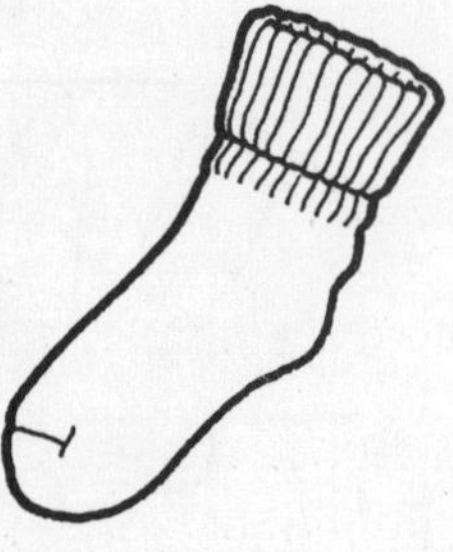  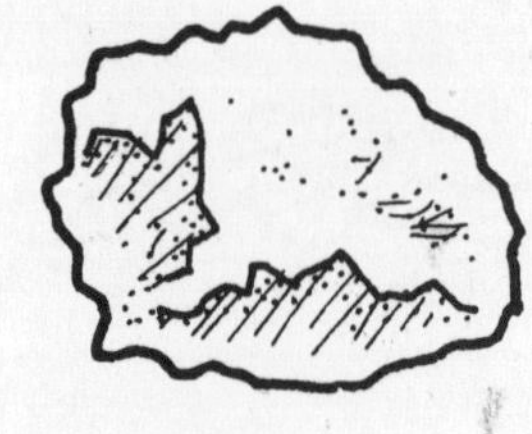 

With your child, make up action rhymes using short *o* words from the page, such as *hop with a mop.*

Name ______________________________

Say the name of each picture. Circle its name.

1.

top pot pack

2.

box fox fog

3.
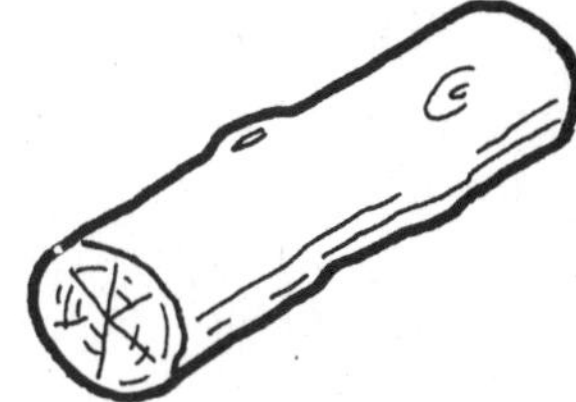
log dog lot

4.

nap map mop

5.

tap tip top

6.

hat hot hit

7.

dog dig dug

8.
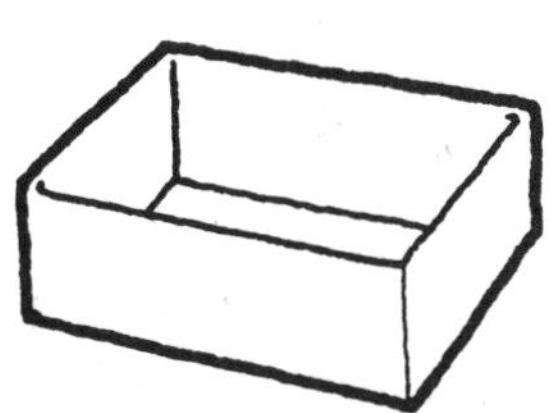
bat box bug

9.

fill duck doll

10.

ox sock ax

11.

rip rack rock

12.
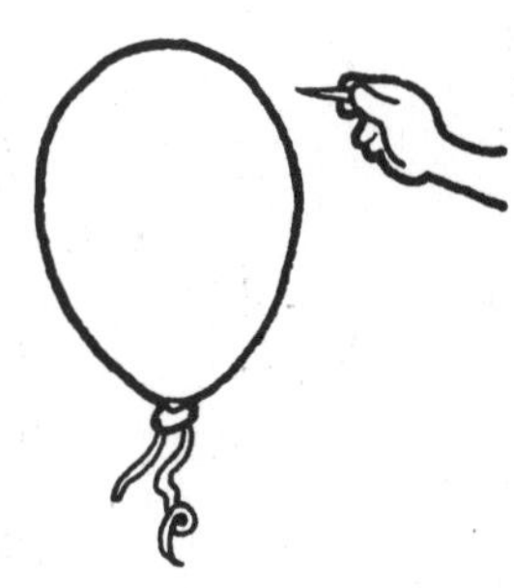
pop pup pat

Color each short o word red. What do you see?

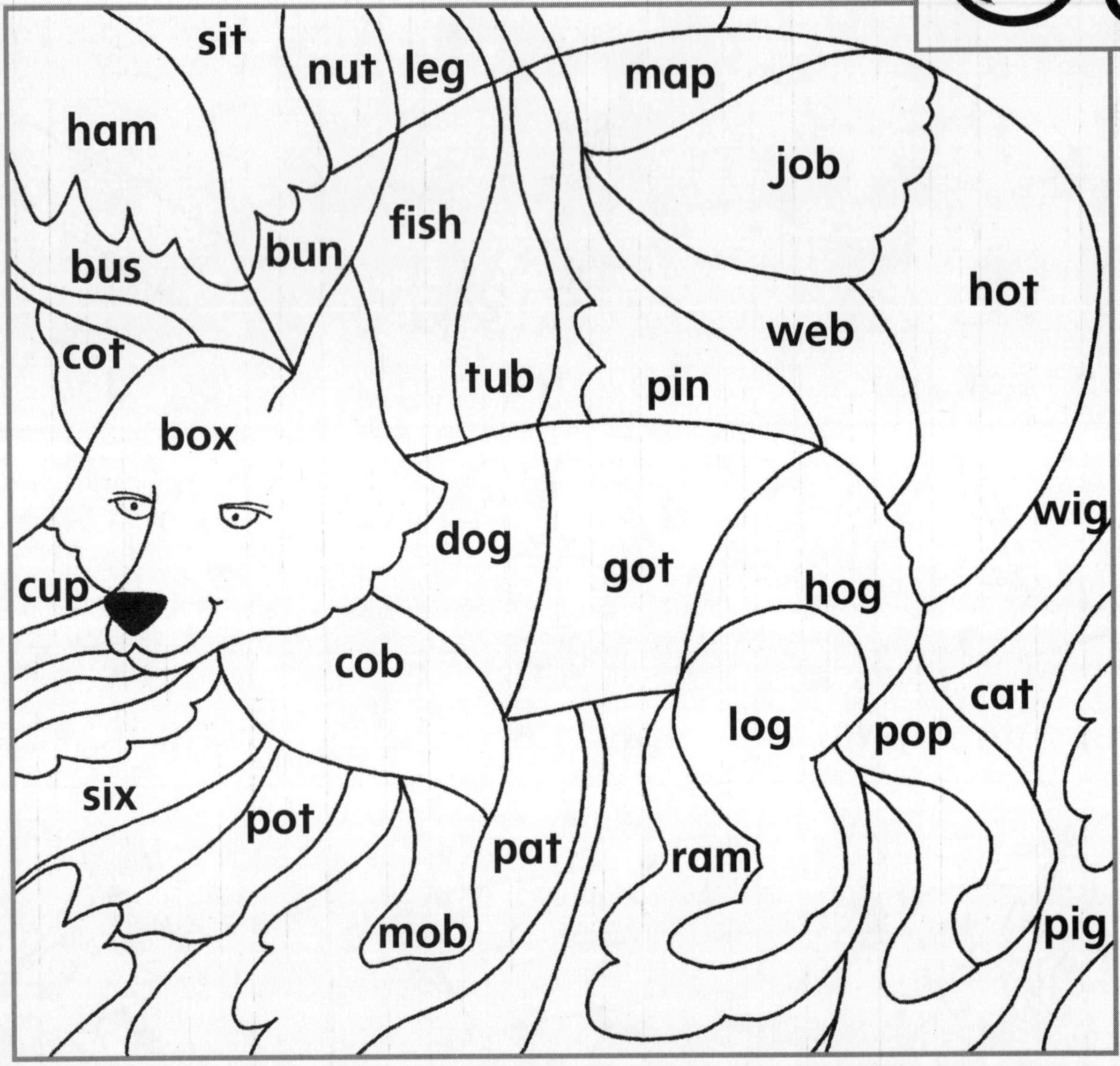

Oo

sit nut leg map
ham job
fish
bun
bus hot
web
cot tub pin
box
wig
dog
got
cup hog
cob
cat
log pop
six
pot
pat ram
mob pig

Use some of the short o words in the puzzle to write a sentence.

Help your child make up a story using some of the short o words on the page.

Name ______________________________

Blend the letter sounds together as you say each word. **Color** the picture it names.

1\. l o g

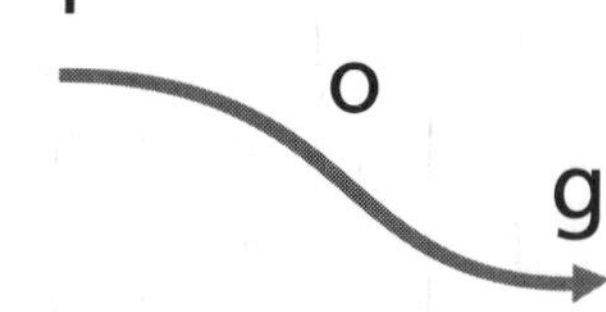

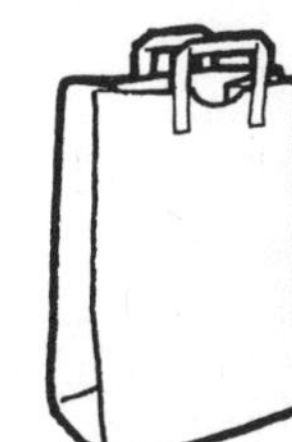

2\. b a t

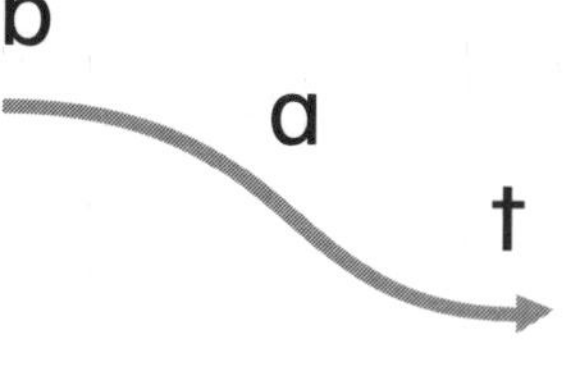

3\. c u b

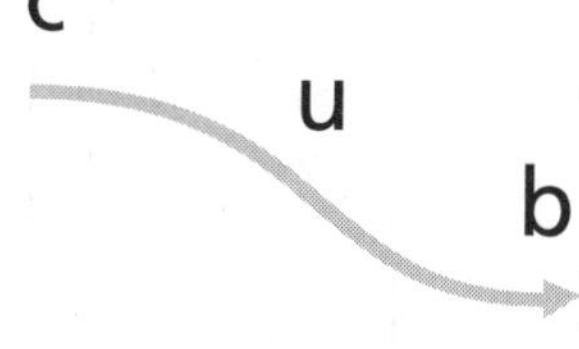

4\. f o x

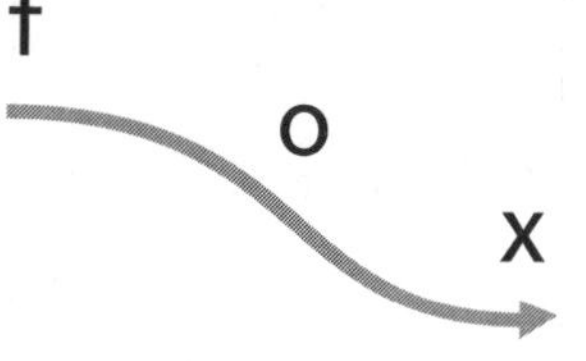

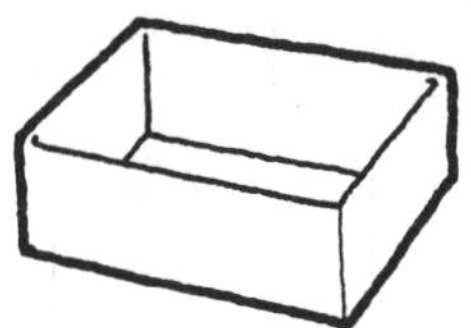

5\. p i n

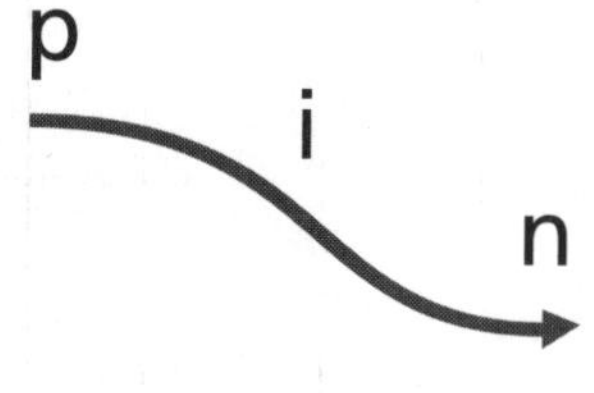

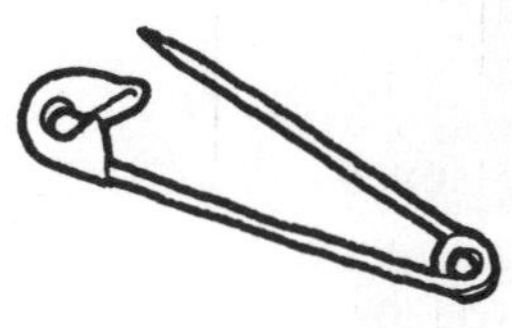

6\. r u g

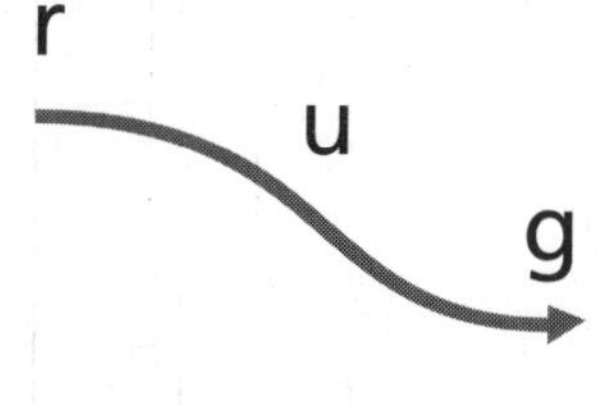

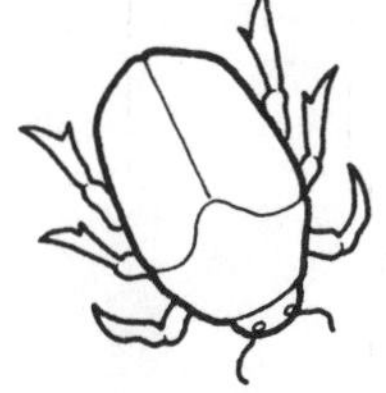

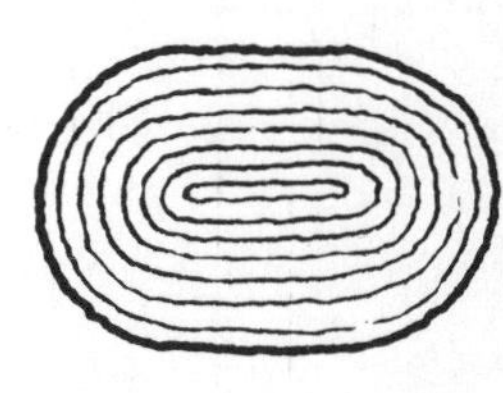

Blend the letter sounds together as you say each word. **Print** the word on the line. **Draw** a line to the picture it names.

1. b ox

2. s ix

3. c up

4. m an

5. d og

6. b us

Name the beginning letter of a word. Ask your child to say a word that starts with that letter.

Name ______________________________

Say the name of each picture. Print the letters for its beginning and ending sounds. Trace the word. In the last box, draw a picture of a short o word. Print the word.

1. mop
2. _o_
3. _o_
4. _o_
5. _o_
6. _o_
7. _o_
8. _oc_
9. _o_
10. _o_
11. _ro_
12. ______

Look at the picture. Circle the word that will finish the sentence. Print it on the line.

1. Bob is ______. hot / got / hop

2. He sits on top of a ______. rock / rack / lock

3. He takes off his ______. sacks / socks / locks

4. The grass is ______. sack / lift / soft

5. He sees a frog in the ______. pond / pot / pod

6. The frog hops on a ______. lock / lost / log

What do you think Bob might do next?

With your child, think of silly sentences using the short *o* words, such as *The frog took off its socks.*

Name ____________________

Say the name of each picture. Print the picture name on the line. In the last box, draw a picture of a short o word. Print the word.

1. 	2. 	3. 
4. 	5. 	6. 
7. 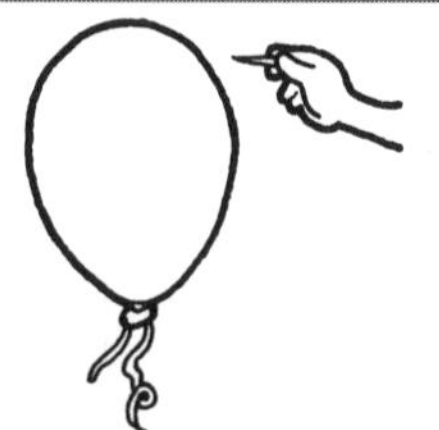	8. 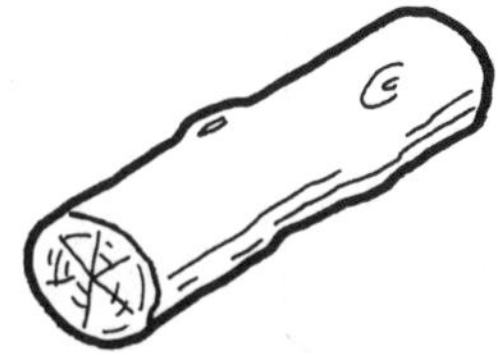	9. 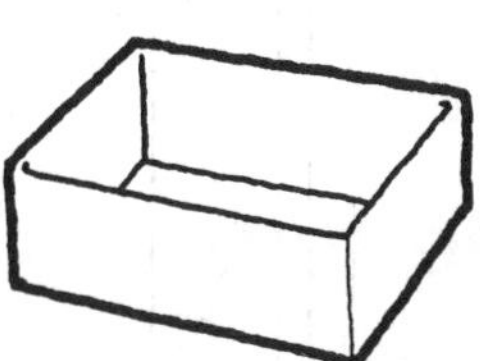
10. 	11. 	12.

Circle the word that will finish the sentence. Print it on the line.

1. Jill likes to ______________. — job / jog / jug

2. She puts on shoes and ______________. — sand / soft / socks

3. She jogs with her ______________. — dot / dock / dog

4. She runs to the ______________ of the hill. — top / tap / mop

5. It gets very ______________. — hog / hit / hot

6. She ______________ to rest. — sips / stops / steps

What sports do you like? Why?

Help your child think of sentences using words from this page to continue the story.

Name ________________________________

Read the story. Print short o words to finish the sentences.

Foxes

Foxes live in many places.
Some foxes live where it is hot.
Some live where it is cold.
Foxes are like dogs.
They have soft fur.
A baby fox is called a cub or a pup.

1. ________________ live in many places.

2. Some foxes live where it is ________________.

3. Foxes are like ________________.

How is a fox like a dog?

Use one of the letters to make a word with **ot** or **og**. Write each real word on a line.

l d v p n

ot

1. ______
2. ______
3. ______
4. ______

l m d h f

og

5. ______
6. ______
7. ______
8. ______

Write a sentence using one of the words you made.

Help your child think of words that end in *on, od, ox,* and *ob.*

Then, the dog and the pup got out and ran!

4

FOLD

Name ____________________

In the Tub

A dog and a pup had a bath in a tub.

1

Six hot bugs said, "Can we hop in the tub?"
The dog said, "You can."

2

FOLD

Six big pigs said, "Can we jump in the tub?"
The dog said, "You can."

3

Name ____________________

Read the words in the box. Write a word to finish each sentence.

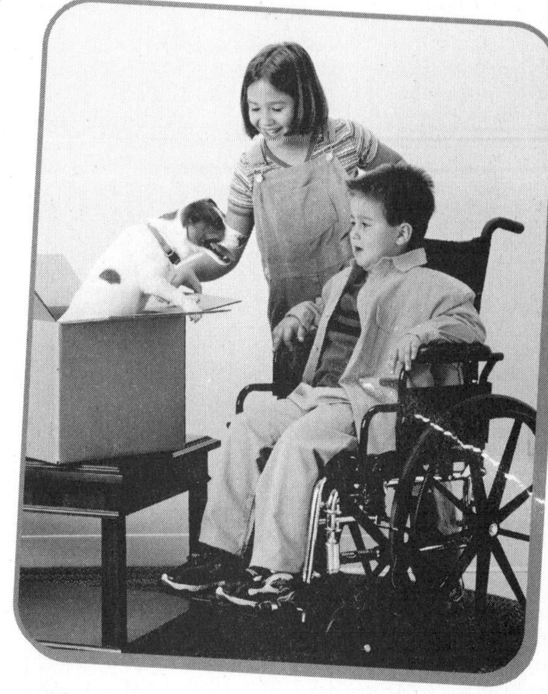

of	her
Our	have
one	come

1. ________ family has a pet.

2. We ________ a dog.

3. Molly is ________ name.

4. We could not find Molly ________ day.

5. I said, "Molly, ________ here!"

6. Molly jumped out ________ a box!

Unscramble the letters to write a word from the box. The word shapes will help you print the words.

have	one	of
our	come	her

1. fo
2. erh
3. uro
4. evha
5. neo
6. moce

CHECKING UP

Put a ✓ next to each word you can read.

☐ one ☐ come ☐ have ☐ of ☐ our ☐ her

HOME

Use some of the words on this page to make up sentences with your child.

Name ___________________________________

"Red Hen, Red Hen,"
Jen said to her hen.
"Red Hen, Red Hen,
Get back to your pen!"

Hen has the short sound of e. Circle each picture whose name has the short sound of e.

1.	2.	3.	4.
5.	6.	7.	8.
9.	10.	11.	12.

Say the names of the pictures in each row.
Color the pictures whose names rhyme.

1.

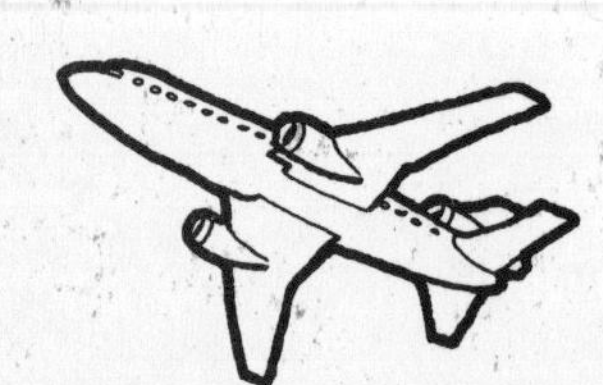  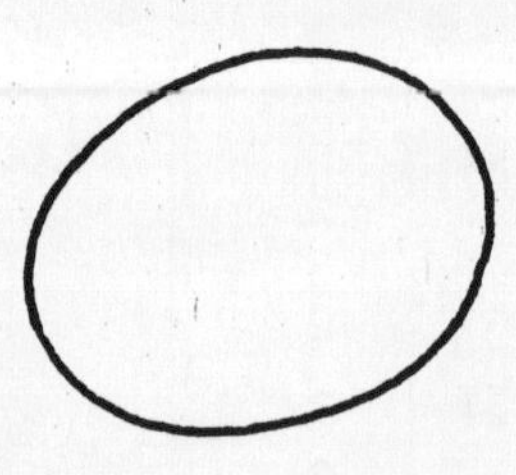 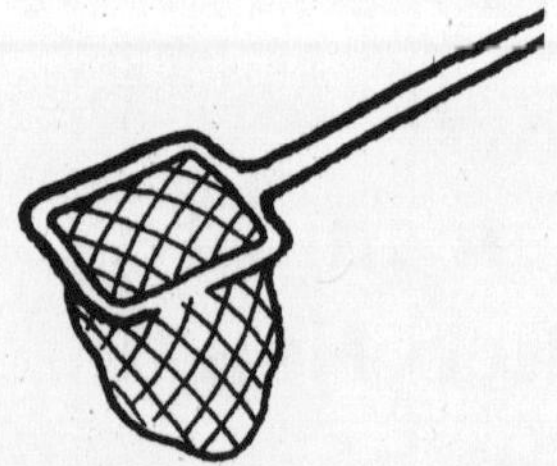

2.

  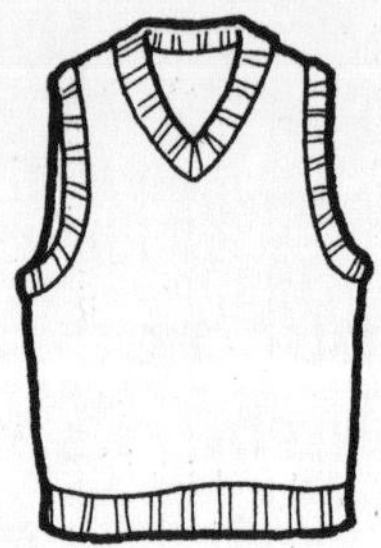 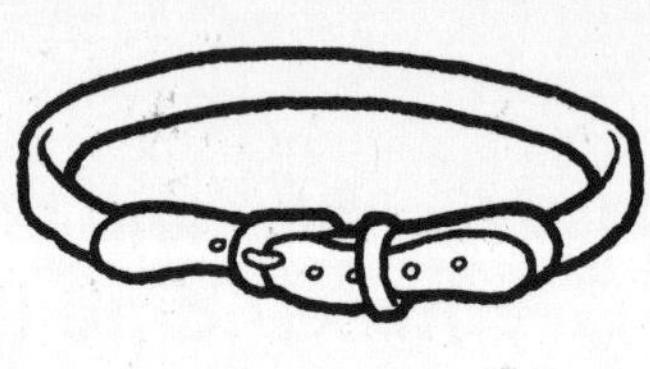

3.

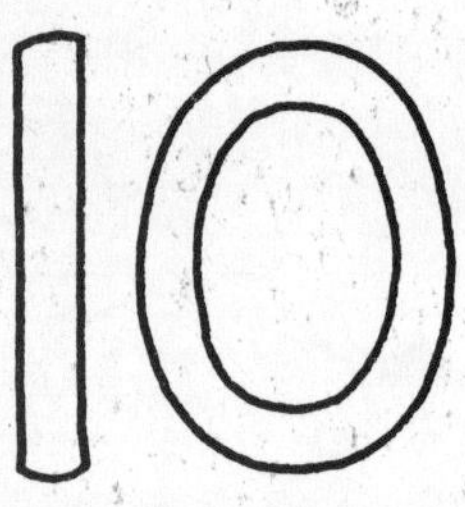  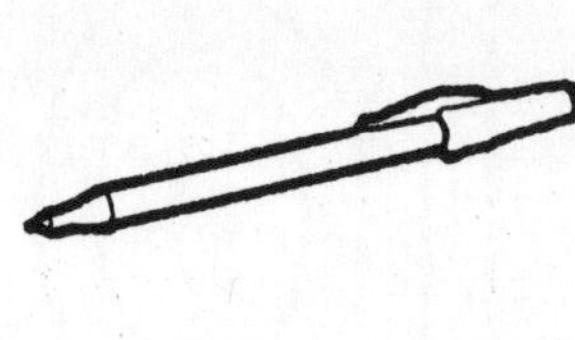 

4.

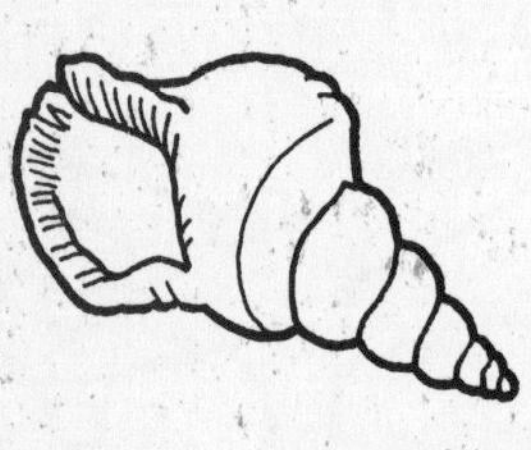   

5.

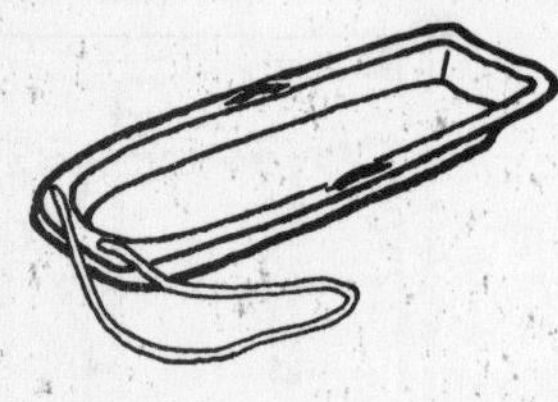  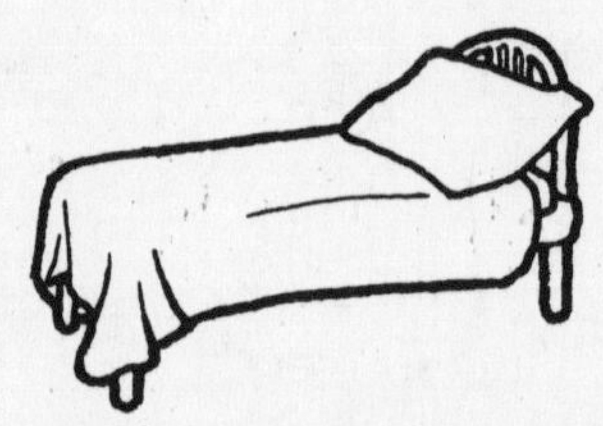 

Name a picture. Ask your child to think of words that rhyme.

Name ______________________________

Say the name of each picture. Circle its name.

1. bed fed led	2. bill sell bell	3. tan ten tin
4.  met net nut	5.  west well web	6. 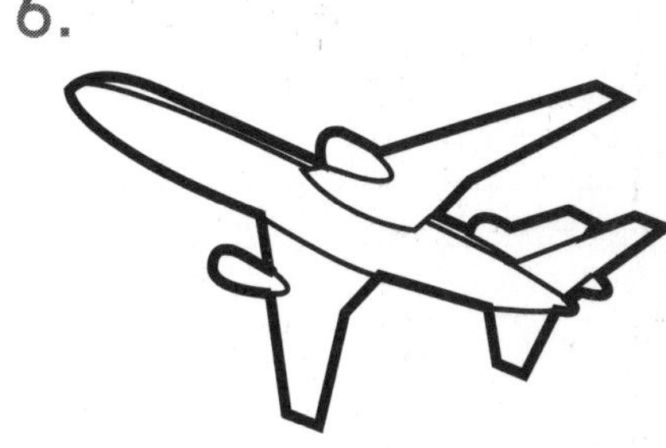 jet pet wet
7.  went man men	8. 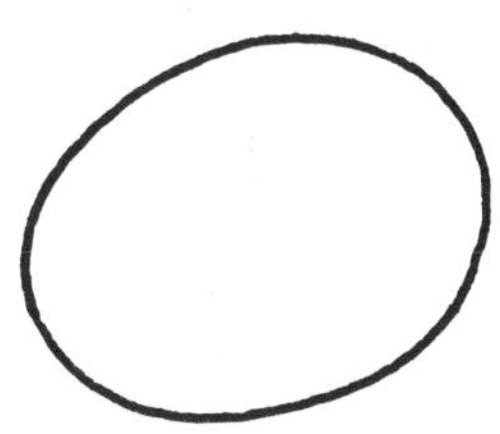 leg egg beg	9. ten tent bent
10. 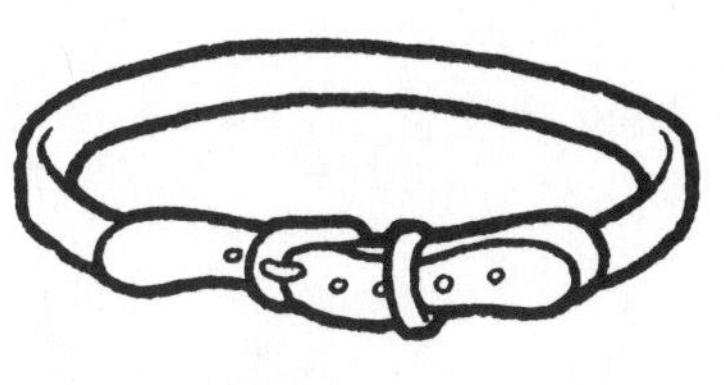 belt bell melt	11.  pin pet pen	12.  nest not just

Four red hens are missing from their pen. Draw a hen in each box. Follow the directions below.

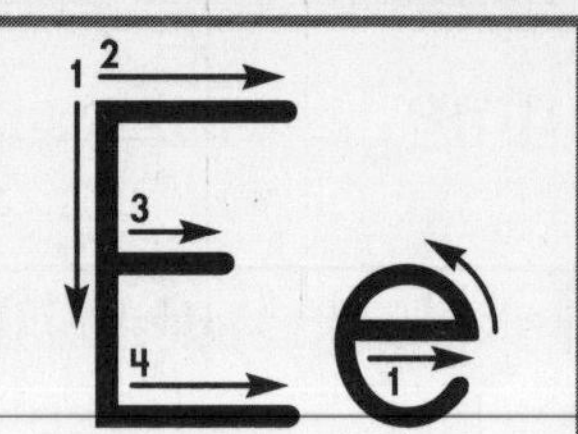

1. Draw a hen in a bed.

2. Draw a hen in a tent.

3. Draw a hen on a sled.

4. Draw a hen in a nest.

hen	bed	tent	sled	nest

Use some of the words from the box to write a sentence.

HOME

Make up riddles using some of the words from the box. Ask your child to guess each word.

Name ____________________________________

Blend the letter sounds together as you say each word. Fill in the bubble under the picture it names.

1. 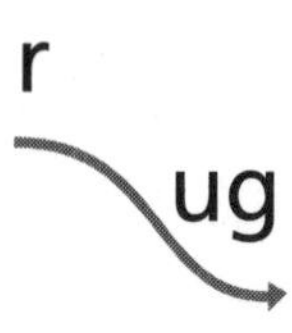

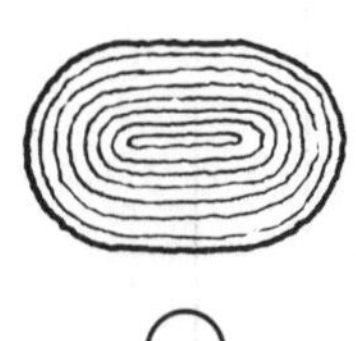 ○  ○  ○

2. 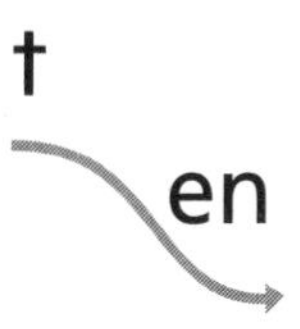

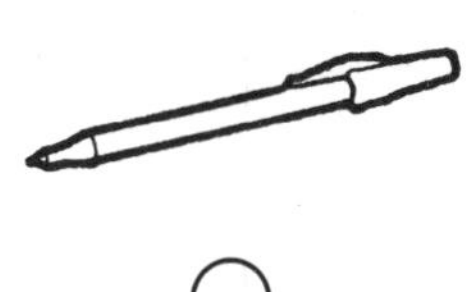 ○  ○ 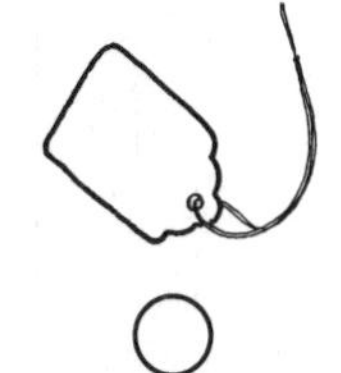 ○

3. 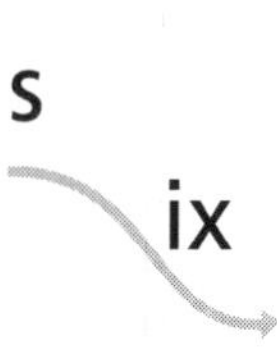

 ○  ○  ○

4. 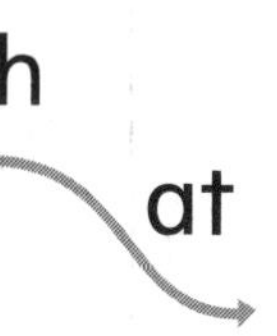

 ○ 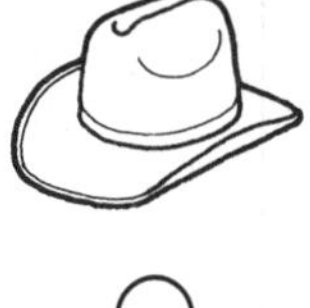 ○  ○

5. 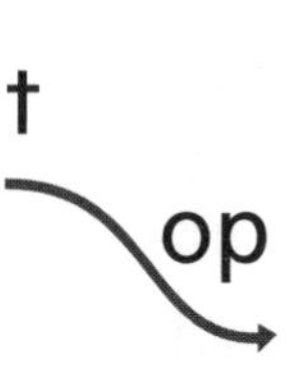

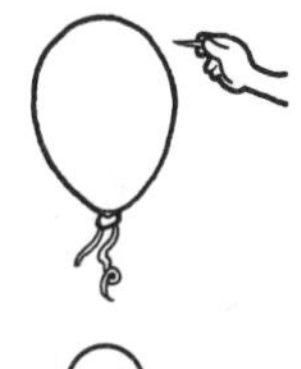 ○  ○ 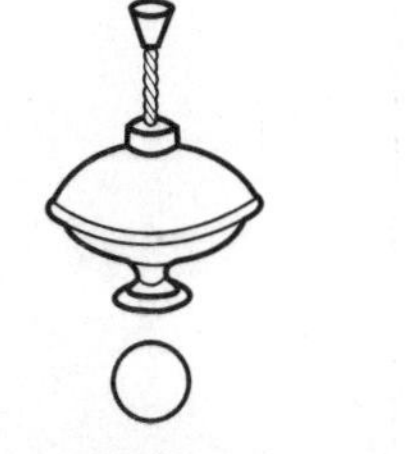 ○

6. 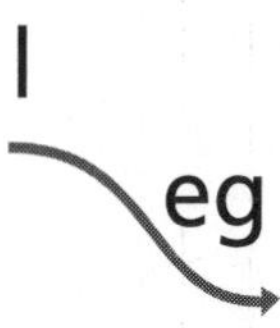

 ○ 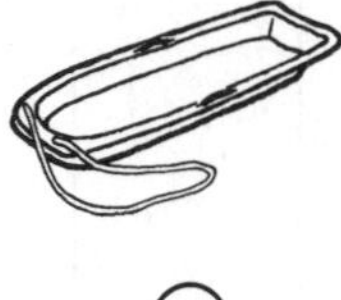 ○ 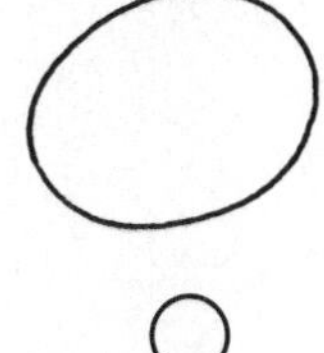 ○

Blend the sounds together as you say each word. Print the word on the line. Draw a line to the picture it names.

1. n et

2. m op

3. s un

4. w ig

5. c at

6. p en

Name a vowel. Ask your child to read a word that has that vowel.

Name ____________________________

Say the name of each picture. Print the letter for its beginning and ending sounds. In the last box, draw a picture of a short e word.

1. net
2. e
3. e
4. e
5.  e
6. 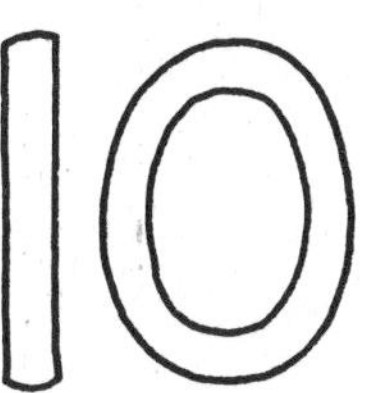 e
7.  e
8.  e
9. 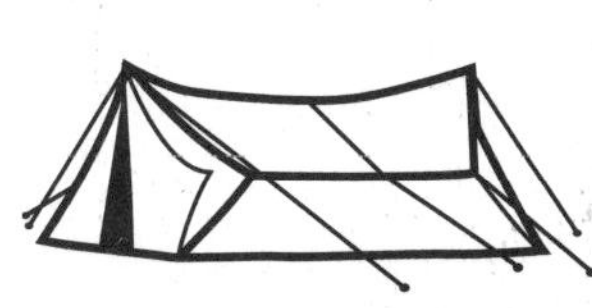 en
10. 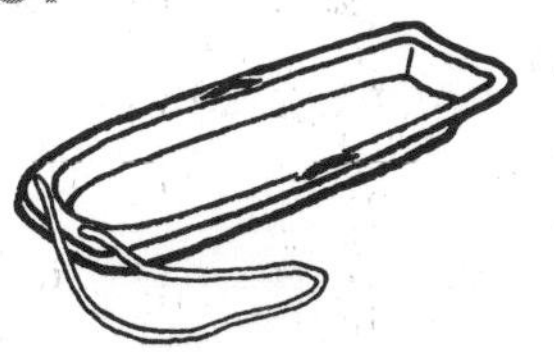 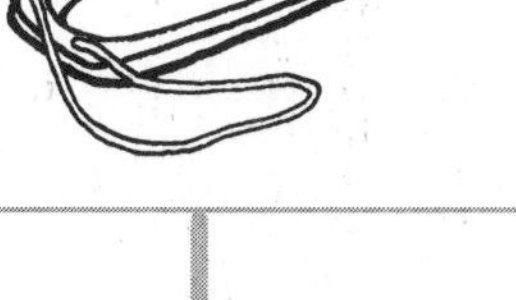 le
11.  es
12. 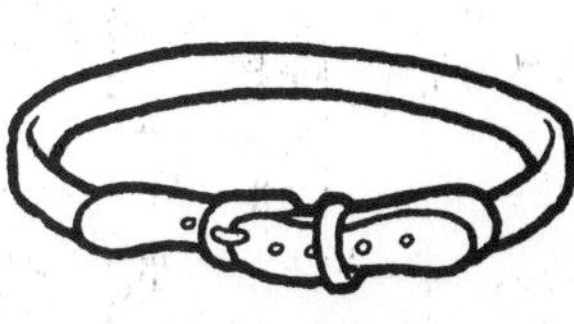  el
13.  es
14.  e
15.  es
16. e

Look at the picture. Circle the word that will finish the sentence. Print it on the line.

1. Meg sits at her ______________. mask / desk / duck

2. She picks up her ______________. pen / pet / pig

3. Meg draws a ______________. best / nest / net

4. Then she draws a big ______________. leg / egg / beg

5. On the nest sits a ______________. hen / ten / pen

6. Meg hangs it by her ______________. belt / bell / bed

What kinds of things do you like to draw?

Point to the picture of the pen and ask your child to name as many words that rhyme with *pen* as possible.

Name ___________________________________

Say the name of each picture. Print the picture name on the line. In the last box, draw a picture of a short e word. Print the word.

1.

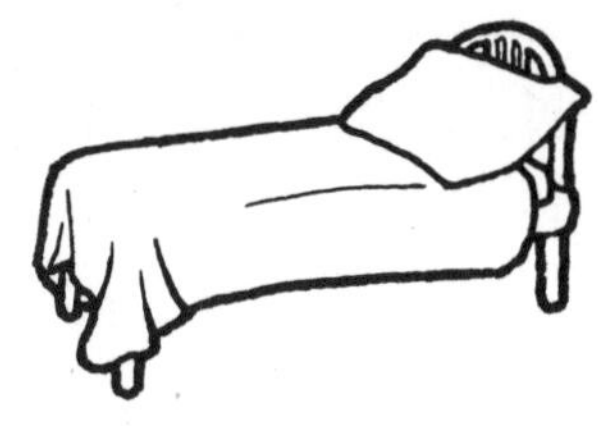

2.

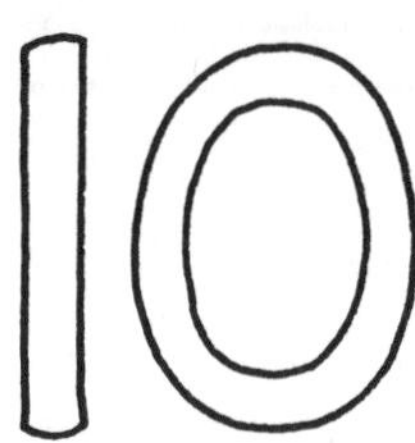

3.

4.

5.

6.

7.

8.

9.

10.

11.

12.

Circle the word that will finish the sentence. Print it on the line.

1. Ted did not have a ______________. sell / sled / sent

2. Ben ______________ Ted use his sled. let / leg / lost

3. It ______________ down the hill fast. went / wet / west

4. Peg let Ted use her sled ______________. exit / nest / next

5. Her sled was as fast as a ______________! just / jet / get

6. Ted liked Peg's sled the ______________. bell / best / bent

Which sled would you like to use? Why?

With your child, think of sentences to continue the story using some of the words on the page.

Name ______________________________

Say the name of each picture. Circle the vowel you hear in its name. Print the word.

bag
bus
lid
map
pig
jet
cup
sock

1. 

a e i o u

____

2. 

a e i o u

____

3. 

a e i o u

____

4. 

a e i o u

____

5. 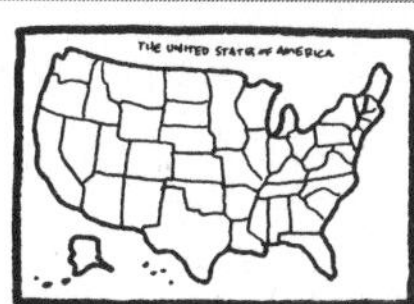

a e i o u

____

6. 

a e i o u

____

7. 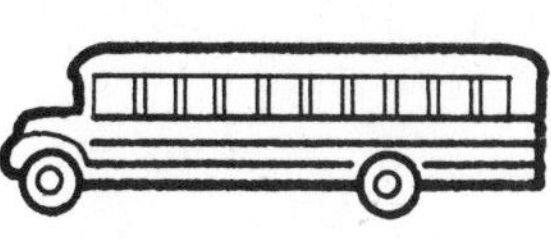

a e i o u

____

8. 

a e i o u

____

Write a postcard to tell a friend about a trip. Some of the words in the box may help you.

cat	map	bed	top	bus
dog	six	jet	did	sun

TO:

My Friend
1 Happy Lane
Yourtown,
USA
12345

Ask your child to use as many of the words in the box as possible in a sentence.

Some fish must hide to get away.
Can you spot a fish here?

4

FOLD

Name ____________________

Fish Food

What do fish like to eat best?

1

This fish likes to eat lots of bugs.

2

FOLD

This fish can fish for small fish.

3

Name ________________________________

Say the name of each picture.
Print the picture name on the line.

1. 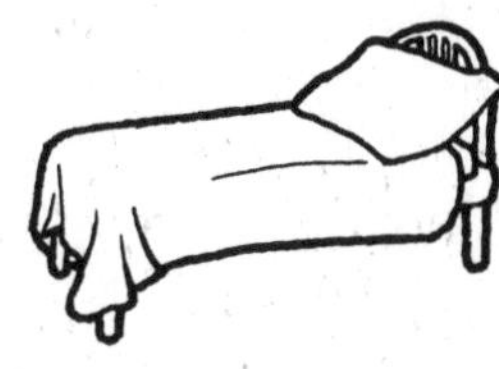 bed

2. 

3. 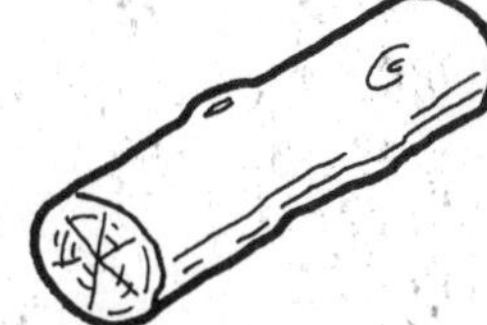

4. 

5. 

6. 

7. 

8. 

9. 

10. 

11. 

12. 

Fill in the bubble beside the sentence that tells about the picture.

1. ○ One pen is in a box.
   ○ One pin is in a bag.

2. ○ The gift is here in the bag.
   ○ The quilt is here on the bed.

3. ○ The man set up the tent.
   ○ The men are on the bus.

4. ○ Miss Beck runs with the dog.
   ○ Jeff hugs the cat on the bed.

Can you read each word? Put a ✓ in the box if you can.

☐ I	☐ are	☐ of	☐ here	☐ like	☐ one
☐ for	☐ my	☐ her	☐ with	☐ down	☐ come
☐ the	☐ you	☐ our	☐ said	☐ have	☐ do

Play

by Frank Asch

Come play with me said the sun,
Come play with me said the earth,
Come play with me said the sky.
What shall we play said I?

Let's fly a kite said the sun,
Stand on me said the earth,
I'll bring the wind said the sky,
I'll hold the string said I.

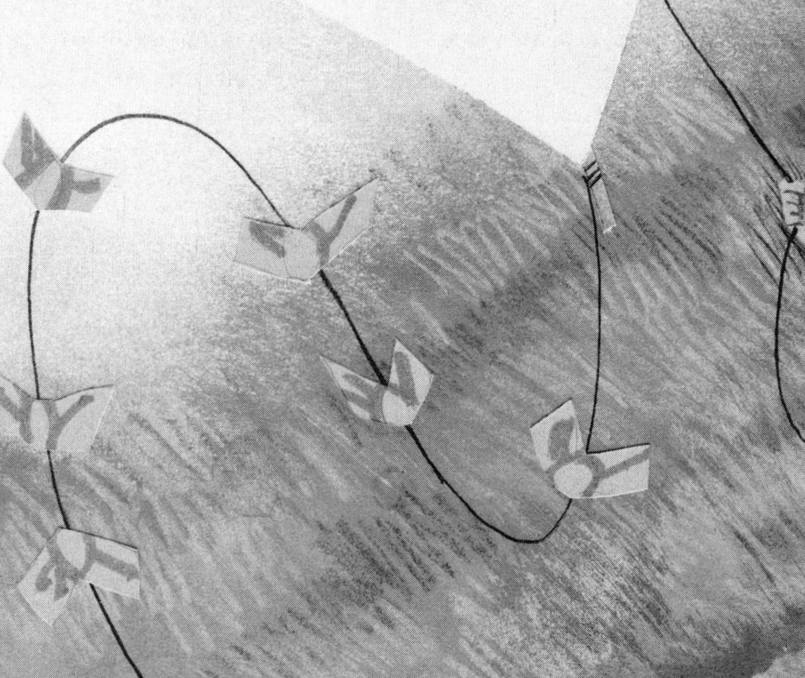

TALK About It: What are other fun ways to play outdoors?

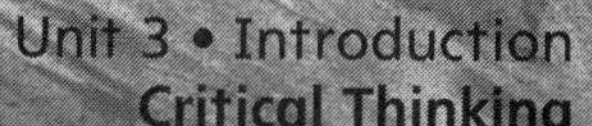

Dear Family,

In this unit called "Let's Play," your child will learn about the sounds of long vowels. Many words related to play contain long vowels, such as skate, feet, bike, boat, and flute. As your child becomes more familiar with vowel sounds, you might try these activities together.

- Look through old magazines and catalogs to find and cut out pictures of toys, games, musical instruments, sports events, or sports equipment whose names have long vowel sounds. Ask your child to group the pictures according to the long vowel sounds.

- Read the poem on page 145 with your child and help him or her to identify the words with long vowel sounds.
- Your child might enjoy reading these books with you. Look for them in your local library.

Ten Minutes Till Bedtime
by Peggy Rathmann

Lentil by Robert McCloskey

Sincerely,

Estimada familia:

En esta unidad, titulada "Juguemos" ("Let's Play"), su hijo/a estudiará los sonidos de las vocales largas en inglés. Muchas palabras relacionadas con actividades de entretenimiento contienen vocales con sonidos largos, como por ejemplo, skate (patín), feet (pies), bike (bicicleta), boat (bote), y flute (flauta). A medida que su hijo/a se vaya familiarizando con los sonidos de las vocales, pueden hacer las siguientes actividades juntos.

- Busquen y recorten en revistas y catálogos viejos ilustraciones de juguetes, juegos, instrumentos musicales, eventos o equipos deportivos cuyos nombres contengan vocales con sonidos largos. Pidan a su hijo/a que agrupe las ilustraciones de acuerdo a los sonidos largos de las vocales.
- Lean el poema en la página 145 con su hijo/a y ayúdenle a identificar las palabras que contengan vocales con sonidos largos.
- Ustedes y su hijo/a disfrutarán leyendo estos libros juntos. Búsquenlos en su biblioteca local.

Ten Minutes Till Bedtime
de Peggy Rathmann

Lentil de Robert McCloskey

Sinceramente,

Name ____________________________

James wants to bake
a big birthday cake.
He plans to make
the cake for Jake.

Bake has the long sound of a. Circle each picture whose name has the long sound of a.

1. 	2. 	3. 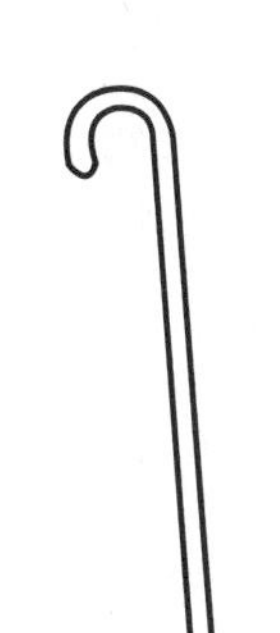	4. 
5. 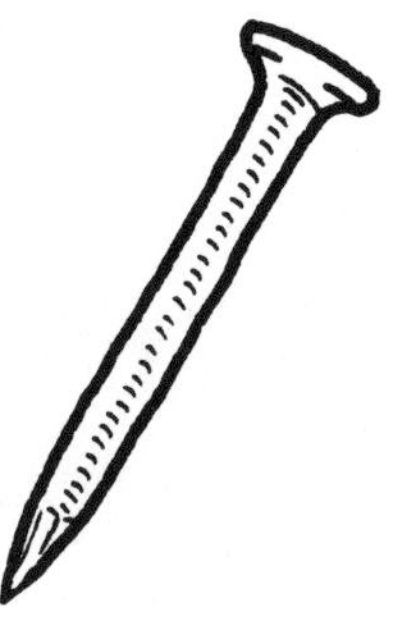	6. 	7. 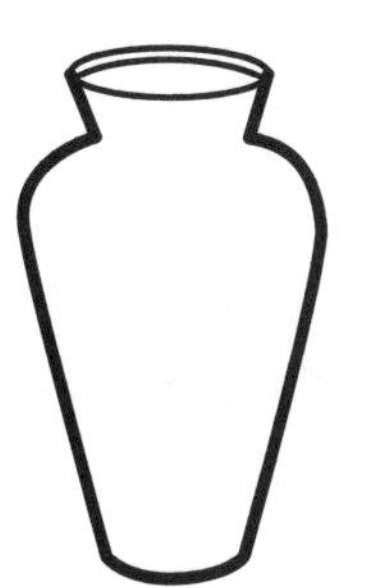	8. 
9. 	10. 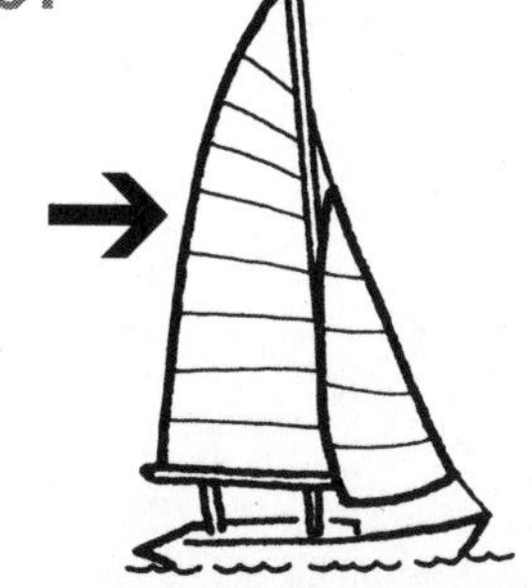	11. 	12. 

Say the names of the pictures in each row.
Color the pictures whose names rhyme.

1.

  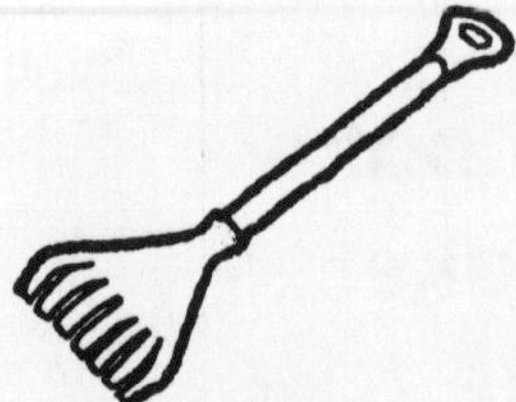 

2.

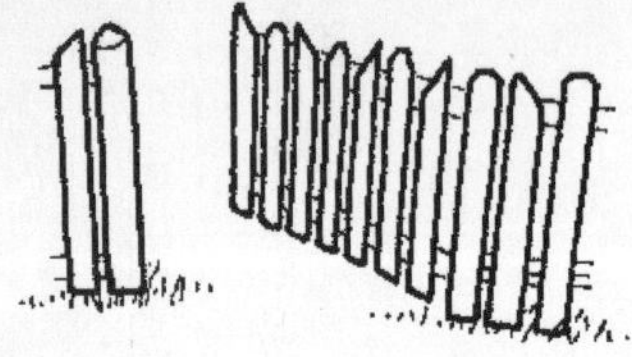   

3.

 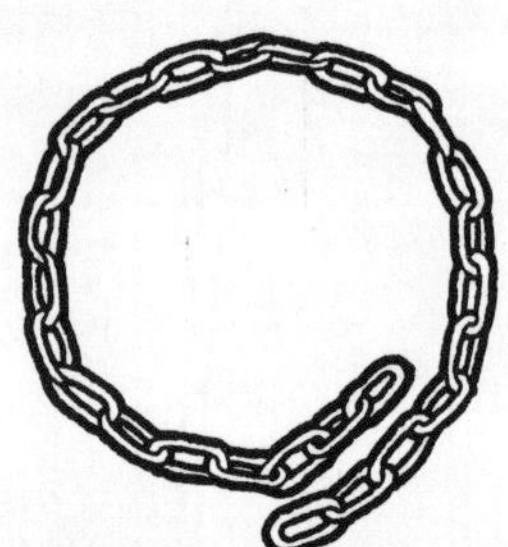  

4.

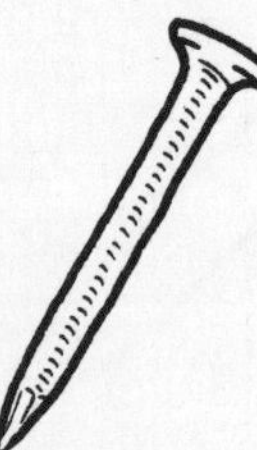   

5.

  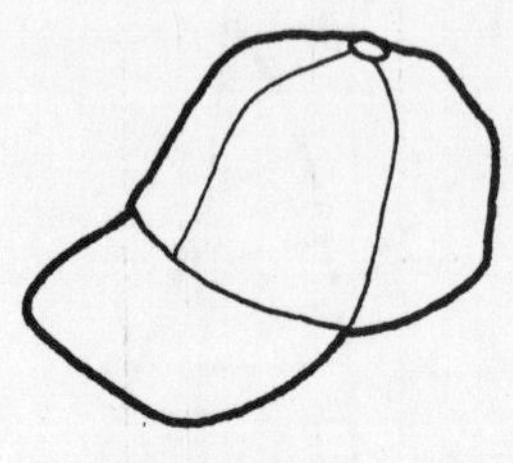 

With your child, make up short rhymes using the rhyming words in each row.

Name ____________________________

Say the name of each picture. Circle its name.

1.  tape tail late	2.  late lake rake	3. 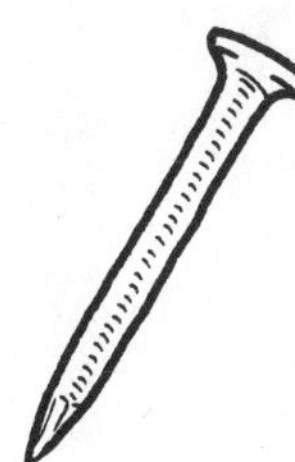 nail rail name
4.  case cap cape	5. 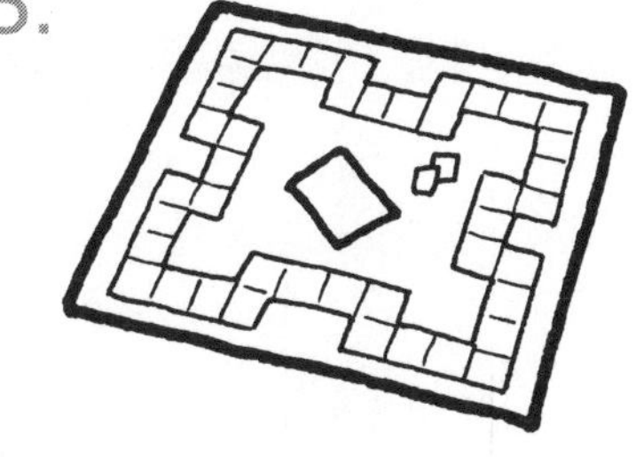 gave game name	6.  pill pail sail
7. 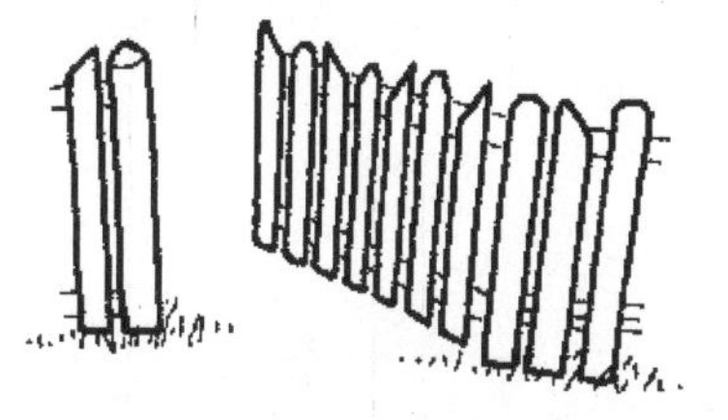 gate game date	8.  pain ran rain	9.  van save vase
10.  may hay way	11.  pail rain Gail	12.  play pay hay

Help Jay get to the game. Read each word. Draw a line to join the long a words.

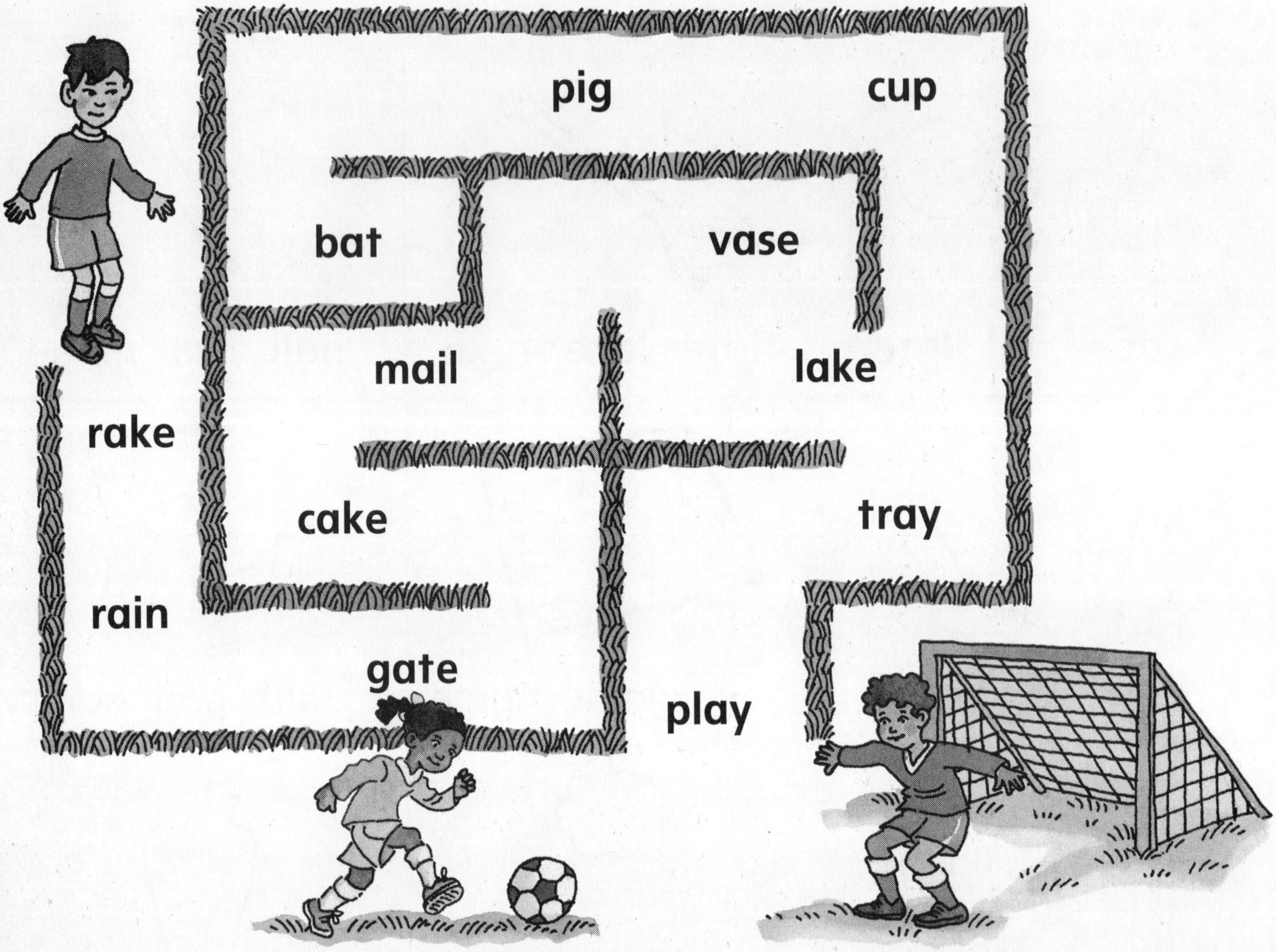

pig
cup
bat
vase
mail
lake
rake
cake
tray
rain
gate
play

Use some of the long a words to write a sentence.

With your child, make up a story using some of the words along the path that leads to the soccer game.

Name ____________________

Say the name of each picture. If the vowel sound is short, color the box with the word **short**. If the vowel sound is long, color the box with the word **long**.

1. 

short long

2. 

short long

3. 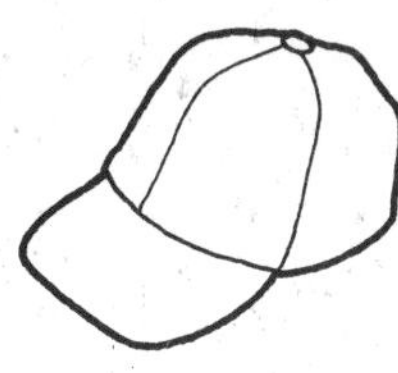

short long

4. 

short long

5. 

short long

6. 

short long

7. 

short long

8. 

short long

9. 

short long

10. 

short long

11. 

short long

12. 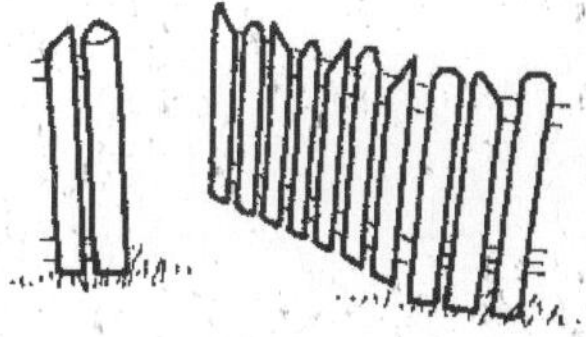

short long

Help Dave, Gail, and Ray find the long a words. Circle each one you find.

1.	at	ate	rake	rack	page
Dave	made	safe	tap	tape	mad
2.	rain	ram	wait	cat	pail
Gail	sat	sail	main	man	pal
3.	May	man	pay	pat	play
Ray	day	hat	say	way	sand

HOME With your child, think of sentences using words that rhyme with *Dave, Gail,* and *Ray,* such as *Ray wants to play today.*

Name ___________________________________

Say the name of each picture. Circle its name.

1.	2.	3.
 rat rate	 pain pan	 tap tape
4.  can cane	5.  can cane	6.  hate hat
7. 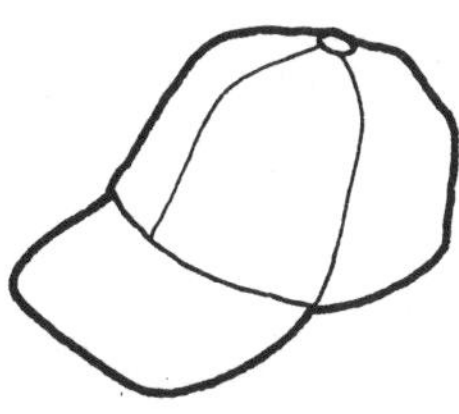 cape cap	8.  cape cap	9.  ran rain
10.  bat bait	11.  hay hat	12.  take tack

Color each balloon that has three rhyming long a words.

1. game tame name
2. take tape ape
3. cane lane mane
4. sail same rail
5. cake rake lake
6. gate date late
7. fade made make
8. cave wave cake
9. bake fake fame
10. nail mail pail
11. rain gain pain
12. hay day pay

Pick a balloon with three rhyming words. Ask your child to name another word that rhymes.

Name ______________________________

Say the name of each picture. Print the missing vowels on the line. In the last box, draw a picture of a long a word. Print the word.

1. 
cape

2. 
c n

3. 
r n

4. 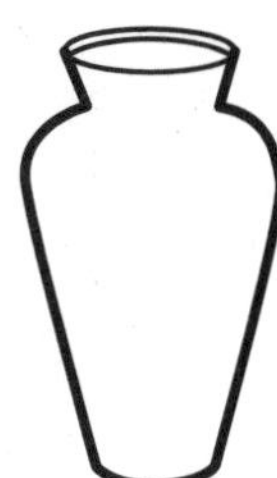
v s

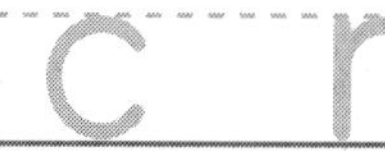

5. 
c k

6. 
l k

7. 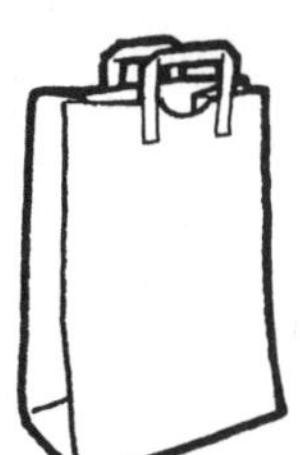
b g

8. 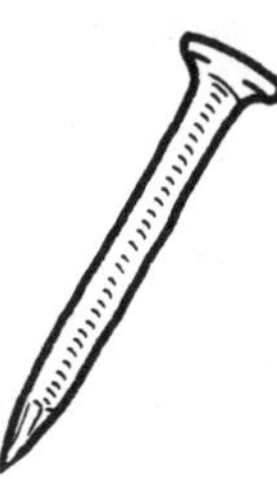
n l

9. 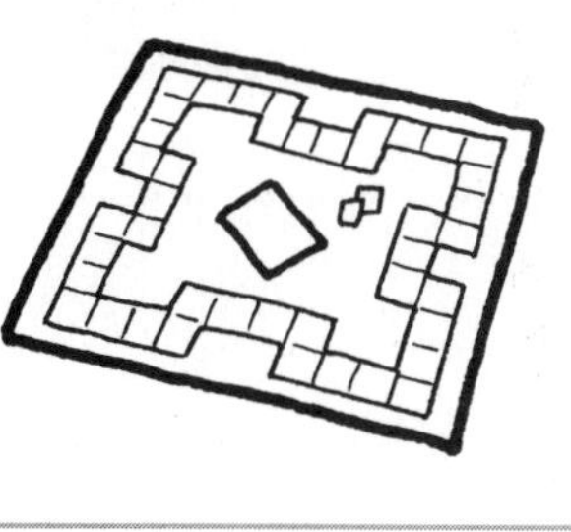
g m

10. 
p l

11. 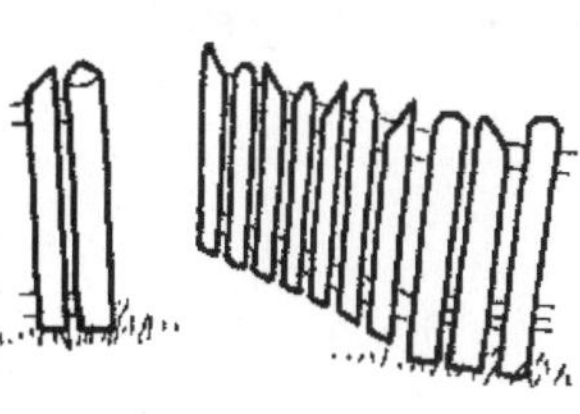
g t

12.

Look at the picture. Circle the word that will finish each sentence. Print it on the line.

1. ______ and Ray go out to play. — Save / Dave / Sand

2. They go to the ______. — lake / make / late

3. They play a ______. — gate / name / game

4. Ray sits by a ______. — save / came / cave

5. Dave sees a boat with a ______. — save / sail / mail

6. They go in when it ______. — rains / cane / ran

What are some things you might do at a lake?

Ask your child to use the words circled on this page in sentences.

Name ____________________

Say the name of each picture. Print the picture name on the line. In the last box, draw a picture of a long a word. Print the word.

1. 

2. 

3. 

4. 

5. 

6. 

7. 

8. 

9. 

10. 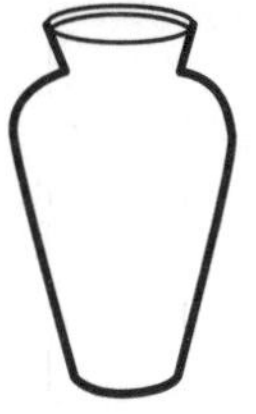

11. 

12.

Circle the word that will finish the sentence. Print it on the line.

1. The bus was __________. lane late lake

2. Mom had to __________. wait wade wake

3. Then, she ran home in the __________. rate rake rain

4. Mom came in by the __________. gain gate game

5. She __________ me a big hug. gave gain gate

6. I gave her the __________. made mail make

Do you think Mom was glad to be home? Why?

With your child, continue the story using some of the words printed on this page.

Name ______________________________

Read the story. Use long a words to finish the sentences.

Hooray For Ray!

It was the day of the big game.
Ray was at bat.
The ball came at him.
Ray gave the ball a big whack!
Ray raced around the bases.
He came to home plate.
"Safe!"
"Hooray for Ray!"

1. It was the day of the big ______________.

2. Ray raced around the ______________.

3. He was ______________ at home ______________.

How do you think Ray felt as he raced around the bases? Why?

Use one of the letters to make a word with **ay** or **ail**. Write each real word on the lines.

d s p h v

ay

1. ______

2. ______

3. ______

4. ______

p m s y n

ail

5. ______

6. ______

7. ______

8. ______

Write a sentence using one of the words you made.

______

______

HOME

Help your child think of other long vowel *a* words, such as *race* and *grape*.

Now you can play!

4

FOLD

Name ______________________

Make a Face

It is fun to make a clown face.

1

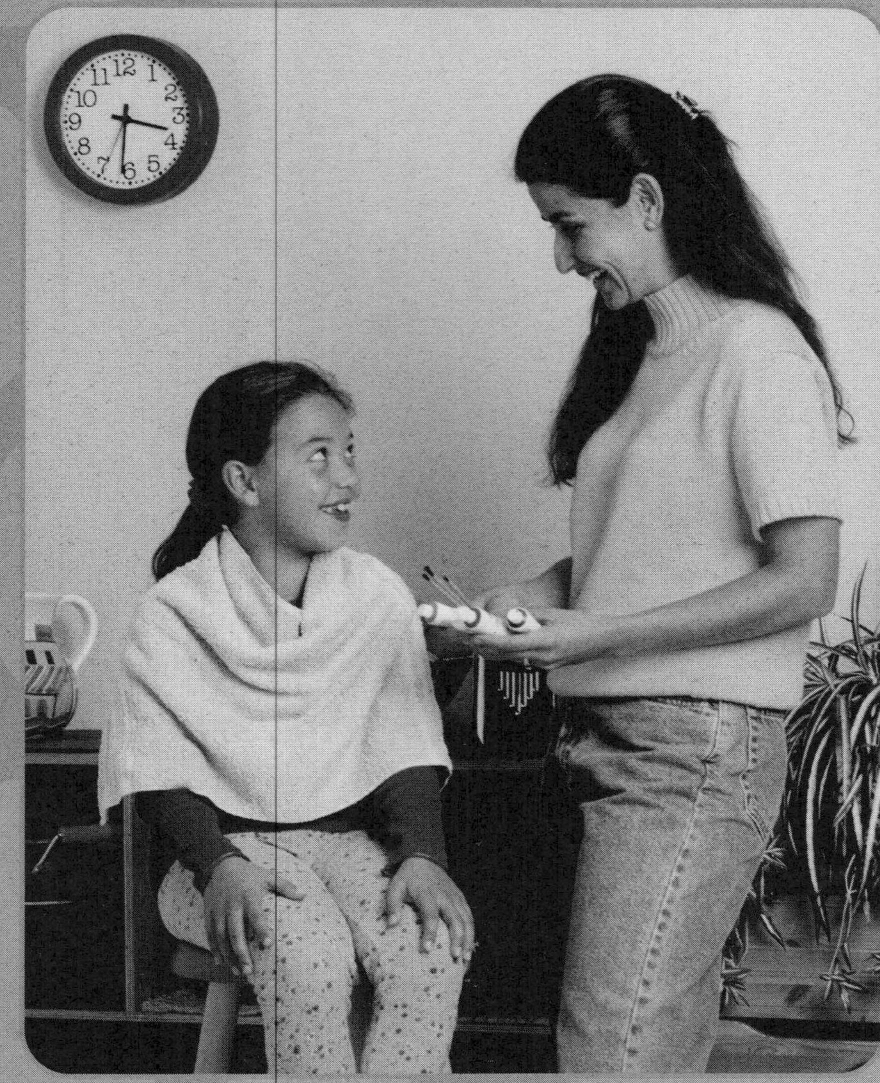

You will need some face paint.

2

FOLD

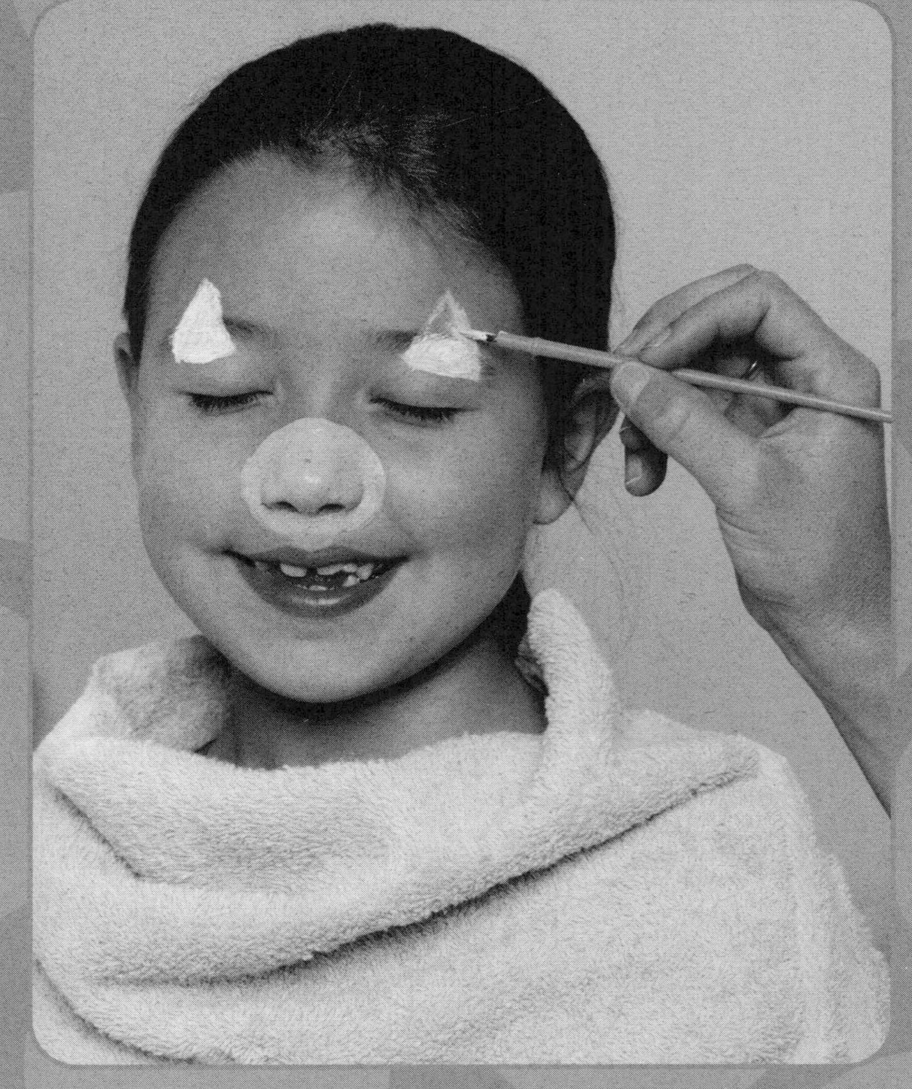

Start by making shapes.

3

Name ______________________________

Read the words in the box. Write a word to finish each sentence.

They	Where
out	two
were	your

1. Kate and Jay ______________ at the beach.

2. Dad took them ______________ to play in the waves.

3. "I see ______________ fish," said Kate.

4. " ______________ are the fish?" Jay said.

5. Dad said, "They are by ______________ feet."

6. ______________ jumped in the waves all day.

Look at the picture. Then, print words from the box to finish the story. The word shapes will help you.

They	were	two
out	Where	your

1. ☐☐☐☐☐ did the cat and dog go to play?

2. ☐☐☐☐ went to the beach.

3. Soon the ☐☐☐ friends ☐☐☐☐ hot.

4. The dog went to swim ☐☐☐ in the waves.

5. "Do not shake ☐☐☐☐ waves on me!" said the cat.

CHECKING UP

Put a ✓ next to each word you can read.

☐ they ☐ were ☐ where ☐ out ☐ two ☐ your

HOME

Help your child retell the story, using some of the new words.

Name ________________________________

I ride my bike.
I fly a kite.
I take a hike.
Then, I say good night!

Ride has the long sound of i. Circle each picture whose name has the long sound of i.

1. 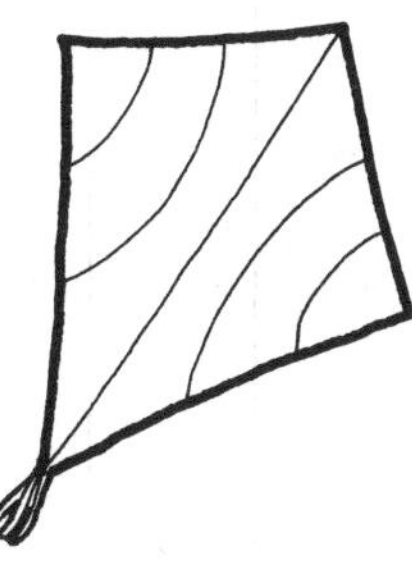

2. 

3. 

4. 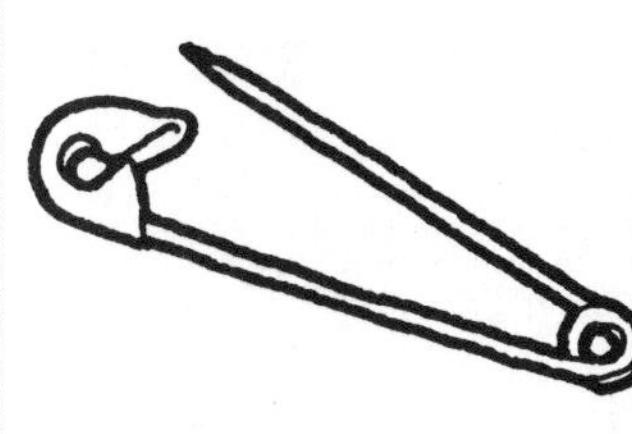

5. 

6. 

7. 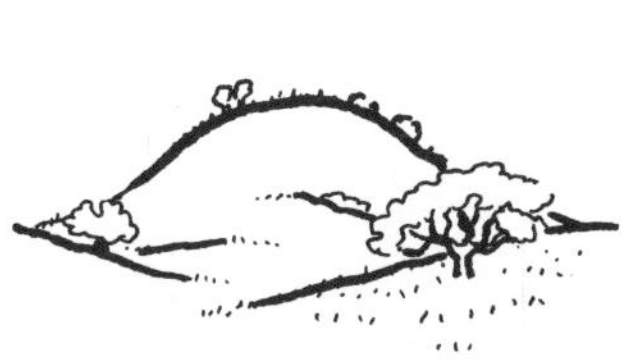

8. 

9. 

10. 

11. 

12.

Say the names of the pictures in each row.
Color the pictures whose names rhyme.

1.

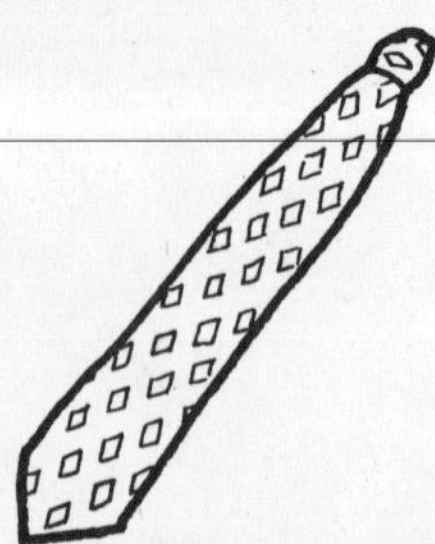

2.

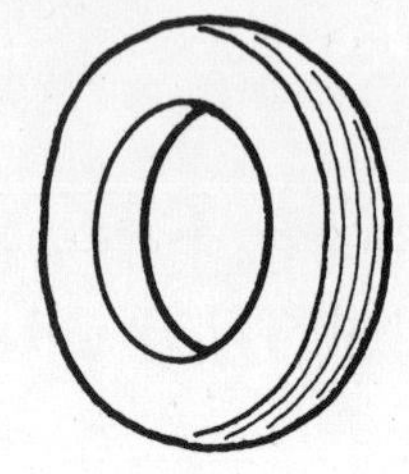

3.

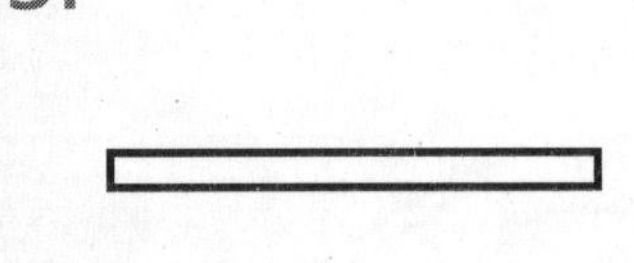

4.

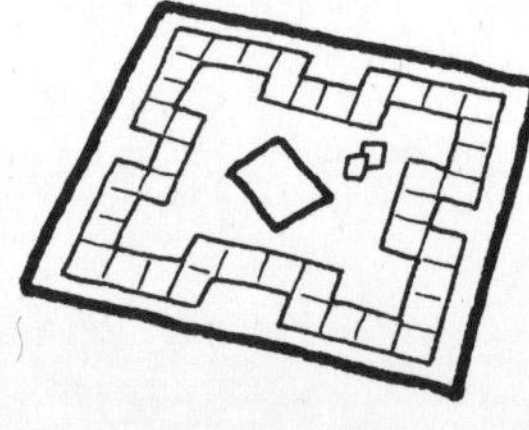

5.

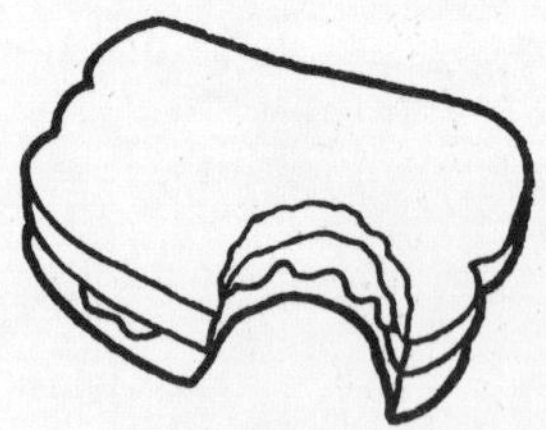
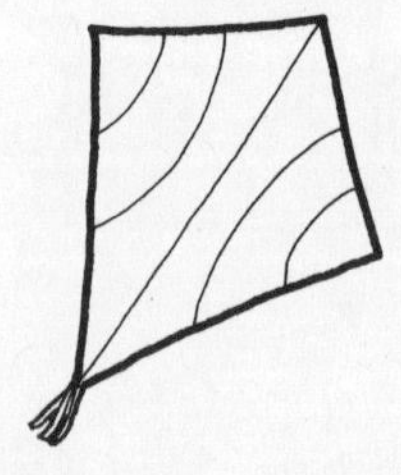
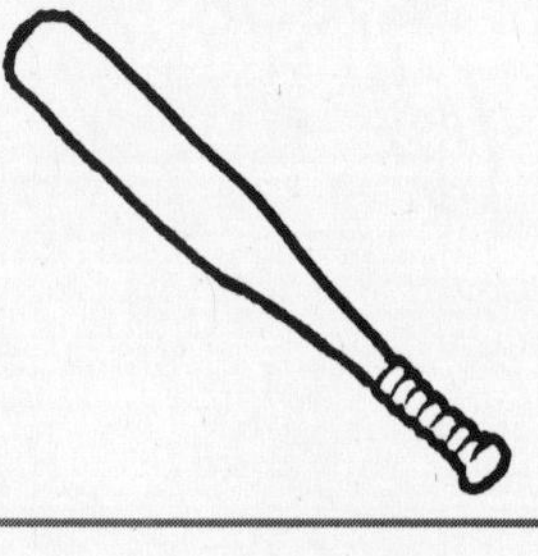

6.

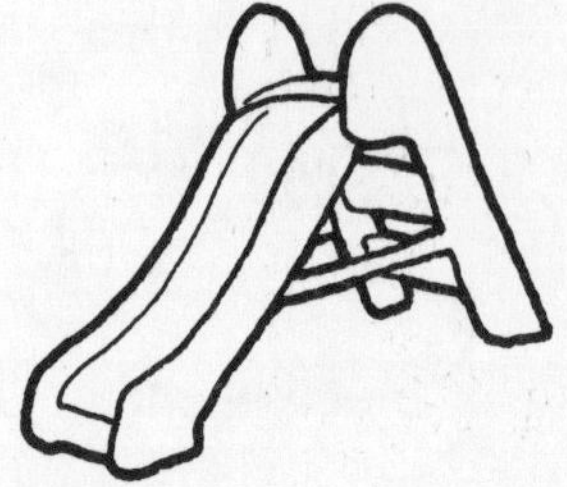

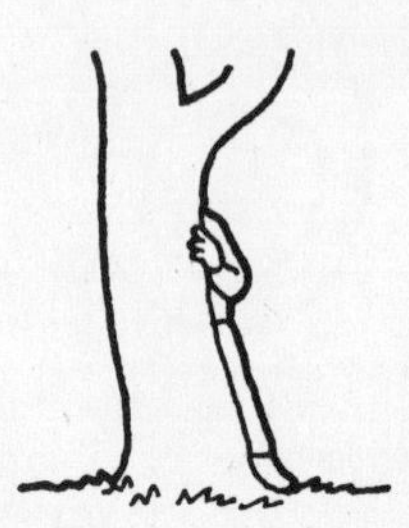

Point to a picture and ask your child to name it. Taking turns, try to say as many rhyming words as you can.

Name ______________________________

Say the name of each picture. Circle its name.

1.

mine nine vine

2.

dive dine dime

3.

pin pie pine

4.

ride hide ripe

5.

bite bike kite

6.

fine fire five

7.
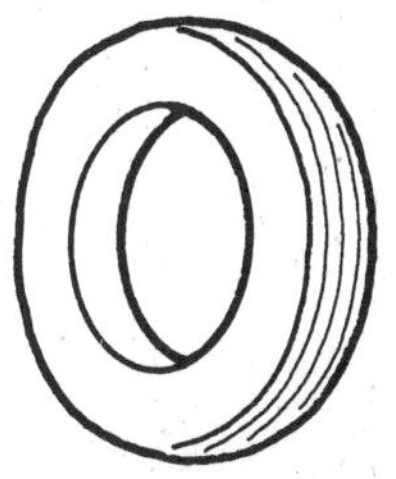
tie ride tire

8.

bite tide bike

9.
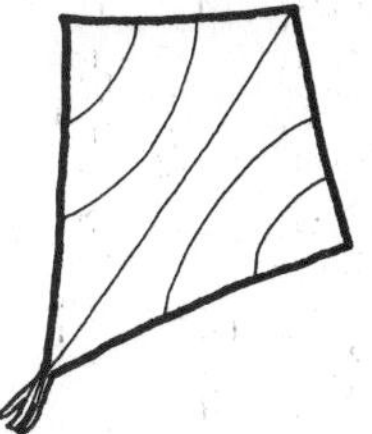
like kite tile

10.
vine wine line

11.

dive dime five

12.
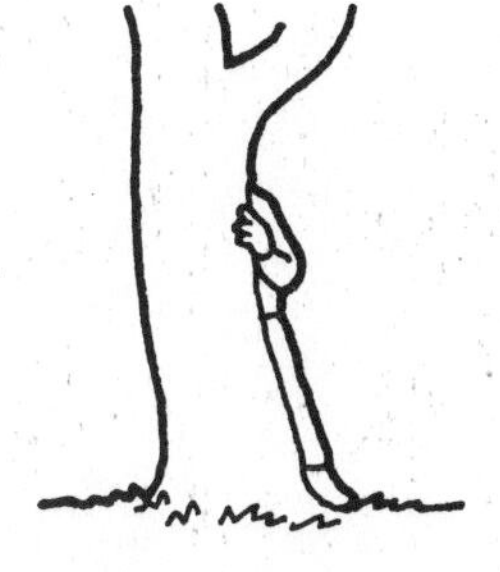
hide ride hit

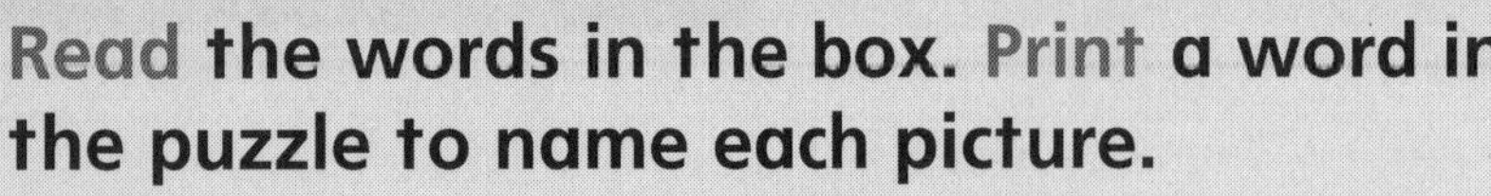
Read the words in the box. Print a word in the puzzle to name each picture.

tie	bike	ride	ice
kite	mice	pie	dime

Across 

1. 

3. 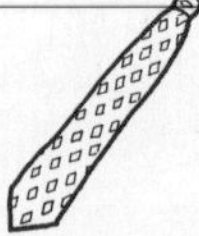

4. 

7. 

8. 

Down 

2. 

5. 

6. 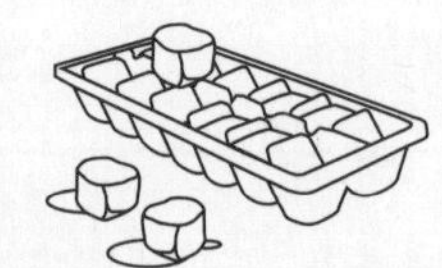

1. 2. 3. 4. 5. 6. 7. 8.

Use some of the words from the box to write a sentence.

HOME

Help your child make up a short poem using some of the long *i* words.

Name ______________________________

Say the name of each picture. If the vowel sound is short, color the box with the word short. If the vowel sound is long, color the box with the word long.

1.

short | long

2.

short | long

3.
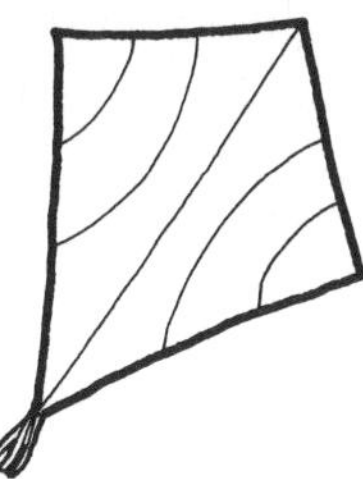

short | long

4.

short | long

5.

short | long

6.

short | long

7.
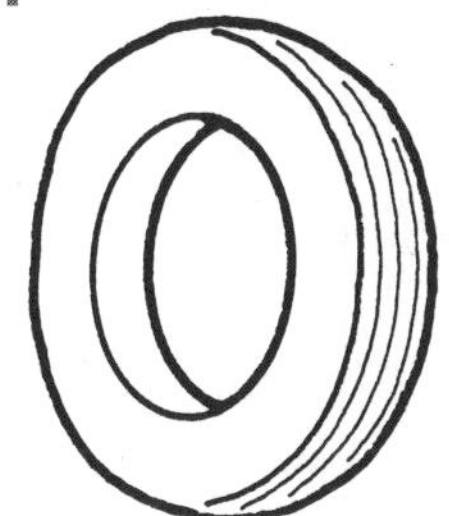

short | long

8.

short | long

9.

short | long

10.

short | long

11.

short | long

12.

short | long

Say the name of each picture. Circle its name.

1. rid ride	2. kit kite	3. pin pine
4. cap cape	5. dim dime	6. rip ripe
7. lid lied	8. ran rain	9. fin fine
10. bit bite	11. Tim time	12. slid slide

With your child, make up sentences using the short and long vowel words, such as *The shark's fin is fine.*

Name ______________________________

Say the name of each picture. Print the missing vowels on the line. Trace the whole word.

1.

r ___ d

2.

p ___ g

3.

d ___ m ___

4.

f ___ r ___

5.

l ___ n ___

6.

h ___ v ___

7.

l ___ d

8.

k ___ t ___

9.

f ___ v ___

10.

b ___ k ___

11.

d ___ v ___

12.

s ___ x

Look at the picture. Circle the word that will finish the sentence. Print it on the line.

1.	Jim has __________ dimes.	fine file five
2.	He will not get a __________.	kite bite bake
3.	He will not get a __________.	lie pie pile
4.	First, Jim waits in __________.	like lied line
5.	He has fun on the __________.	rise ripe ride
6.	He rides home on his __________.	take bike bite

Why do you think Jim chose the ride?

Help your child think of sentences using words from the page to continue the story.

Name ____________________

Say the name of each picture. Print the name on the line. In the last box, draw a picture of a long i word. Print the word.

1. 
bike

2. 

3. 

4. 

5. 

6. 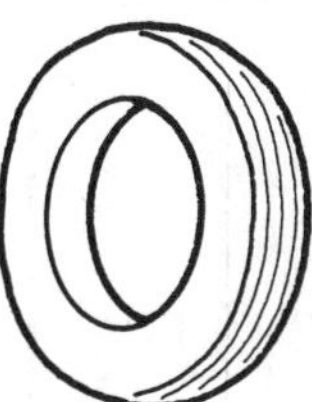

7. 

8. 

9. 

10. 

11. 

12.

Circle the word that will finish the sentence. Print it on the line.

1. Mike likes his ______________. bite / bike / bake

2. It has a nine on the ______________. side / sale / sand

3. It is the same size as ______________. miss / mine / mitt

4. Mike will ______________ it in the race. ride / ripe / rake

5. The race is six ______________ long! miss / mills / miles

6. Last time it ended in a ______________. tie / tide / tip

How does it feel when you win a race?

Help your child make up a sentence that uses any two circled words, then draw a picture that goes with it.

Name ________________________________

Read the story. Use long i words to finish the sentences.

Flying a Kite

Children in many places like
to fly kites.
In Japan, children fly kites
on New Year's day.
The kites can come in many
shapes and sizes.
Children tie on a string.
The kites dive and glide.
Hold on to the line!

1. Children in many places like to fly ______________.

2. Children ______________ on a string.

3. The kites ______________ and glide.

Can you think of more shapes and sizes for kites?

Use one of the letters to make a word with **ide** or **ine**. Write each real word on the lines.

r s w h y

ide

1. ____________

2. ____________

3. ____________

4. ____________

n m b f l

ine

5. ____________

6. ____________

7. ____________

8. ____________

Write a sentence using one of the words you made.

____

____

HOME

Help your child make up a sentence using as many long vowel *i* words as you can.

Dad hiked a mile, and Di took a ride. That made Ray smile!

4

FOLD

Name ______________________

Di Tries

"I can hike a mile," said Ray.

1

FOLD
"I may hike a mile, too," said Di.
2
"You can try," Ray said.
"Fine," said Di. "Make way!"
3

Name ______________________________

Read the words in the box. Write a word to finish each sentence.

long	there
Why	little
could	about

1. ______________ was Maya smiling?

2. She was thinking ______________ her pets.

3. She had two ______________ white mice.

4. The mice had ______________ tails.

5. Maya ______________ hold them in her hands.

6. The mice liked to be ______________.

Look at the picture. Then, print words from the box to finish the story. The word shapes will help you.

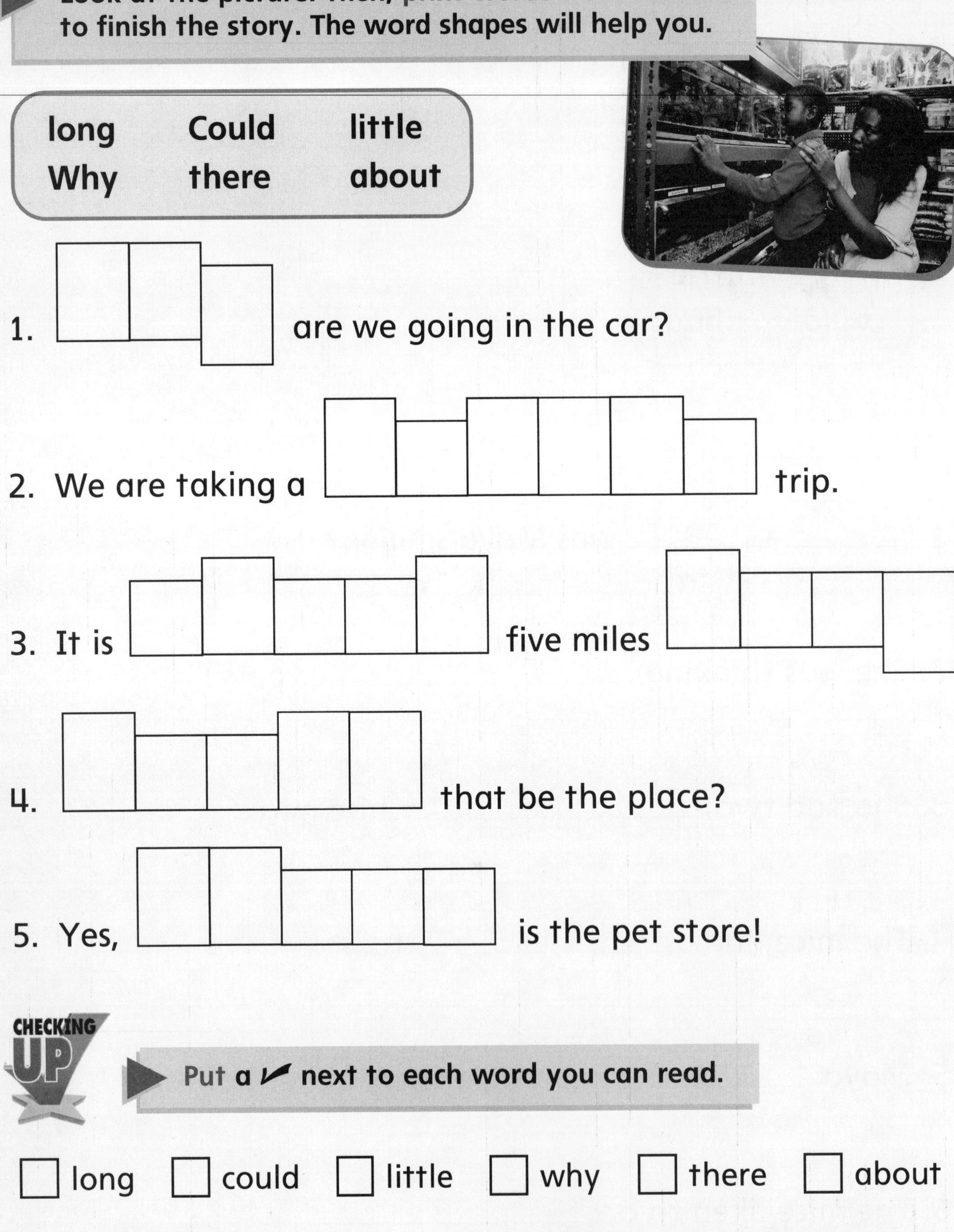

long	Could	little
Why	there	about

1. ______ are we going in the car?

2. We are taking a ______ trip.

3. It is ______ five miles ______.

4. ______ that be the place?

5. Yes, ______ is the pet store!

CHECKING UP

Put a ✓ next to each word you can read.

☐ long ☐ could ☐ little ☐ why ☐ there ☐ about

HOME

Help your child use the boxed words to make up sentences, such as *The little mouse is nice.*

Name ____________________________________

Lu used a tube
Of strong white glue
To paste her cube
On top of Sue's.

Tube has the long sound of u. Circle each picture whose name has the long sound of u.

1. 

2. 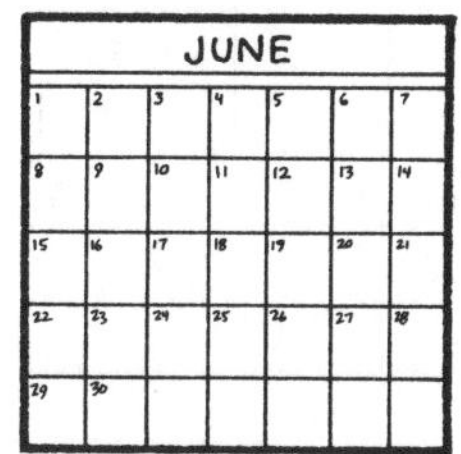

3. 

4. 

5. 

6. 

7. 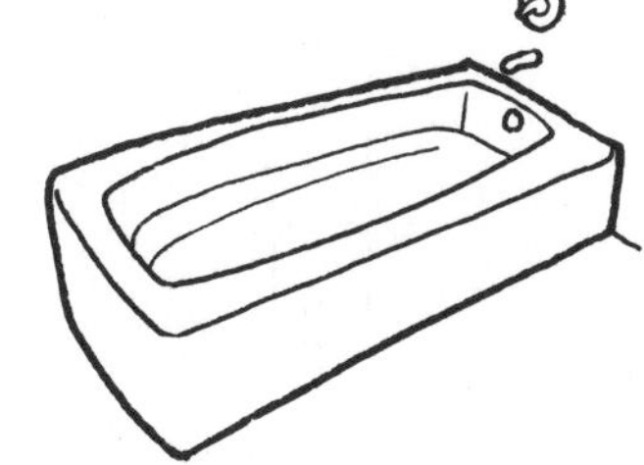

8. 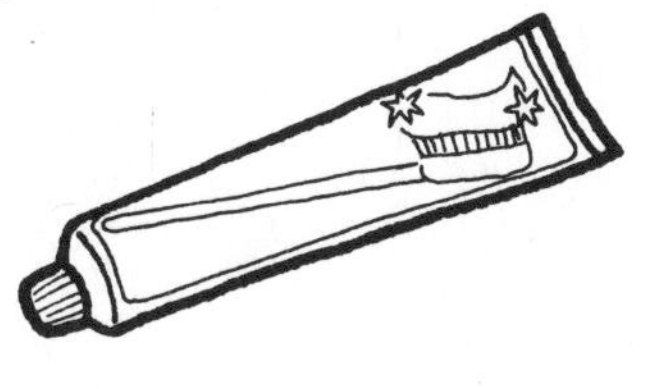

9. 

10. 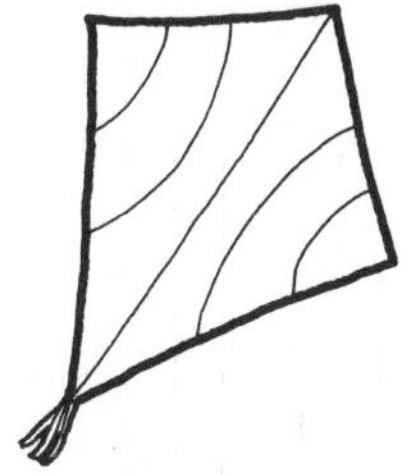

11. 

12. 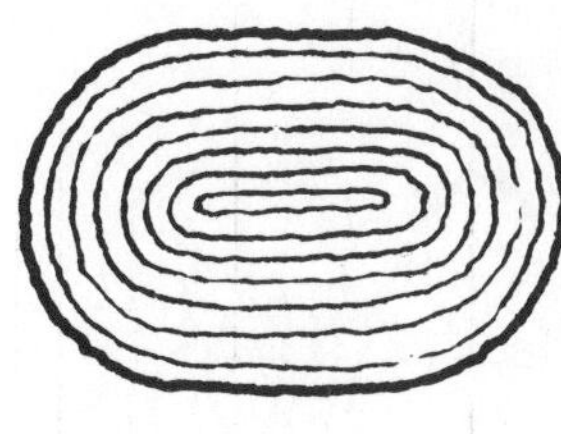

Say the names of the pictures in each row. Color the pictures whose names rhyme.

1.

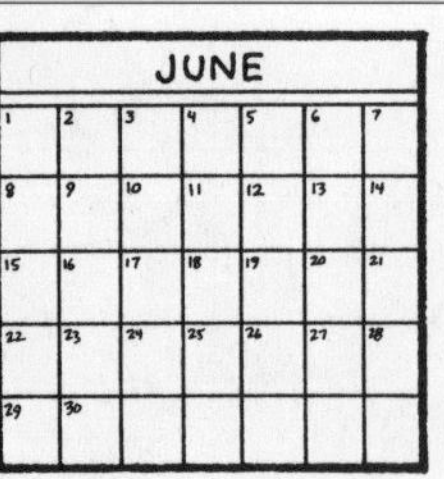

2.

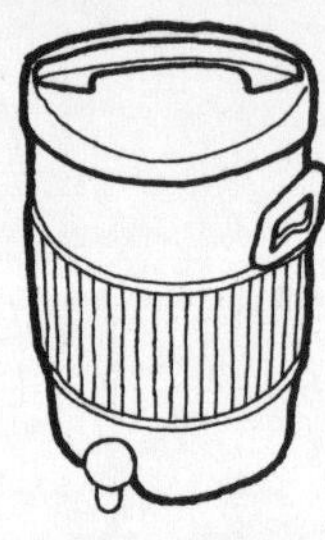

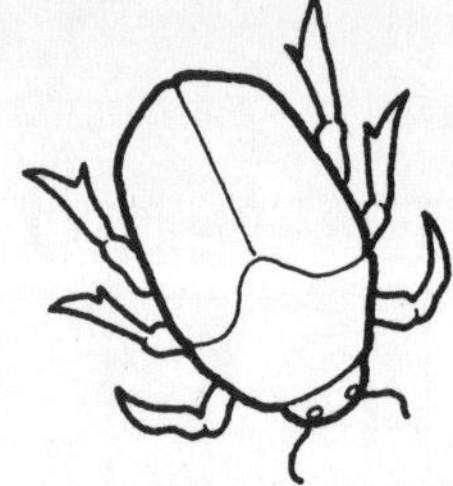

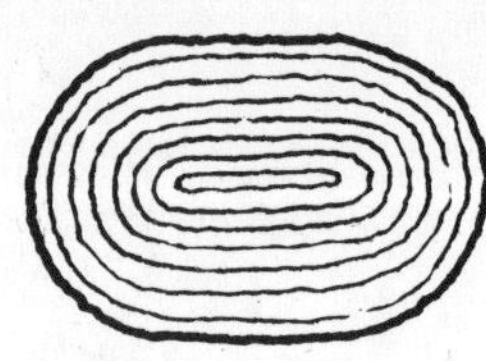

3.

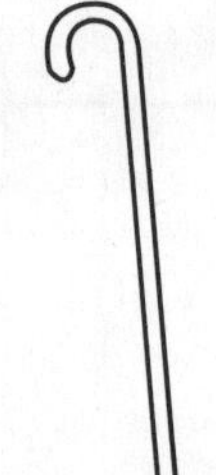

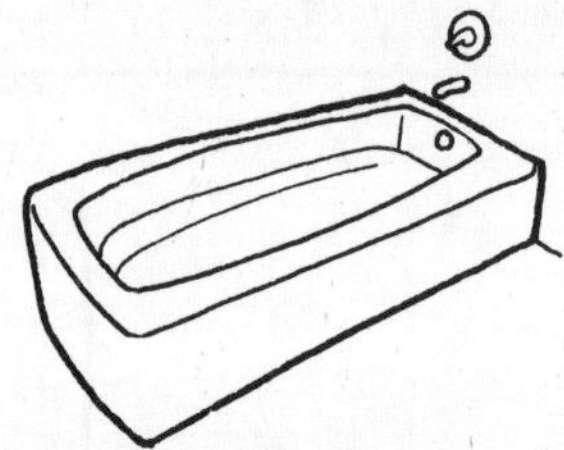

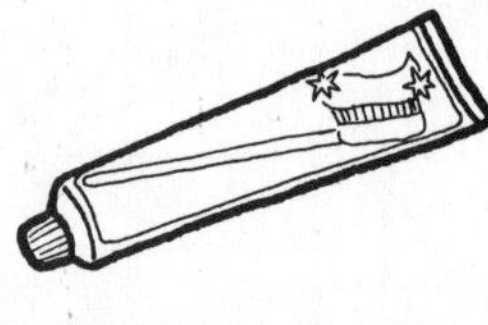

4.

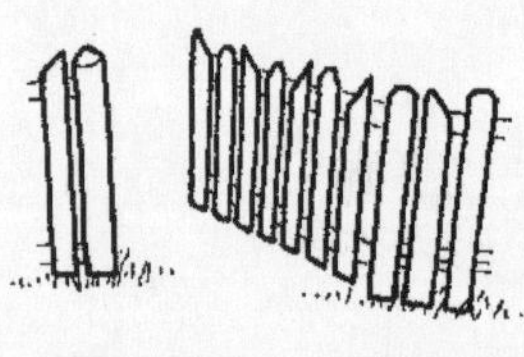

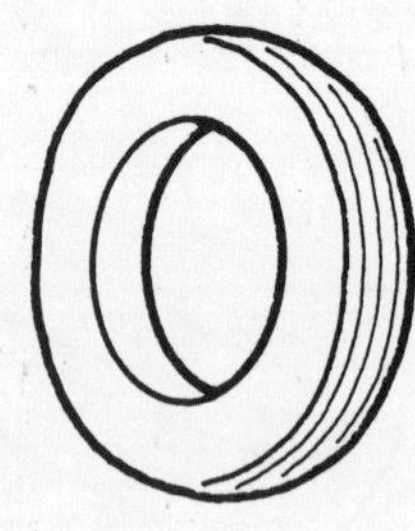

5.

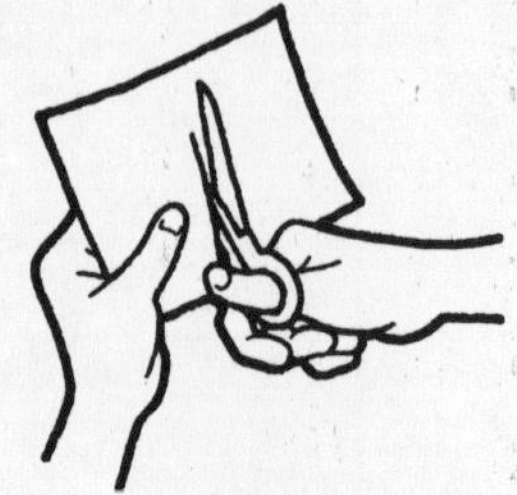

With your child, make up a sentence that rhymes for each row of rhyming pictures, such as *I sang a tune in June.*

Name ______________________________

Say the name of each picture. Circle its name.

1.

rule mule rude

2.

cup cube cub

3.

cute cube cub

4.
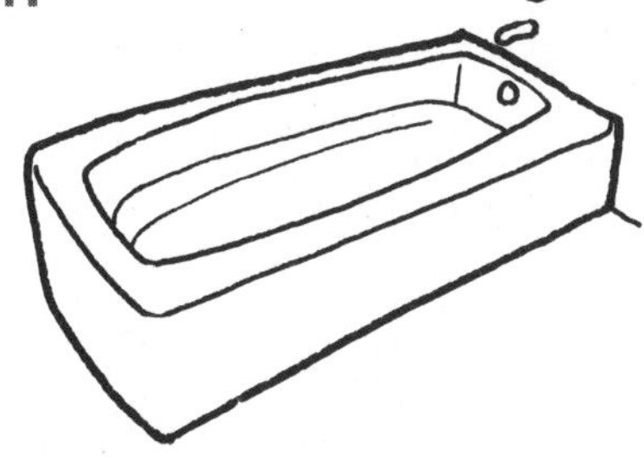
tub tube tug

5.
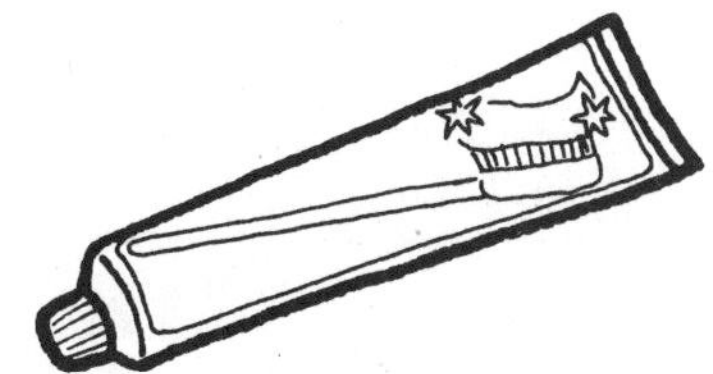
tune tube tub

6.

Sue due fuss

7.

use sit suit

8.
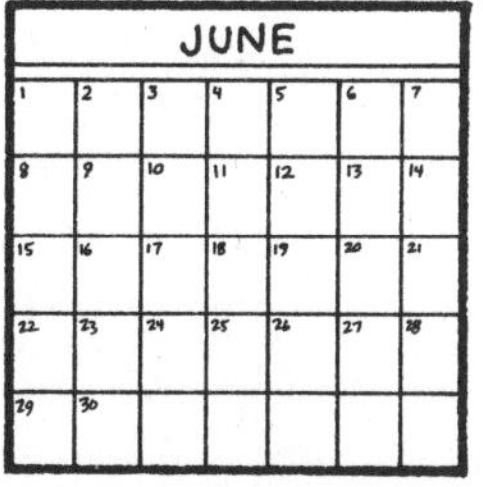

June tune nuts

9.

use sun suit

10.

tune tube tuck

11.

run bun rude

12.

fun suit fruit

Read each sentence. Use the code to make each pair of words. Print them on the lines. Then, circle the word that finishes the sentence.

1 = a	2 = e	3 = i	4 = u	5 = b	6 = c
7 = f	8 = l	9 = m	10 = r	11 = s	12 = t

1. June plays the ______ ______.
   12 4 5 1 — 10 4 8 2

2. Luke will feed his ______ ______.
   7 8 4 12 2 — 9 4 8 2

3. Sue likes to eat ______ ______.
   6 4 5 2 — 7 10 4 3 12

4. Ben got a new ______ ______.
   11 4 3 12 — 6 8 4 2

5. Duke's house is ______ ______.
   12 10 4 2 — 5 8 4 2

Make up riddles using the long vowel *u* words from the page. Ask your child to guess each word.

Name ______________________________

Say the name of each picture. If the vowel sound is short, color the box with the word short. If the vowel sound is long, color the box with the word long.

1.

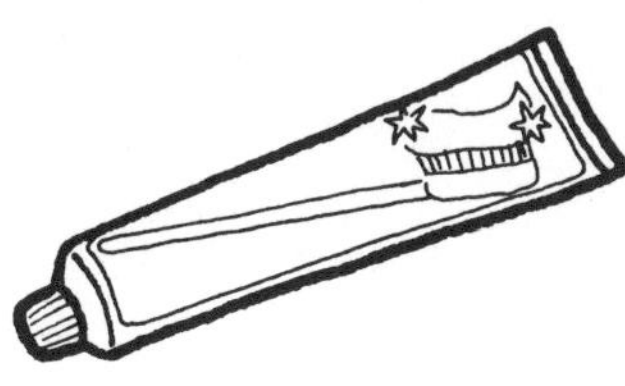

short | long

2.

short | long

3.

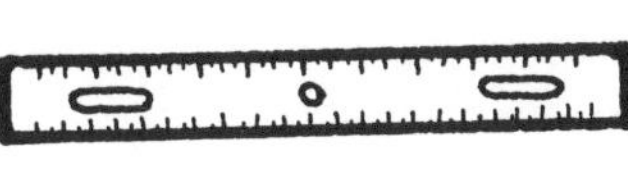

short | long

4.

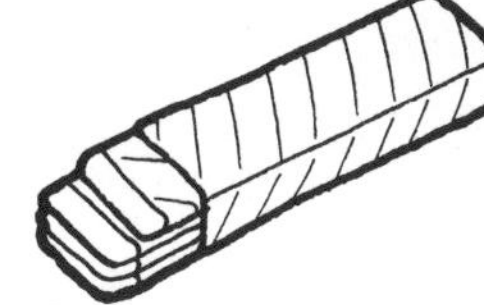

short | long

5.

short | long

6.

short | long

7.

short | long

8.

short | long

9.

short | long

10.

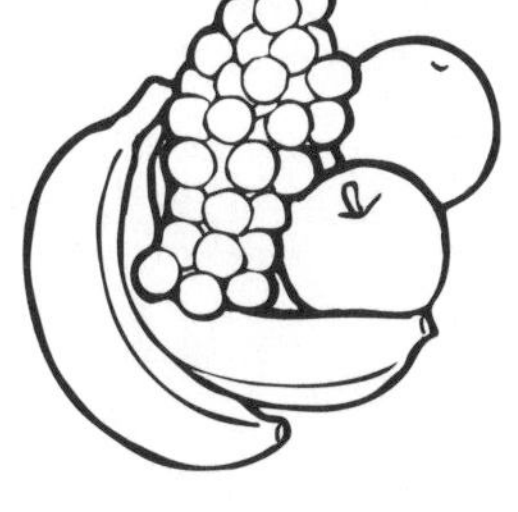

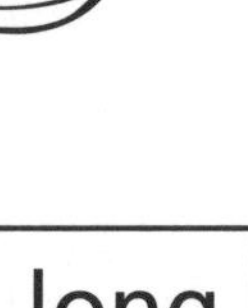

short | long

11.

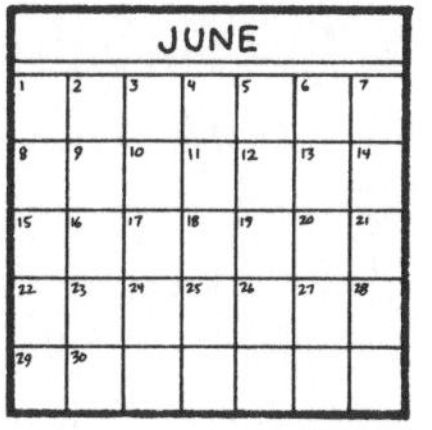

short | long

12.

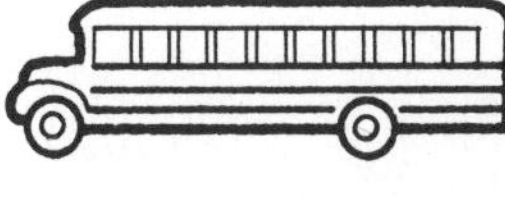

short | long

Color the bubble blue if it has three long u words in it.

1. rude Sue tune
2. suit tune fruit
3. mule use cube
4. fire tire ride
5. blue rule Sue
6. cute mute cube
7. pail sail tail
8. mile file pile
9. rug tug mug

Use some of the long vowel u words on this page to write a sentence.

HOME

Point to a bubble and say the words inside. With your child, take turns naming other words with the long or short vowel sound.

Name ___________________________________

Say the name of each picture. Circle its name.

1. 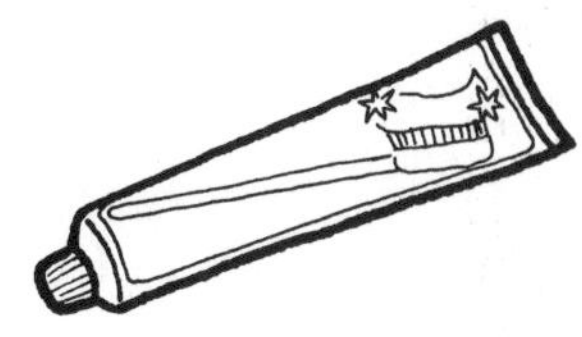 tub tube	2. 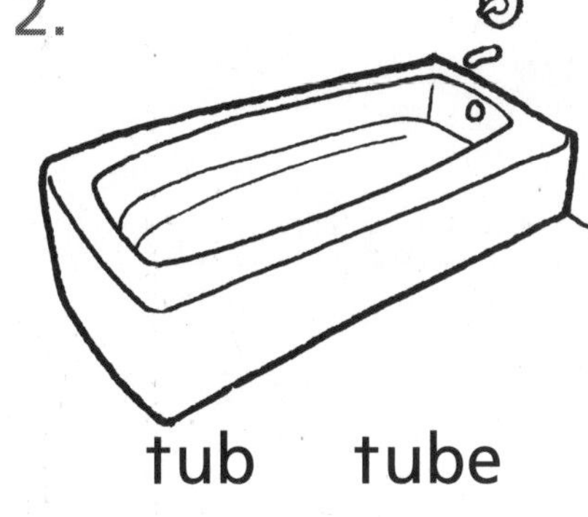 tub tube	3.  pin pine
4.  dim dime	5. 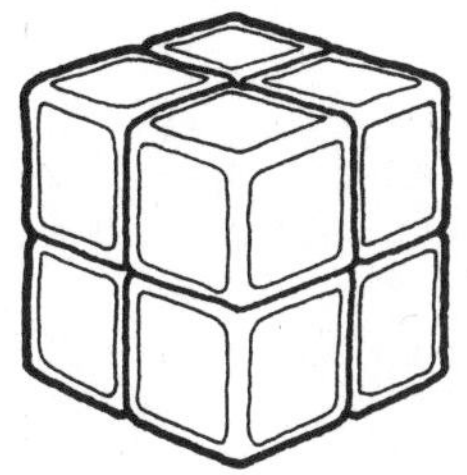 cub cube	6.  cub cube
7.  ran rain	8. 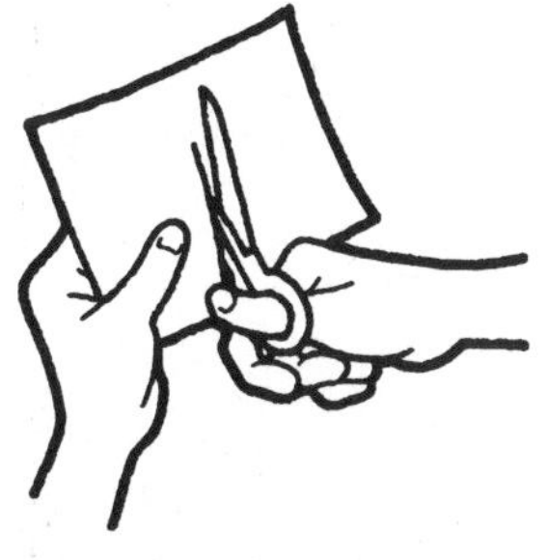 cut cute	9.  rid ride
10.  hat hate	11.  cape cap	12. 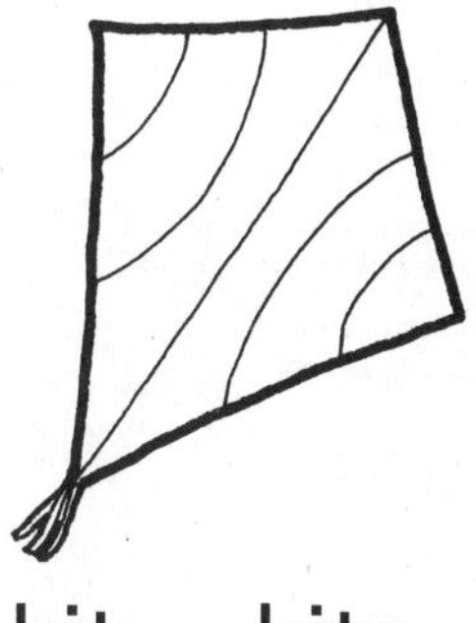 kit kite

Look at the picture. Circle the word that will finish the sentence. Print it on the line.

1. Luke will __________ a box. — us / use / tune

2. The box looks like a __________. — cute / cube / cub

3. He got it from __________. — rule / Sue / due

4. Luke has a __________ of glue in it. — tune / tub / tube

5. He will put a __________ in it, too. — ruler / rude / rubs

6. Luke will take it on the __________. — suit / bun / bus

Where do you think Luke is taking the box?

Help your child to think of a sentence that uses some of the long *u* words on the page.

Name ______________________________

Say the name of each picture. Print the missing vowels on the line. Trace the whole word.

1. c b	2. t l	3. J n	4. f v
5. l k	6. t b	7. k t	8. s t
9. g m	10. c p	11. m l	12. t n

**Circle the word that will finish the sentence.
Print it on the line.**

1. Sue has a ________________. — must / mule / mile

2. Is a mule a ________________ pet? — cute / cube / cut

3. Will she ride it in ________________? — jug / tune / June

4. Does the mule like to eat ________________? — fun / fruit / rule

5. I do not have a ________________. — cute / clue / cuts

6. I want to ask ________________. — sun / Sue / suit

**Where do you think Sue lives?
Why do you think that?**

Help your child to continue the story using some of the circled words on the page.

Name ____________________

Say the name of each picture. Print the name on the line. In the last box, draw a picture of a long u word. Print the word.

1. 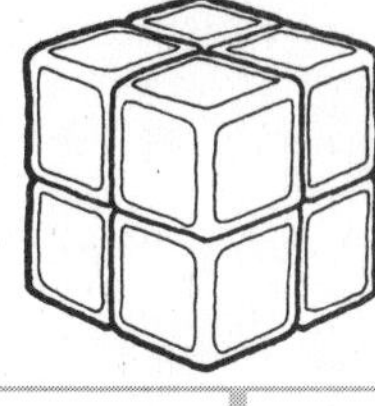

cube

2. 

3. 

4. 

5. 

6. 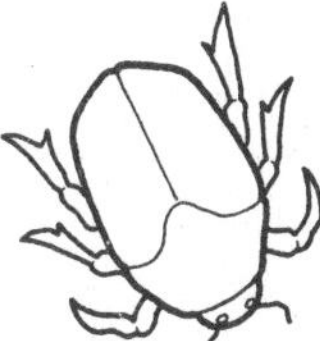

7. 

8. 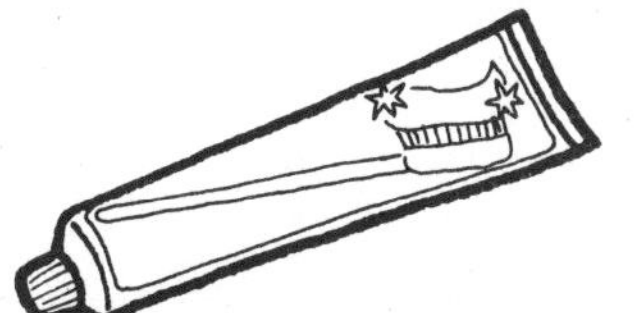

9. 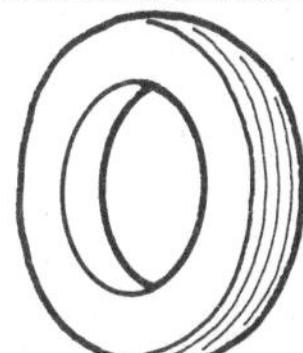

10. 

11. 

12.

Circle the long **a**, long **i**, and long **u** words in the puzzle. The words in the box will help you.

r	a	i	n
s	u	i	t
r	a	c	a
t	i	e	p
m	u	l	e

rain	ice	tape
suit	tie	mule

Print the word from the box that names each picture.

1. ______________________

2. ______________________

3. ______________________

4. ______________________

5. ______________________

6. ______________________

HOME

Ask your child to use three of the words from the box in a sentence.

Name ____________________

Read the story. Use long **u** words to finish the sentences.

The Blue Suit

A cute cub saw some fruit.
The fruit was blue.
"This fruit looks good,"
said the cub.
He ate the fruit.
He hummed a tune.
Blue juice got all over him.
"Look!" said the cub's dad.
"You have a new blue suit!"

1. The ____________ was blue.

2. Blue ____________ got on the cub.

3. The cub had a new ____________ ____________.

What kind of fruit did the cub eat?

Use one of the letters to make a word with une or ule. Write each real word on the lines.

j d b t

une

1. ______

2. ______

3. ______

m l r v

ule

4. ______

5. ______

Write a sentence using one of the words you made.

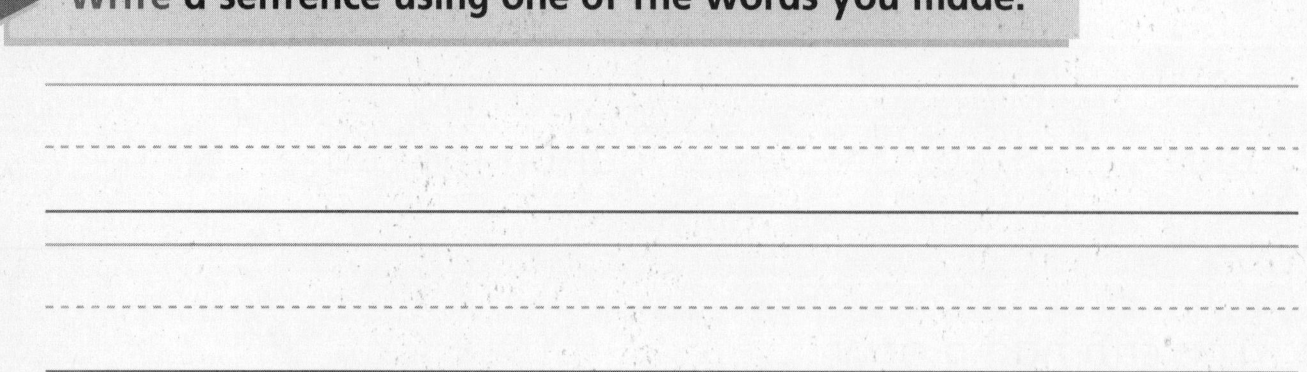

HOME

Ask your child questions that can be answered with long *u* words, such as *"What word means song?" (tune)*

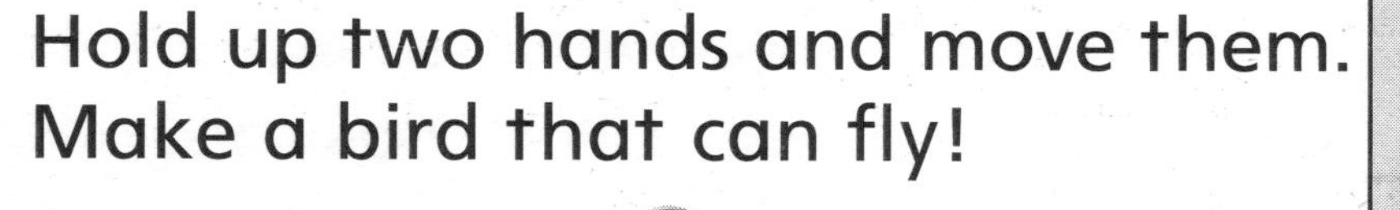

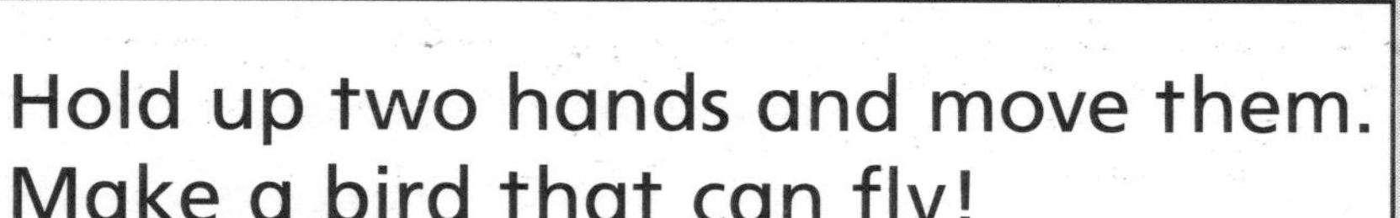

Hold up two hands and move them.
Make a bird that can fly!

FOLD

Name ______________________

Hand Games

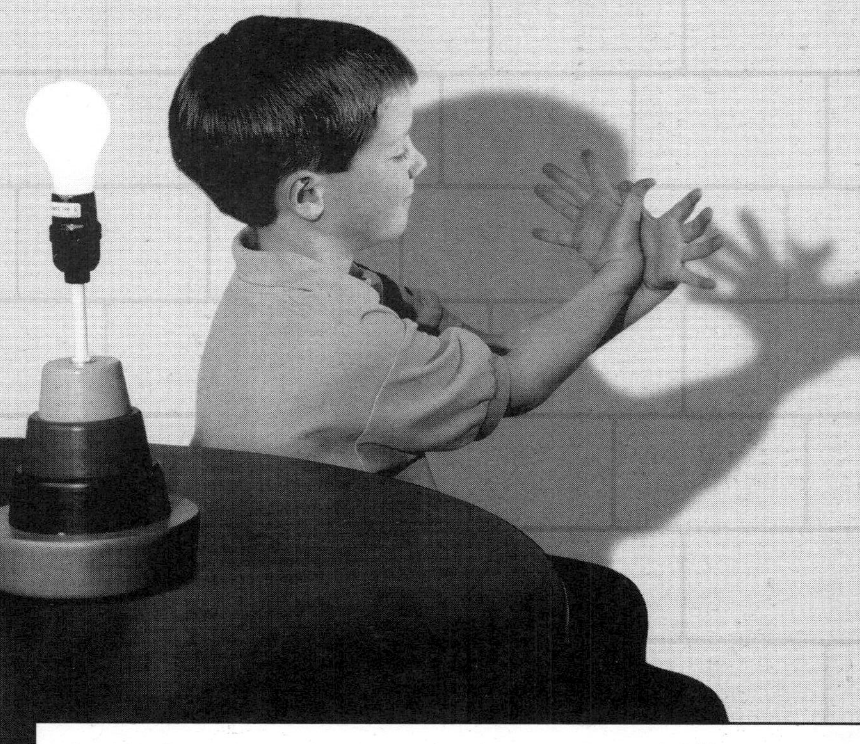

You can use your hands to make pictures. Shine a light on a wall.

Make a cute rabbit. Hold up one hand this way.

2

FOLD

Make a huge white swan. Hold up two hands like this.

3

Name ____________________

Turn the jump rope,
High, low, fast, slow!
Put on a show!
Come on, let's go!

Rope has the long sound of o. Circle each picture whose name has the long sound of o.

1.	2.	3.	4.
	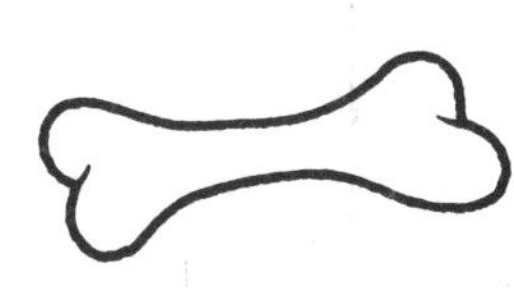		
5.	6.	7.	8.
		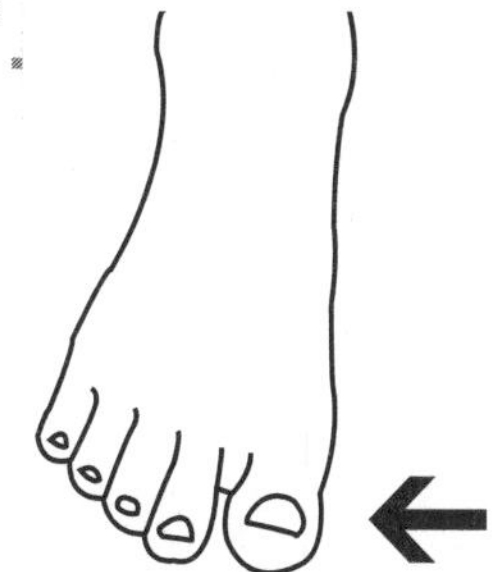	
9.	10.	11.	12.
	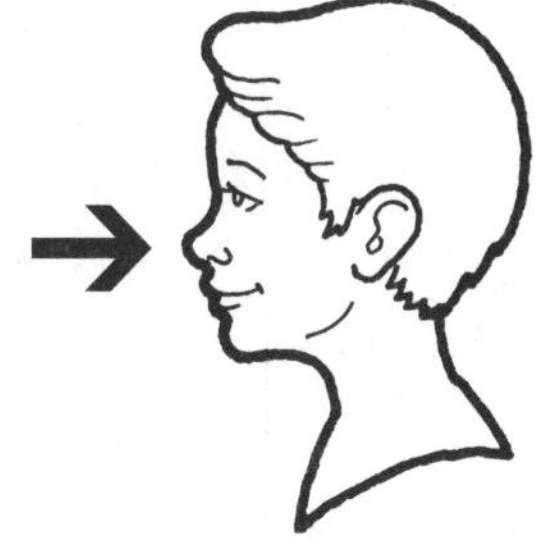	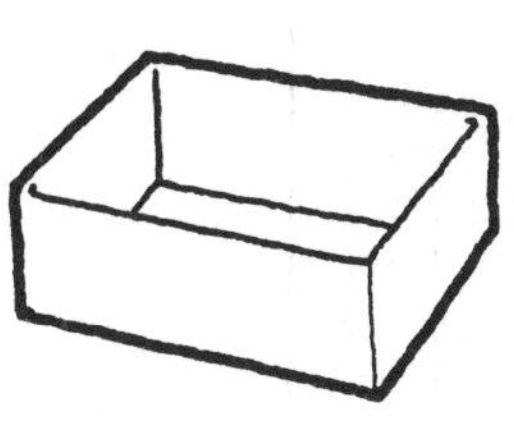	

Say the names of the pictures in each circle. Color the parts of the circle that have pictures with long o names.

1.

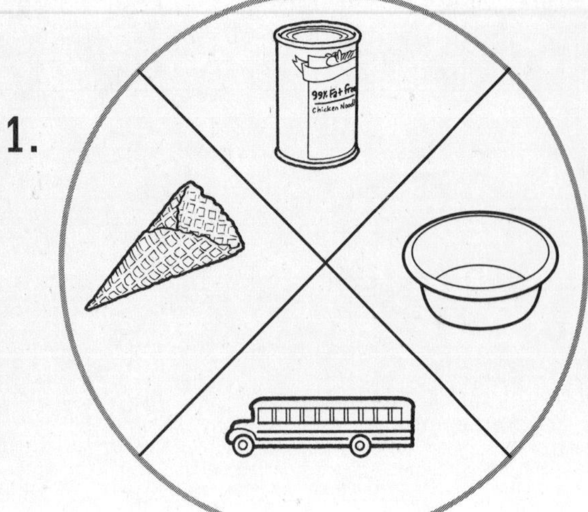

2.

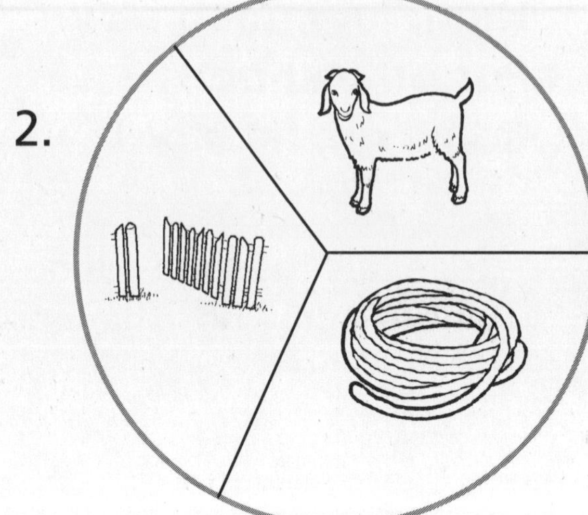

3.

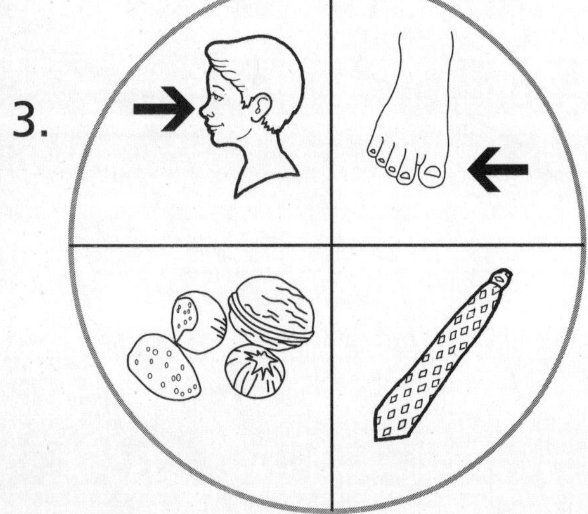

4.

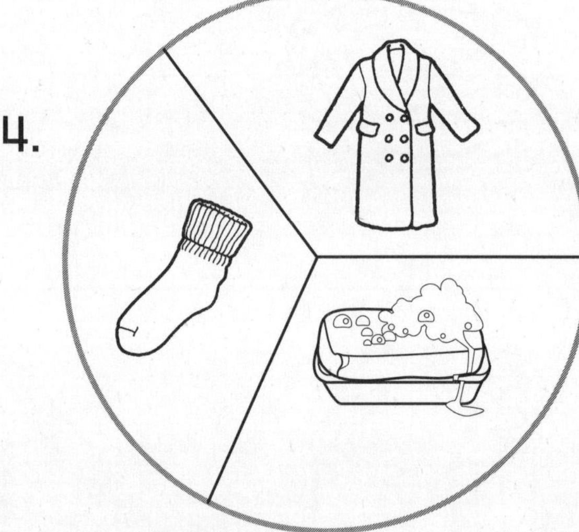

Use some of the long o words to write a sentence.

HOME With your child, take turns saying all the long *o* words you can name.

Name ___________________________

▶ **Say** the names of the pictures in each row.
Color the pictures whose names rhyme.

1. 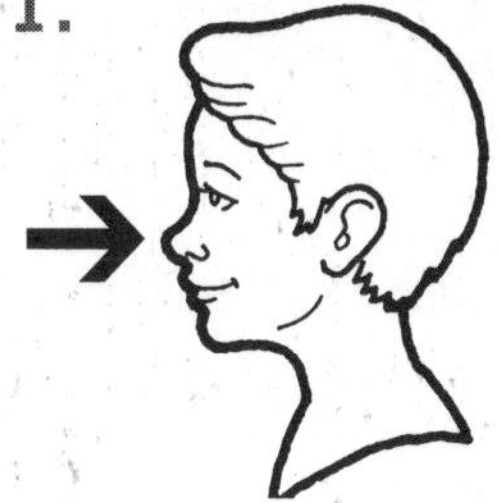 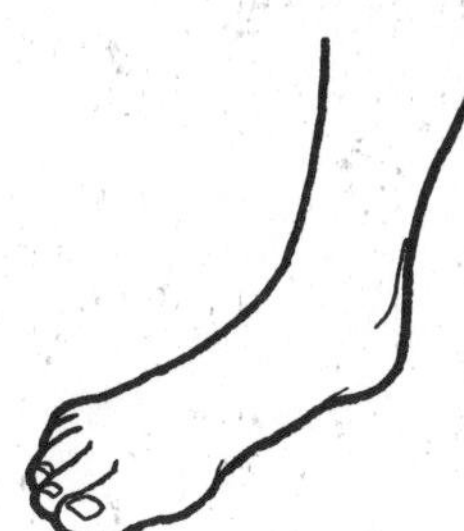 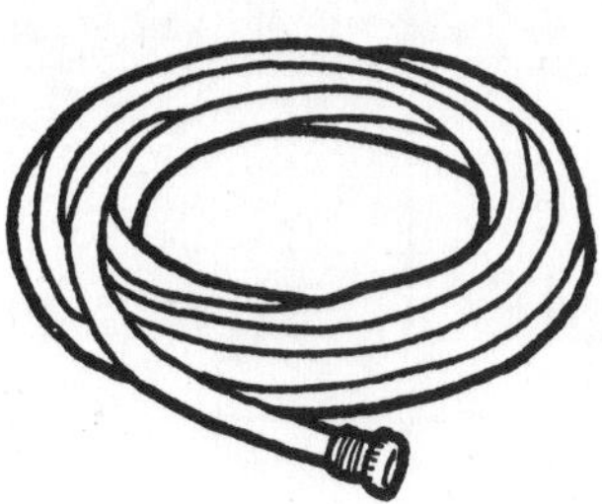 

2. 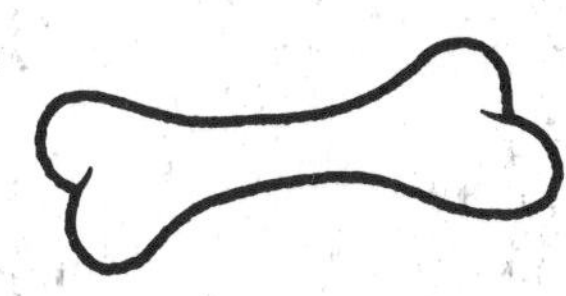 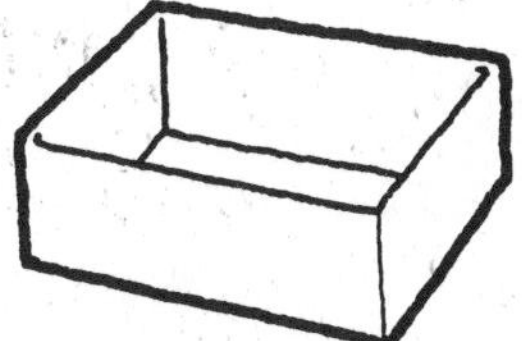  

3.   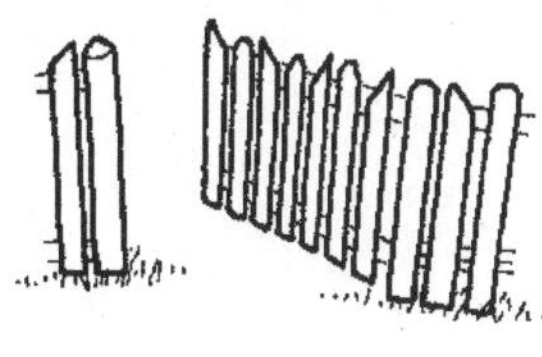 

4.    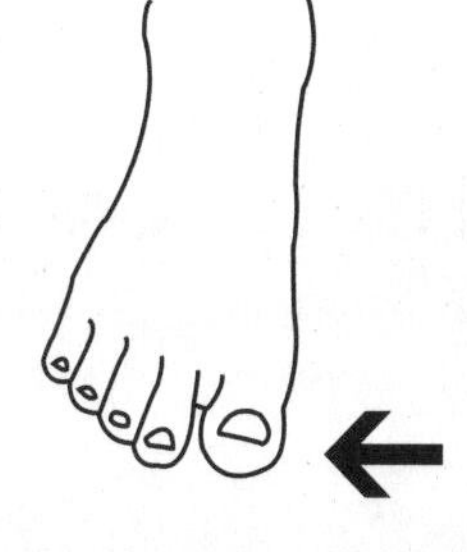

5.    

Say the name of each picture. Circle its name.

1.	2.	3.
	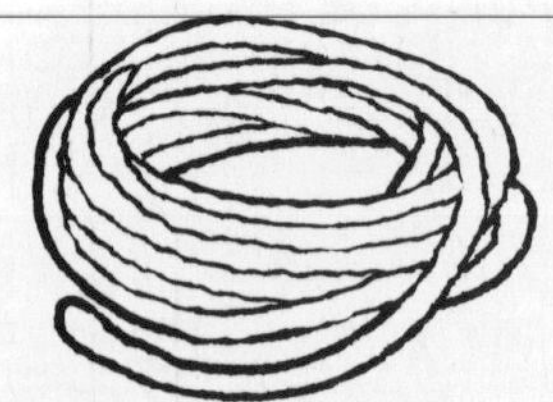	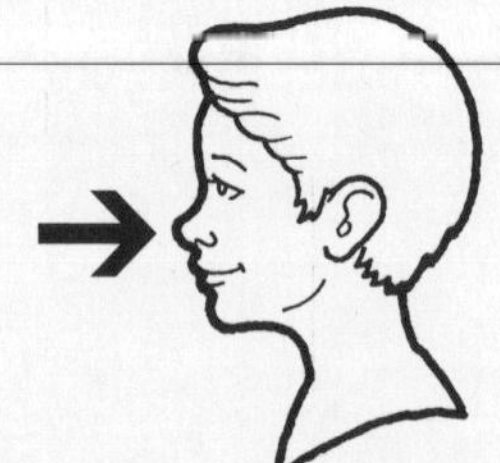
coat cat coal	ripe rope rip	name rose nose
4.	5.	6.

sap soap sop	boat bat toad	robe rob bone
7.	8.	9.
	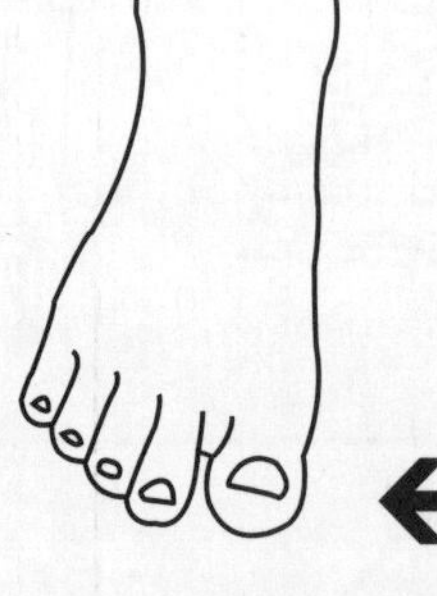	
rain cone cane	doe hoe toe	gate goat got
10.	11.	12.
	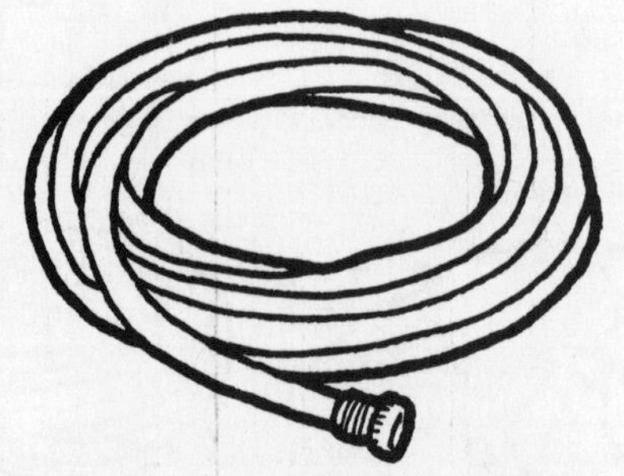	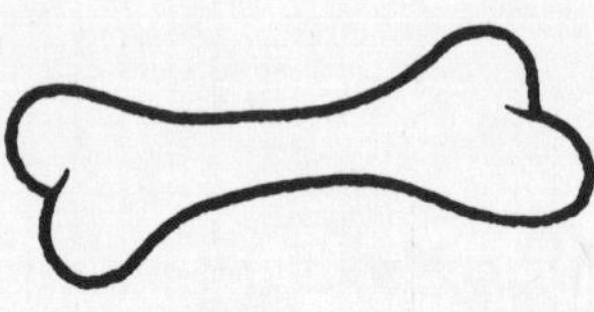
row bow toe	hose hope hot	cone boat bone

Help your child think of other words that rhyme with the names of the pictures on this page, such as *nose, rose, toes.*

Name ______________________________

Say the name of each picture. Circle the letters that make the long sound of **o**.

1.  goat	2.  bow	3. 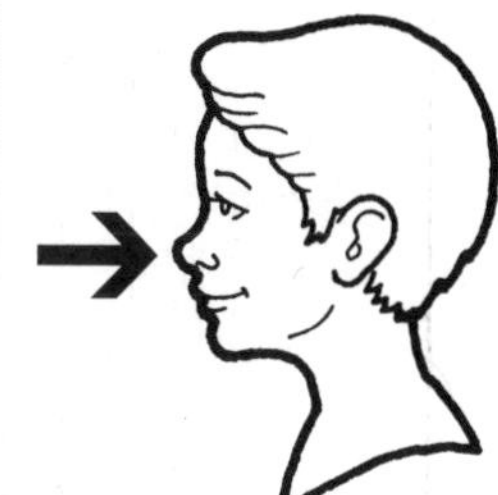 nose	4.  cone
5.  rope	6.  boat	7. 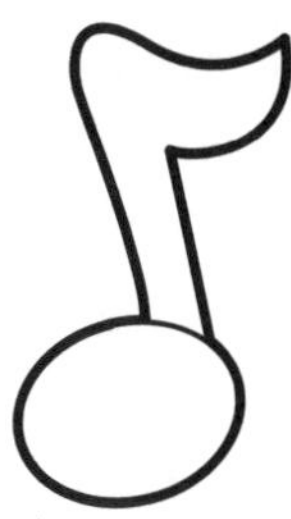 note	8.  row
9.  soap	10. 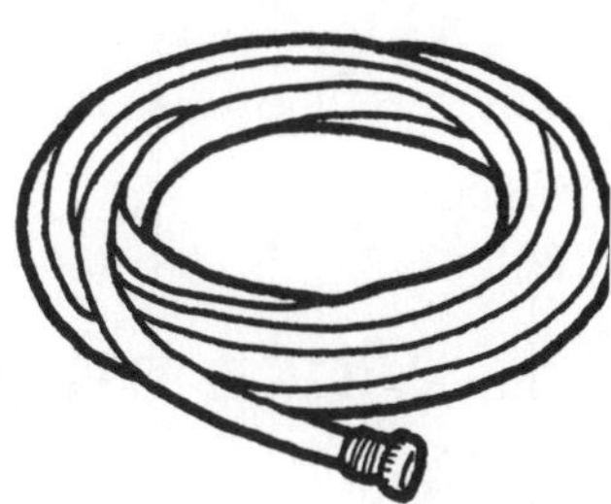 hose	11.  coat	12. 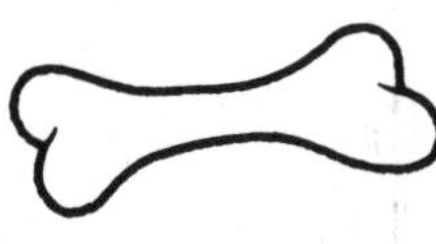 bone

Look at the picture. Then, follow the directions below.

Directions

1. Color the hose green.
2. Color the boat blue.
3. Circle the girl who will row.
4. Draw a toad on the stone.
5. Make an X on the hoe.
6. Color the roses red.
7. Draw a hole for the mole.
8. Draw a rope on the goat.

With your child, make up a story about the picture using the long *o* words.

Name ____________________________

Say the name of each picture. If the vowel sound is short, **color** the box with the word **short**. If the vowel sound is long, **color** the box with the word **long**.

1.

short | long

2.

short | long

3.

short | long

4.

short | long

5.

short | long

6.

short | long

7.

short | long

8.

short | long

9.

short | long

10.

short | long

11.

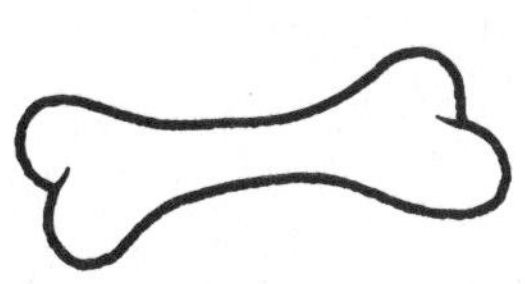

short | long

12.

short | long

Say the name of each picture. Circle the words in the boxes that rhyme with the picture name.

1.	bone	cane	loan	moan	can
	Joan	tone	run	zone	coat
2.	got	boat	coat	note	vote
	rate	cute	tote	gate	moat
3.	snow	doe	tip	top	slow
←	go	tube	row	foe	tail
4.	rope	slow	blow	rip	snow
	low	ride	bow	tow	rock

Help your child to make up sentences using the rhyming words, such as *I wore a coat in the boat.*

Name ______________________________

Say the name of each picture. Circle its name.

1.

cat coat

2.

not note

3.

mop mope

4.

kit kite

5.

bat boat

6.

rob robe

7.

got goat

8.
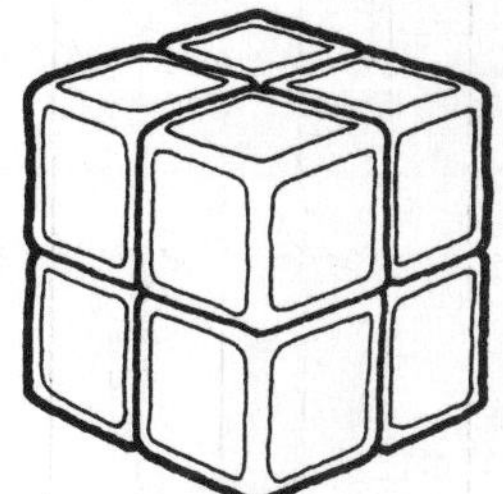
cub cube

9.

sap soap

10.

rat rate

11.

moan man

12.
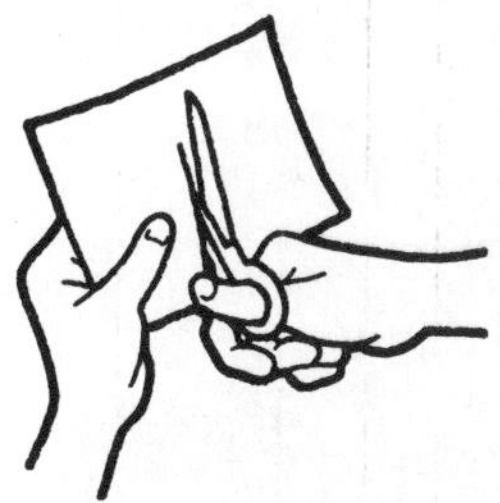
cute cut

Look at the picture. Circle the word that will finish the sentence. Print it on the line.

1. A mole hides in a ______________. hose hole hope

2. A fish swims in a ______________. box bone bowl

3. A goat eats a ______________. bone cone cane

4. A cat goes up a ______________. poke pole loan

5. A dog begs for a ______________. bone robe boat

6. A fox cleans its ______________. cone coal coat

Which animals make good pets? Why?

Ask your child to use the words circled on this page in sentences.

Name ______________________________

Say the name of each picture. Print the missing vowels on the line. Trace the whole word.

1. c n	2. h s	3. r b	4. t p
5. r p	**6.** c t	**7.** n t	**8.** n s
9. s p	**10.** p t	**11.** m p	**12.** b t

Circle the word that will finish the sentence. Print it on the line.

1. The store is up the ______________. road robe role

2. Joan goes in and smells the ______________. song soak soap

3. It gets on her ______________. not nose hope

4. Joan sees a red ______________. boss bow row

5. She sees a blue ______________, too. robe rob ripe

6. She will pay and take them ______________. hose hole home

What kind of store did Joan visit?

With your child, think of other sentences using these long *o* words.

Name ______________________________

Say the name of each picture. Print the name on the line. In the last box, draw a picture of a long o word. Print the word.

1.

bone

2.

3.

4.

5.

6.
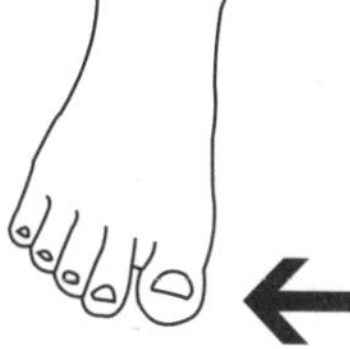

7.

8.

9.

10.

11.
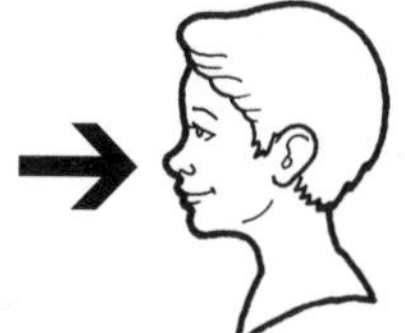

12.

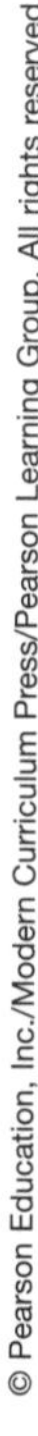

Say each picture name. Draw a line through the three pictures in a row that have the same long vowel sound.

1.

2.

3.

4.

Ask your child to think of more words using the long vowel *a, i, u,* or *o* that "won" in each puzzle.

Name ______________________________

Read the story. Use long o words to finish the sentences.

Joe's Show

Joe wanted to put on a show.
"My dog Bo will be in the show," he said.
"Bo can catch a bone."
Joe's friend Rose came by.
"Can my dog Moe be in your show?" Rose asked.
"He knows how to roll over," she said.
"Yes," said Joe.
Moe and Bo were stars!

1. Joe wanted to put on a ______________.

2. Bo can catch a ______________.

3. Moe knows how to ______________ over.

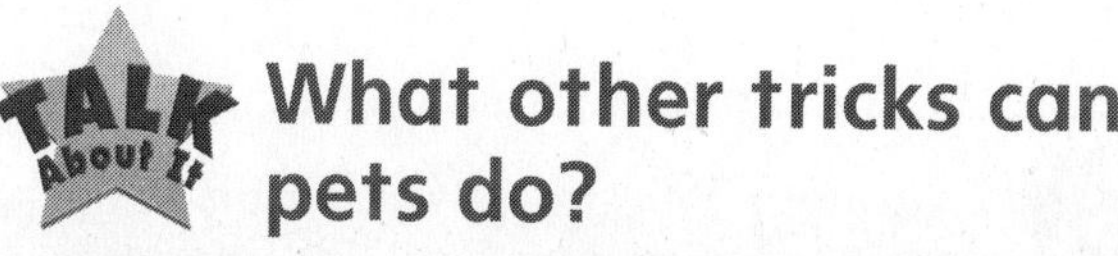

What other tricks can pets do?

Use one of the letters to make a word with **ose** or **old**. Write each real word on the lines.

r h n f p

ose

1. ____________
2. ____________
3. ____________
4. ____________

g s c p h

old

5. ____________
6. ____________
7. ____________
8. ____________

Write a sentence using one of the words you made.

____

____

Ask your child to put two thumbs up for a rhyming pair; then, say word pairs such as *rose–hose* or *sold–stop*.

Children in many places like to jump rope. What kind of games do you like to play?

4

FOLD

Name ____________________

Games Around the Globe

Children around the globe like to play games.

1

Some children play ball games. They must know the rules of the game.

2

FOLD

Some children like to play clapping games. They can clap and sing a tune.

3

Name ____________________

Read the words in the box. Write a word to finish each sentence.

from	which
them	because
Their	want

1. Joe could not go out ____________ of the rain.

2. "Do you ____________ to call Cody or Flo?" Mom said.

3. Joe did not know ____________ friend to call.

4. Mom said Joe could call both of ____________.

5. They played a game ____________ Mexico.

6. ____________ game was fun!

Look at the picture. Then, print words from the box to finish the story. The word shapes will help you.

from	**their**	**because**
them	**Which**	**want**

1. Lin and Lola know Joel ______ school.
2. They ______ him to be ______ friend.
3. Joel used to say, "______ twin is which?"
4. Now he can tell ______ apart.
5. He knows ______ Lin has a gold cap.

CHECKING UP

Put a ✓ next to each word you can read.

☐ them ☐ want ☐ because ☐ which ☐ from ☐ their

HOME Help your child to make up a sentence using some of the words in the box.

Name ______________________________

Here in my tree
Is the best place to be.
I can see down,
But the green leaves
Hide me!

Tree has the long sound of e. Circle each picture whose name has the long sound of e.

1.

2.

3.

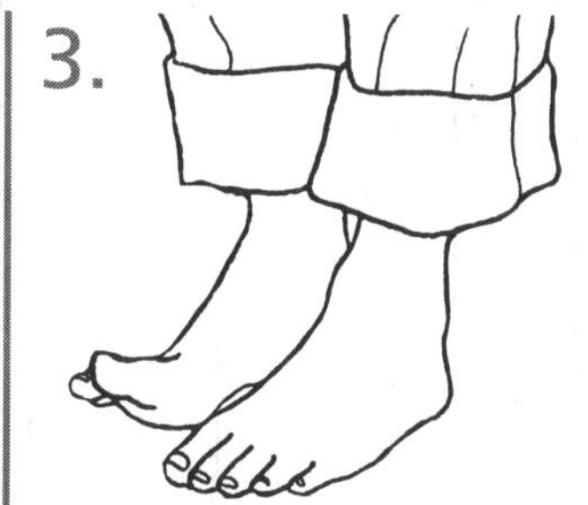

4.

5.

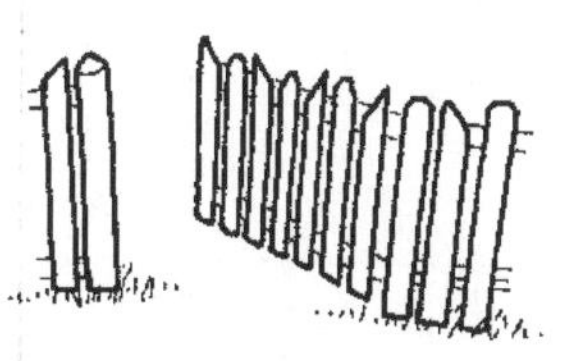

6.

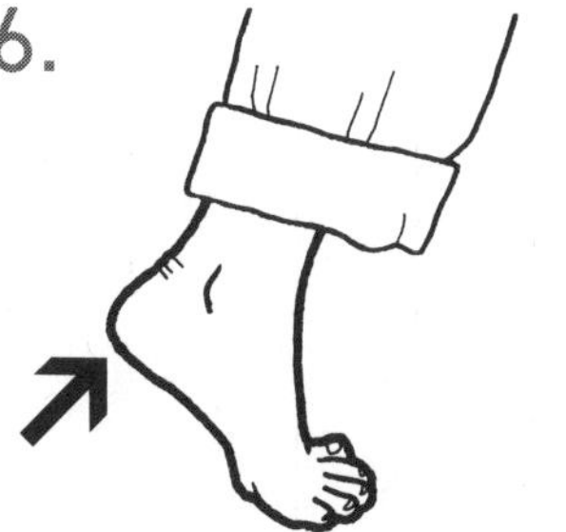

7.

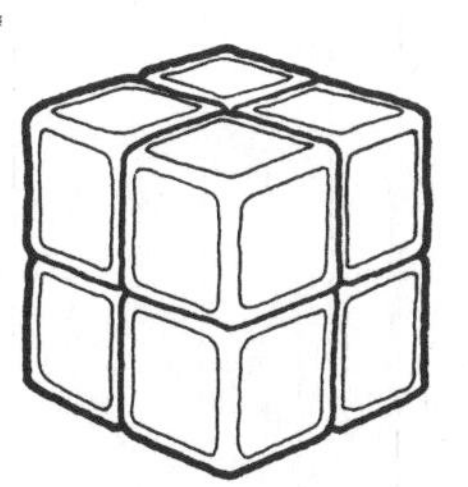

8.

9.

10.

11.

12.

Say the names of the pictures in each row.
Color the pictures whose names rhyme.

1.

2.

3.

4.

5.

With your child, take turns naming the first picture in a row and saying a new word that rhymes, such as *wheel, feel.*

Name ______________________________

Say the name of each picture. Circle its name.

1. 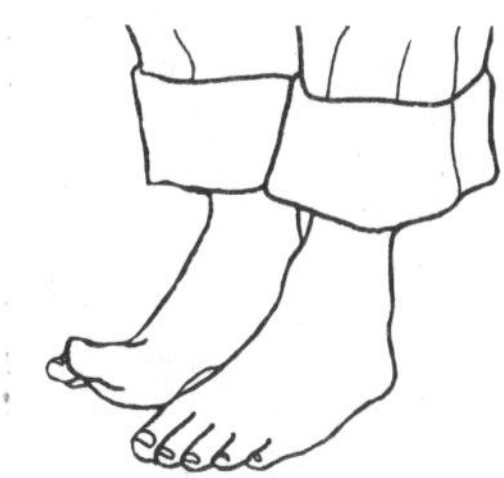

beet feed feet

2. 

leaf lead feel

3. 

meat seat seed

4. 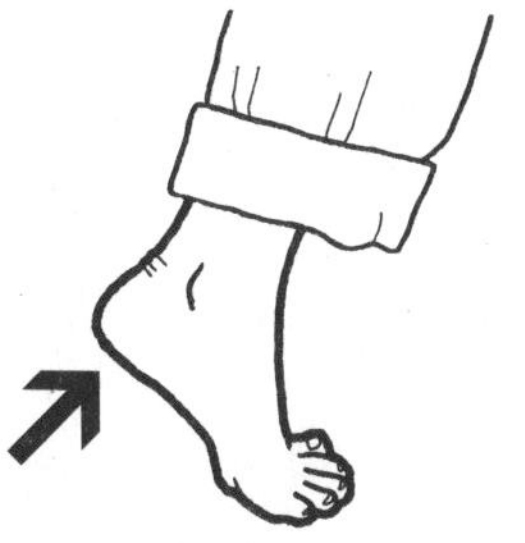

feel heel heat

5. 

see tea bee

6. 

real seat seal

7. 

jeep Jean peep

8. 

beep peel reel

9. 

beam seem team

10. 

bead jeans bean

11. 

need seed seal

12. 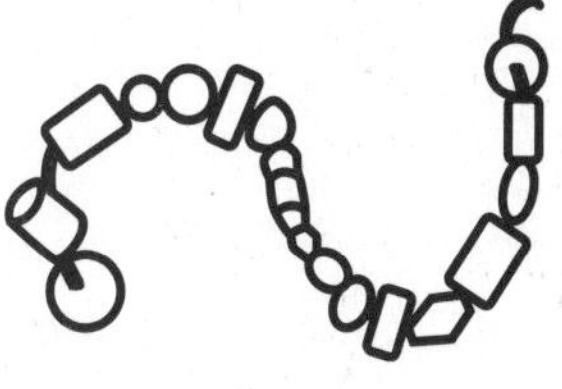

beads bean beep

Help Jean and Lee find the seals at the zoo. Read each word. Draw a line to join the long e words.

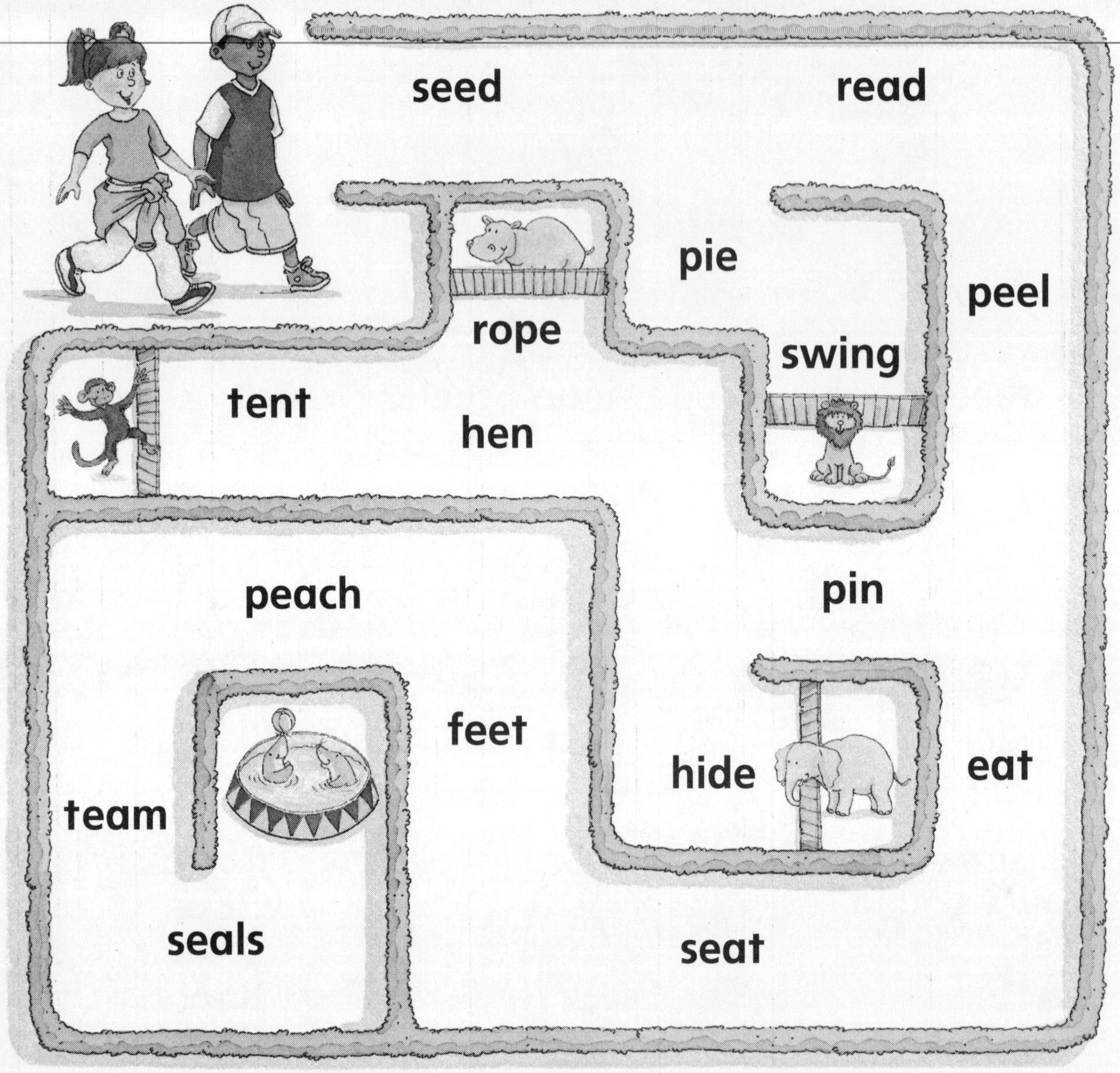

seed
read
pie
peel
rope
swing
tent
hen
peach
pin
feet
hide
eat
team
seals
seat

Use some of the long e words to write a sentence.

HOME

Help your child to use some of the words along the path to make up a short story.

Name ______________________________

Say the name of each picture. If the vowel sound is short, color the box with the word short. If the vowel sound is long, color the box with the word long.

1.

short long

2.

short long

3.

short long

4.

short long

5.

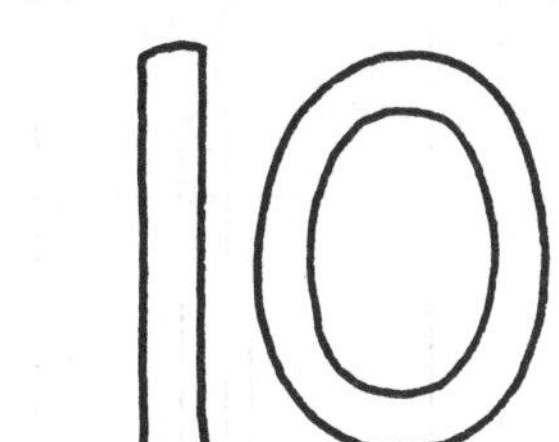

short long

6.

short long

7.

short long

8.

short long

9.

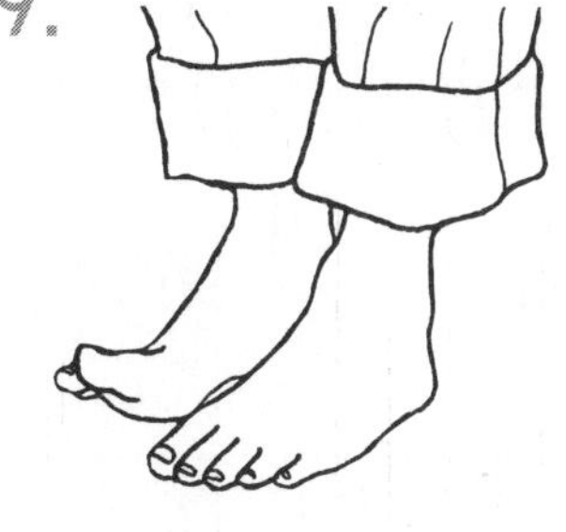

short long

10.

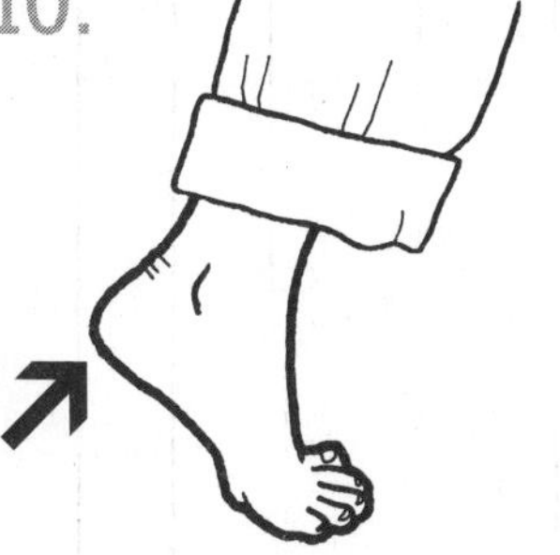

short long

11.

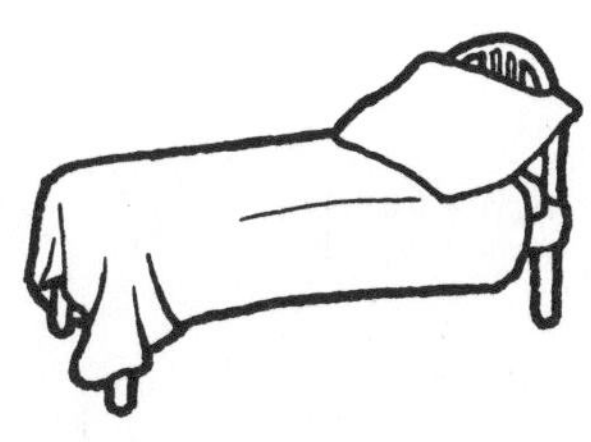
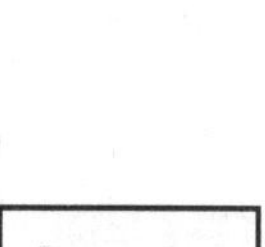

short long

12.

short long

Say the name of each picture. Circle the words in the boxes that rhyme with the picture name.

1.	me	team	see	met	bean
	he	we	fee	tea	seed
2.	feel	seal	sell	deep	deal
	men	meal	real	leaf	help
3.	feet	beat	bet	heat	set
	seat	net	neat	peat	wet
4.	please	pegs	feet	meats	fleas
	seals	teas	begs	deep	team

HOME

Ask your child to clap for a rhyming pair; then, say word pairs from the page, such as *me, see* and *tea, met*.

Name ______________________________

Say the name of each picture. Circle its name.

1.
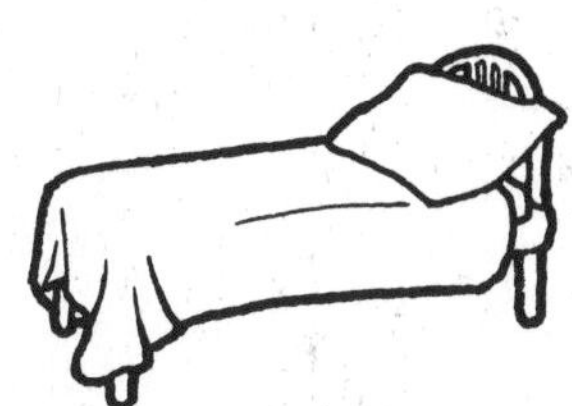
bed bead

2.

met meat

3.

neat net

4.
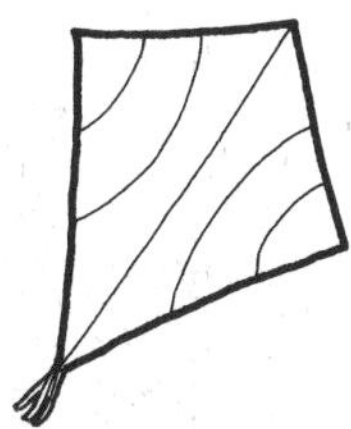
kite kit

5.
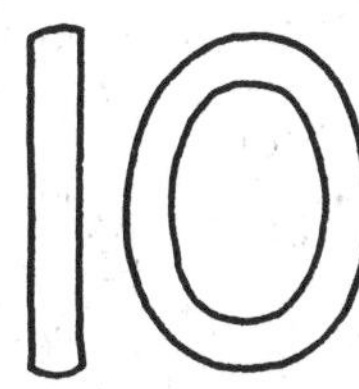
ten teen

6.

set seat

7.

mean men

8.

cube cub

9.
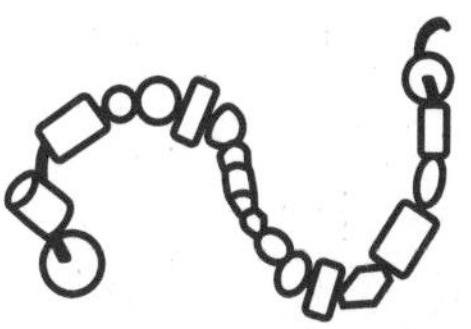
beds beads

10.

cape cap

11.

bit bite

12.

eat at

Look at the picture. Circle the word that will finish the sentence. Print it on the line.

1. I sit in my ____________. seal / seed / seat

2. It feels nice to rest my ____________. feet / feel / feed

3. Dean heats up the ____________. met / team / meat

4. Mom piles on more ____________. peak / peas / pens

5. Can I eat a heap of ____________? beds / beans / beads

6. After I eat I brush my ____________. teeth / team / ten

What food do you like best? Why?

Help your child make up a story using some of the circled words on the page.

Name ______________________________

Say the name of each picture. Print the missing vowels on the line. Trace the whole word.

1.	2.	3.	4.
f t	h n	s l	b d
5.	6.	7.	8.
n t	s t	t m	m t
9.	10.	11.	12.
j p	w b	l f	h l

Circle the word that will finish the sentence. Print it on the line.

1. We rode to Lee's game in the ______________. jeans jeep peep

2. We sat in a row with many ______________. seats seals seems

3. The Seals beat the Bees last ______________. well week keep

4. The Bees are in the ______________. lead leap leak

5. The Seals ______________ to win. neat need seed

6. Will Lee's ______________ win the game? tent tame team

Which team do you think will win?

With your child, make up a silly sentence using some of the circled words.

Name ______________________________

Say the name of each picture. Print the name on the line. In the last box, draw a picture of a long e word. Print the word.

1. 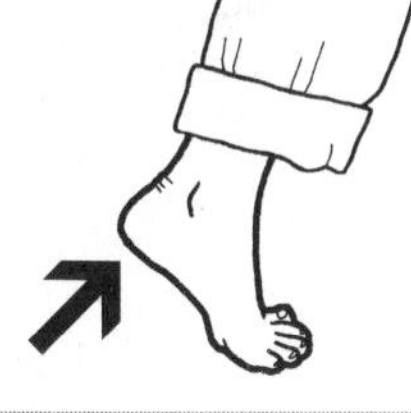
heel

2. 

3. 

4. 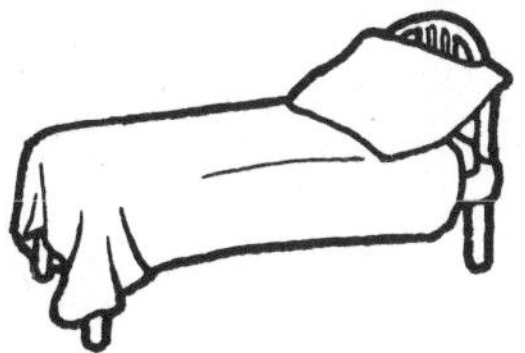

5. 

6. 

7. 

8. 

9. 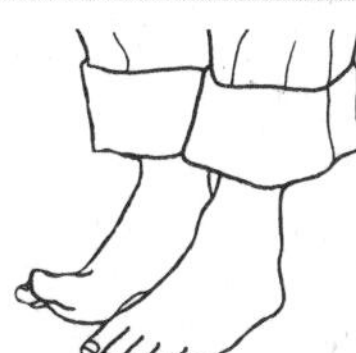

10. 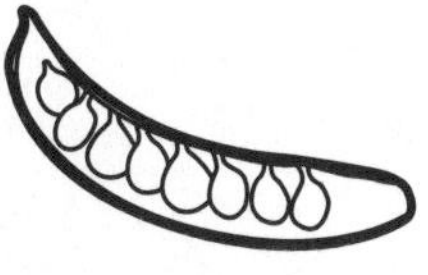

11. 

12.

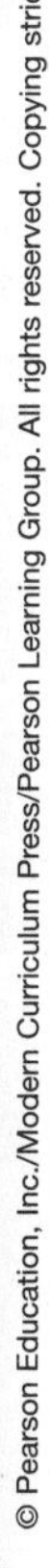

Look at the vowel sound. Color the pictures in each row whose names have that vowel sound.

1. **Long a**	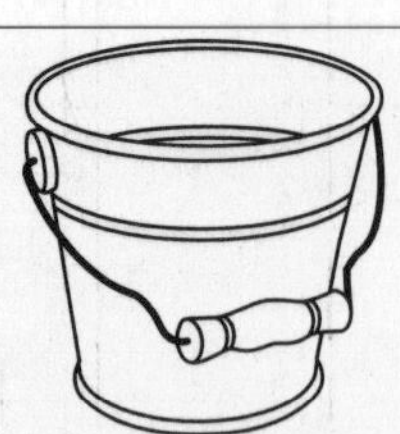			
2. **Long i**				
3. **Long u**	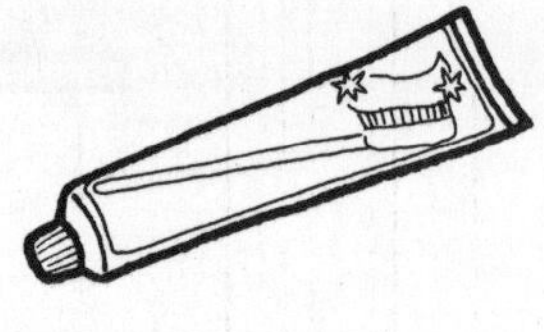			
4. **Long o**			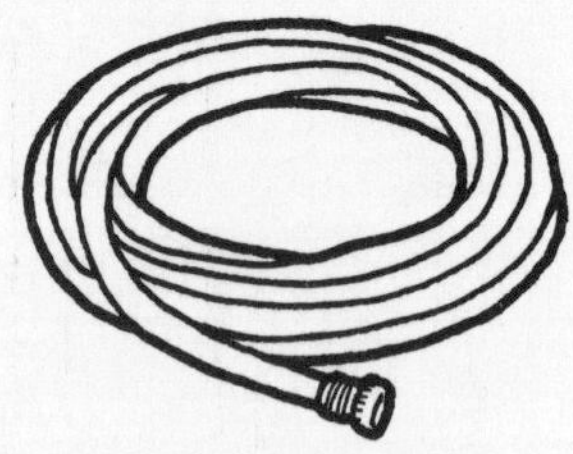	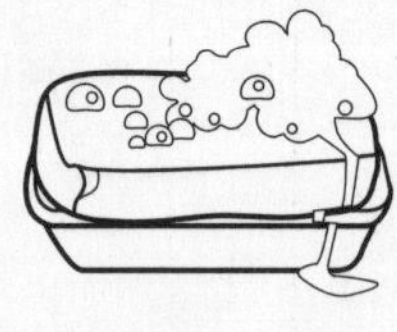
5. **Long e**	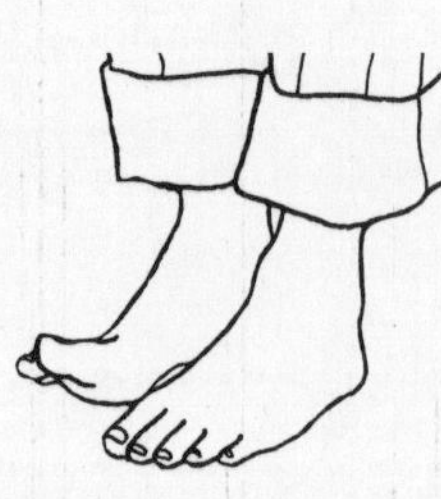			

Ask your child to think of rhyming words for three of the picture names.

Name ____________________

Blend the letter sounds together as you say each word. Then color the picture it names.

1. c a n e

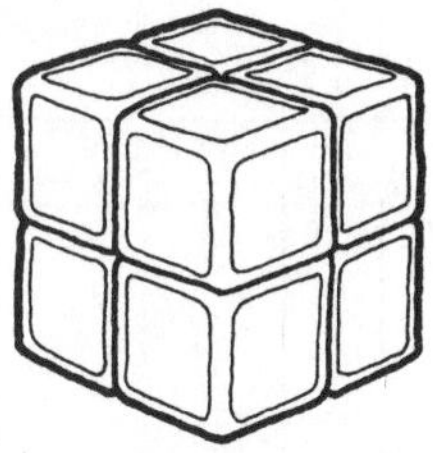

2. h o s e

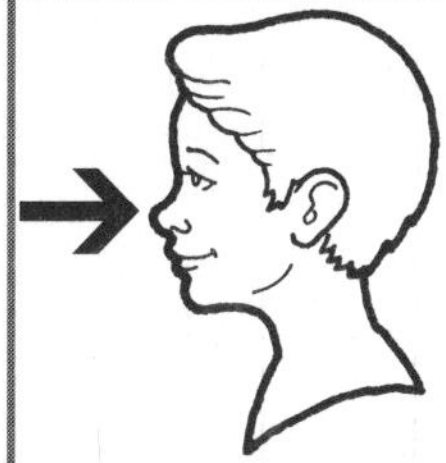

3. t u b

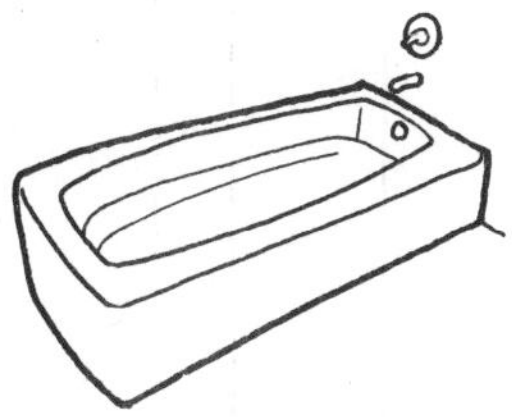

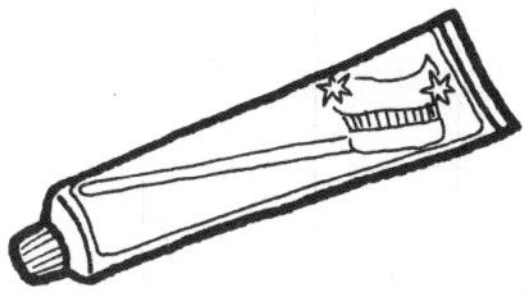

4. s e a t

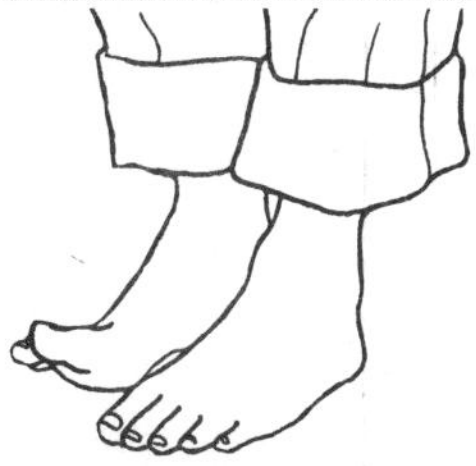

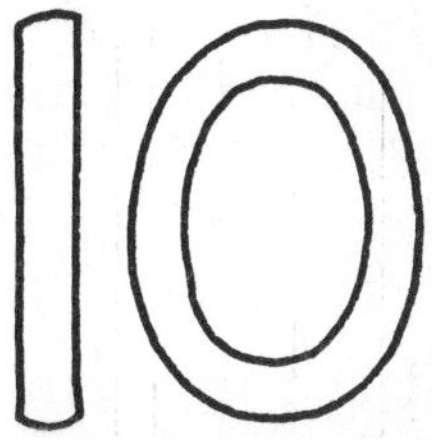

5. p i n

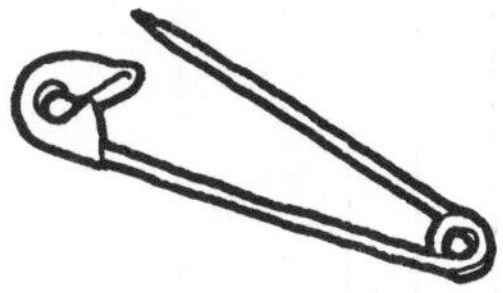

6. d o g

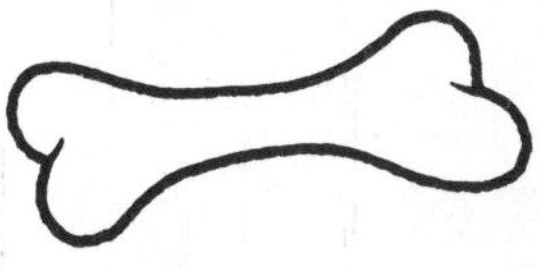

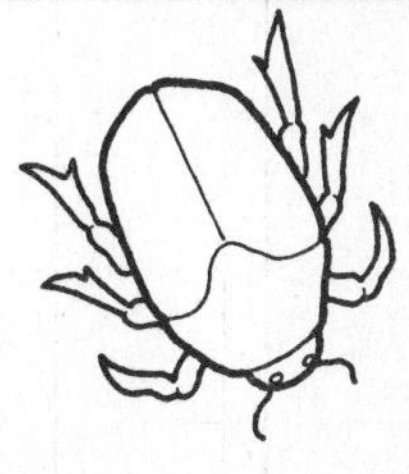

Blend the letter sounds together as you say each word. Print the word on the line. Draw a line to the picture it names.

1. c ub

2. m eat

3. r ain

4. p ig

5. m op

6. t ube

Help your child make up silly rhymes for picture names, such as *Hop on a mop*.

Name ________________________________

Say the name of each picture. Print the missing vowels on the lines. Trace the whole word.

1. c _ _ t	2. t _ r _	3. f _ _ t	4. r _ b _
5. t _ b _	6. b _ _	7. d _ m _	8. h _ _
9. l _ _ f	10. c _ k _	11. s _ _ t	12. n _ _ l

Read the word in the box. Add an e to make a long vowel word. Write it on the first line. Then change the vowel of the word in the box to make a short vowel word. Write it on the second line.

	Long Vowel	Short Vowel
1. tap	tape	top
2. pin		
3. cut		
4. hop		
5. not		
6. pan		
7. hid		

Help your child think of sentences using short and long vowel word pairs, such as *I did not get a note.*

Name ______________________________

Say and spell each long vowel word. Print each word on a line in the box that shows its long vowel sound.

fruit	rain	pie	bean	bike
bone	hay	soap	seal	glue

Long a ______________ ______________

Long i ______________ ______________

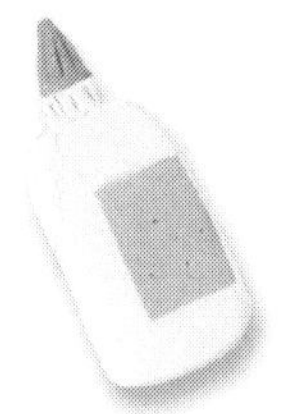

Long u ______________ ______________

Long o ______________ ______________

Long e ______________ ______________

Write a letter to a friend. Tell about a game, sport, or hobby you like. The words in the box may help you.

kite	rope	feet
bike	flute	day

Dear ____________________,

Your friend,

You may want to help your child address an envelope and mail the letter to a friend.

Mom closed the window. Good night, Mike! Good night, Bruce!

4

FOLD

Name ____________________

No Sleep

One night Mike was fast asleep.

1

Bruce licked Mike's face. That woke him up.
2
Next came a blue jeep. It made a loud BEEP.
3

Name ______________________________

Say the name of each picture. Fill in the bubble beside the picture name.

1.
- ○ cake
- ○ rake
- ○ coat
- ○ keep

2.
- ○ mile
- ○ mail
- ○ ruler
- ○ mule

3.
- ○ wave
- ○ vase
- ○ five
- ○ dive

4.
- ○ bone
- ○ cone
- ○ cane
- ○ tune

5.
- ○ jeans
- ○ jeep
- ○ deep
- ○ game

6.
- ○ sail
- ○ seem
- ○ rose
- ○ suit

7.
- ○ tie
- ○ toe
- ○ lie
- ○ tire

8.
- ○ rail
- ○ road
- ○ read
- ○ rain

9.
- ○ bait
- ○ goat
- ○ boat
- ○ toad

10.
- ○ tile
- ○ tube
- ○ tape
- ○ time

11.
- ○ mate
- ○ moat
- ○ boat
- ○ meat

12.
- ○ rope
- ○ soap
- ○ pole
- ○ robe

Circle the word that will finish the sentence. Print it on the line.

1. Sue had a ________ blue kite. — net / neat

2. The kite did ________ have a tail yet. — not / note

3. Joe ________ up rags to make a tail. — cut / cute

4. Then they sailed the ________. — kit / kite

Can you read each word? Put a ✓ in the box if you can.

☐ long	☐ their	☐ where	☐ want	☐ out	☐ little
☐ your	☐ could	☐ about	☐ two	☐ from	☐ why
☐ they	☐ which	☐ them	☐ were	☐ there	☐ because

Read Aloud

Everybody Eats Bread

People came to America from all over the world. They brought many ways to make bread.

French Americans make long, skinny loaves. The crust is crisp and brown. Mexican Americans wrap a flat bread around beans and meat. Jewish Americans bake bread with eggs and milk. They twist the loaf into a braid.

It does not matter what shape bread is. Every shape tastes good!

TALK About It

What kind of bread do you like best?

Dear Family,

In this unit called "Everybody Eats," your child will learn about words that begin and end with consonant blends and words with **y** as a vowel. Many food names, such as **gr**apes, **pl**um, **str**awberr**y**, mi**lk**, and cherr**y**, begin or end with consonant blends or end with **y** as a vowel. As your child becomes familiar with consonant blends and words with **y** as a vowel, you might try these activities together.

- Talk with your child about a favorite food. Have him or her draw a picture of the food. Then, help him or her to write a sentence about the food.
- Read the article on page 239 together. Ask your child to identify words with consonant blends and **y** as a vowel.
- Your child might enjoy reading these books with you. Look for them in your local library.

The Giant Carrot by Jan Peck

Blueberries for Sal by Robert McCloskey

Sincerely,

____

Estimada familia:

En esta unidad, titulada "Todos comemos" ("Everybody Eats"), su hijo/a estudiará palabras en inglés que comienzan y terminan con combinaciones de consonantes y palabras con y como una vocal. Muchos nombres de alimentos, como por ejemplo, **gr**apes (uvas), **pl**um (ciruela), **str**awberr**y** (fresa), mi**lk** (leche) y cherr**y** (cereza), comienzan o terminan con grupos de consonantes o terminan con **y** como una vocal. A medida que su hijo/a se vaya familiarizando con los grupos de consonantes y las palabras con **y** como una vocal, pueden hacer las siguientes actividades juntos.

- Conversen con su hijo/a sobre una comida favorita. Pídanle que haga un dibujo de dicha comida y después, con su ayuda, que escriba una oración que describa la comida.
- Lean juntos el artículo en la página 239. Pidan a su hijo/a que identifique palabras con combinaciones de consonantes e **y** como una vocal.
- Ustedes y su hijo/a disfrutarán leyendo estos libros juntos. Búsquenlos en su biblioteca local.

The Giant Carrot de Jan Peck

Blueberries for Sal de Robert McCloskey

Sinceramente,

____

Name ____________________________

I love to munch
Fresh fruit for brunch
And have a bunch
Of grapes with lunch.

Say the name of the first picture in the row. Circle each picture in the row whose name begins with the same blend.

1\.

grapes

2\.

tree

3\.

brush

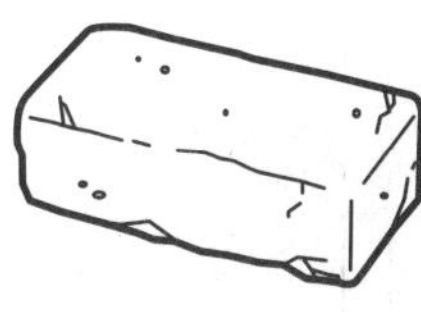

4\.

crib

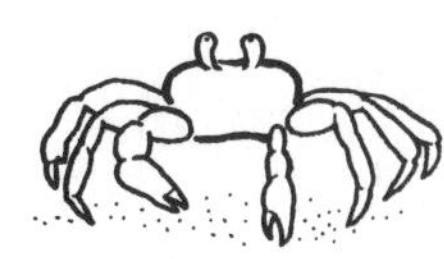

Say the name of the first picture in the row. Color each picture in the row whose name begins with the same blend.

1. prize

2. frog

3. dress

4. train

5. crab

Ask your child to say the name of each picture and name the first two letters of each word.

Name ___________________________________

Say the name of each picture. Circle its name.

1.  free tree	2. 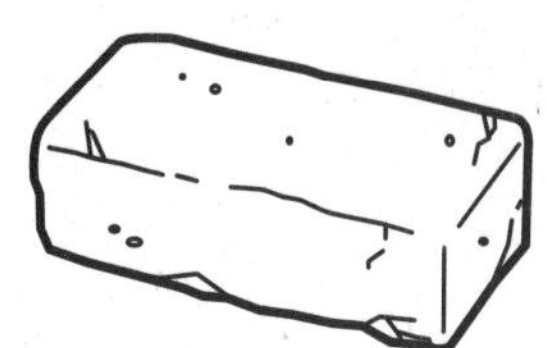 trick brick	3.  prize cries
4.  frog frame	5.  crab crib	6.  drive dress
7.  braid bride	8.  grapes grass	9.  crane crown
10.  drum drip	11.  frown frame	12.  grass grab

Say the name of each picture. Print its beginning blend on the line. Trace the whole word.

1. crab
2. ain
3. ide
4. uit
5. ick
6. ess
7. ize
8. ane
9. ee
10. um
11. ass
12. og

Point to a picture and ask your child to think of another word that begins with the same sound.

Name ____________________________________

Slice the plum.
Place it on a plate.
You take some.
I'll be glad to wait.

Say the name of the first picture in the row. Circle each picture in the row whose name begins with the same blend.

1.  plug |   

2.  block |    

3.  club | 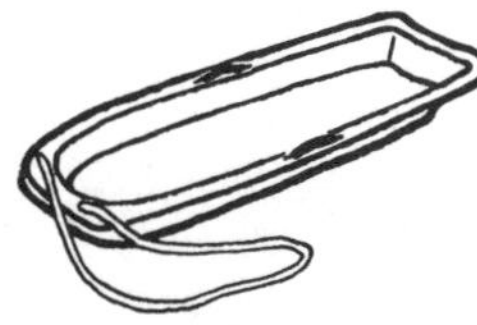   

4.  flag | 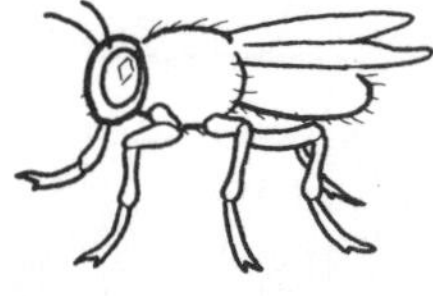 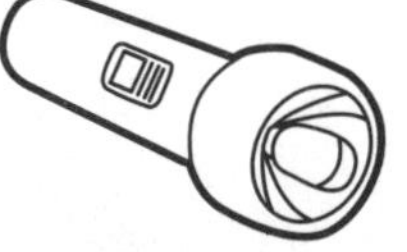  

5.  glass |    

Say the name of each picture. Circle its name.

1. block flock	2. grape plate	3. class glass
4. drag flag	5. clue glue	6. plug plum
7. crack clock	8. plant plan	9. flat float
10. grass glass	11. club clap	12. fly cry

Play a word game with your child by saying, "I say *fly*, you say fl___." Your child supplies a word with the blend.

Name ____________________________________

Say the name of each picture. Print its beginning blend on the line. Trace the whole word.

1. 

club

2. 

____ant

3. 

____ag

4. 

____ate

5. 

____ock

6. 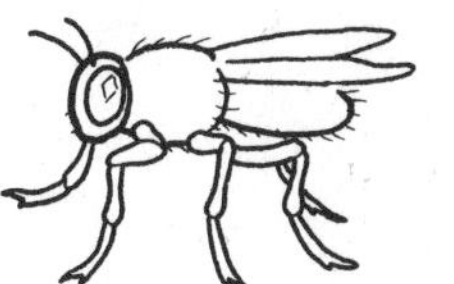

____y

7. 

____at

8. 

____ass

9. 

____ock

10. 

____obe

11. 

____ug

12. 

____ue

Say the name of each picture. Circle the word that will finish the sentence. Print it on the line.

1. Take a peek into my ______. — clap / class / grass

2. Bruce draws a funny ______. — clock / clown / frown

3. Fran makes a clock from a paper ______. — plate / prank / plum

4. Mr. Glen lets us grow ______. — plans / plates / plants

5. We play with clay and ______. — braids / drives / blocks

6. We look at the ______. — globe / glass / grape

Would you like to do what Bruce and Fran did in school? Why?

Point to the words *Bruce, Fran, Glen, grow, play, clay* and ask your child to think of more words that begin with the same sounds.

Name ___________________________________

Spice smells nice,
And tastes good, too.
But too much spice
Can spoil the stew.

► Say the name of the first picture in the row. Circle all the pictures in the row whose names begin with the same blend.

1. 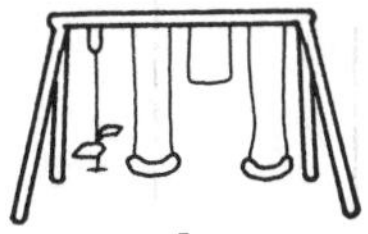 swing

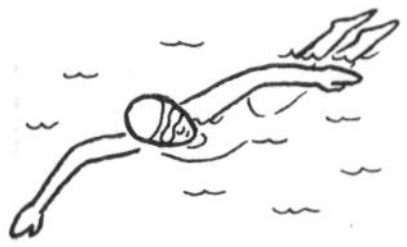

2.  spill

3.  skate

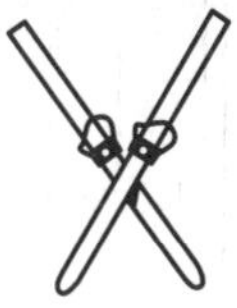

4. 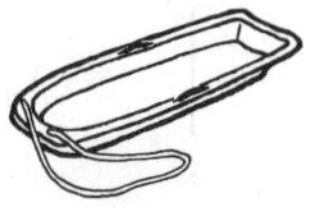 sled

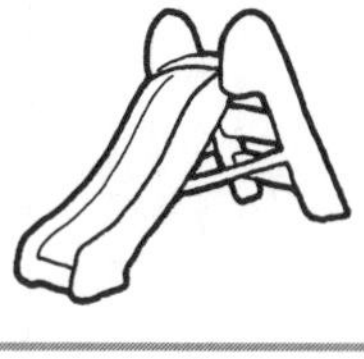

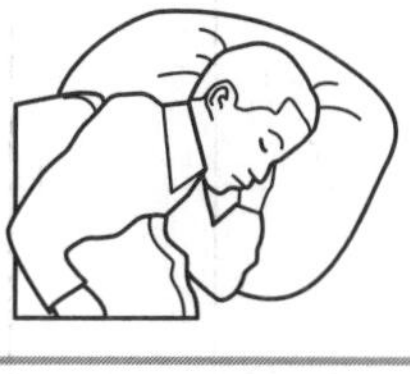

5.  snail

6.  stop

Say the name of each picture. Circle its name.

1. sled slide	2. stops steps	3. spill spade
4. skunk spunk	5. spin swim	6. scrap scrub
7. sweet street	8. smoke spoke	9. square scare
10. swing string	11. snake skate	12. spot spoon

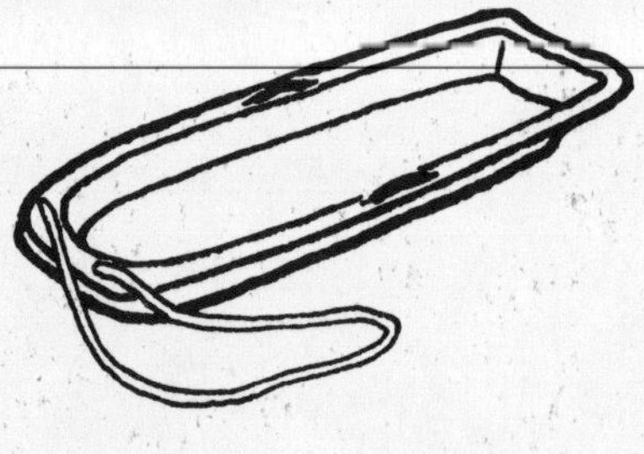

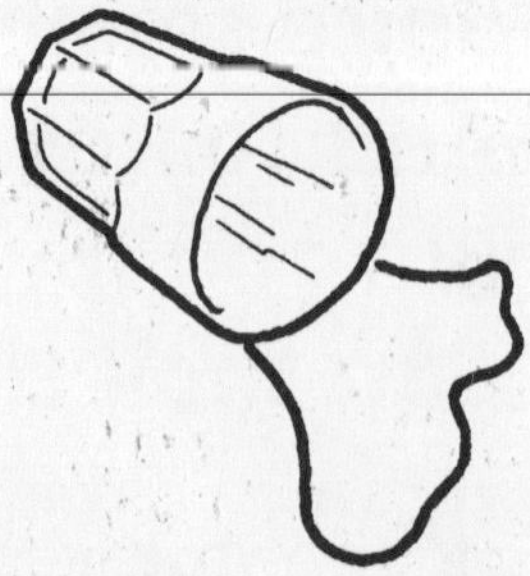

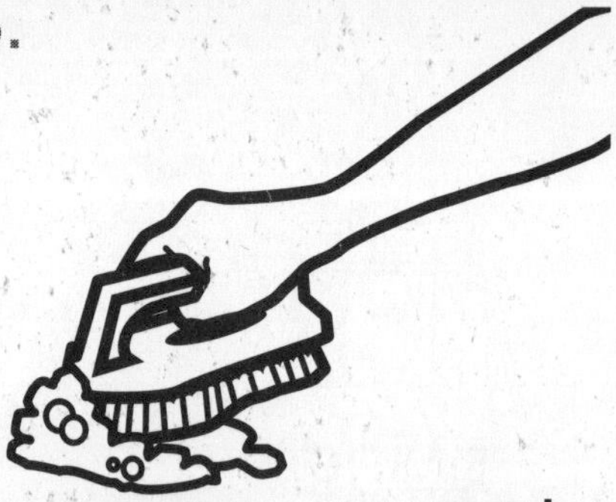

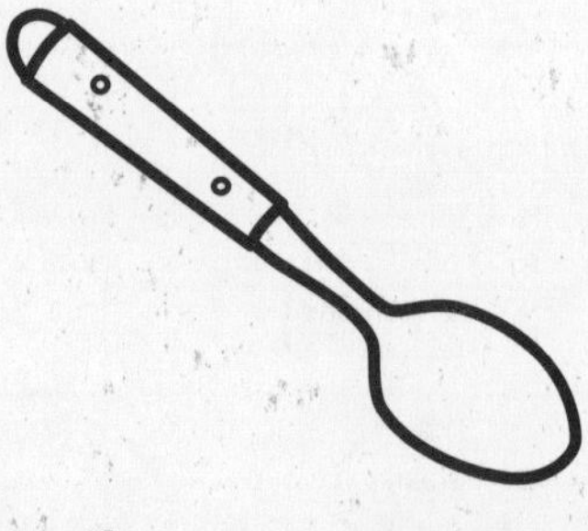

Say "*s-l, sl.*" Ask your child to name a word that begins with the *sl* sound. Repeat for *st, sp, sk, sw, sm.*

Name ______________________________

Say the name of each picture. Print its beginning blend on the line. Trace the whole word.

1. 
______ skate

2. 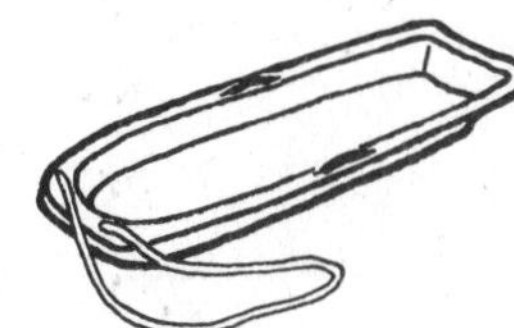
______ ed

3. 
______ ub

4. 
______ ar

5. 
______ ail

6. 

______ op

7. 
______ oke

8. 
______ irt

9. 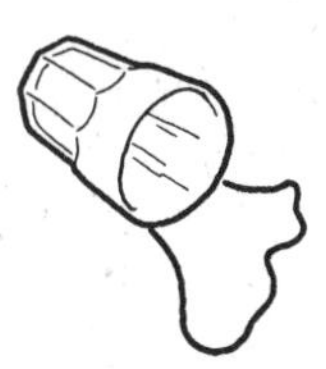
______ ill

10. 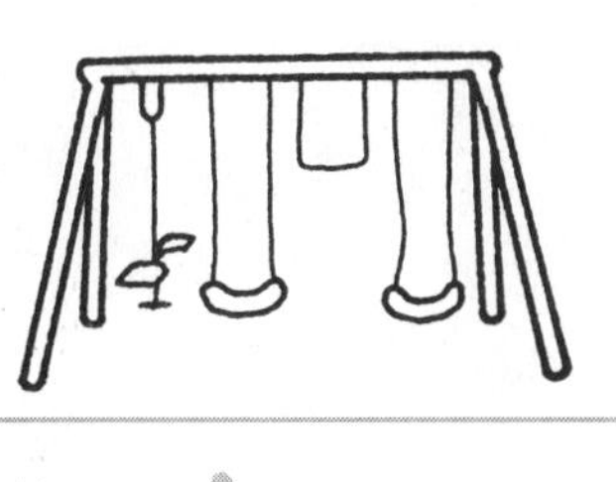
______ ing

11. 
______ are

12. 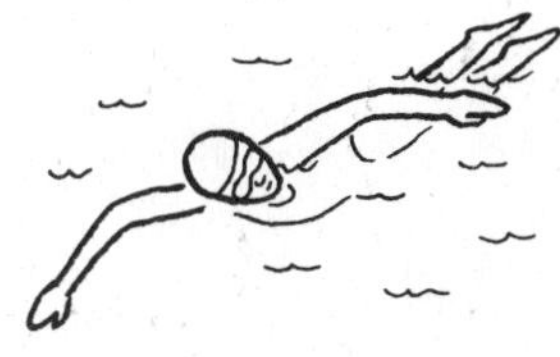
______ im

Say the name of the picture. Circle the word that will finish the sentence. Print it on the line.

1. Be sure to ________ and read each rule! — spill / stop / star

2. Take turns on the ________. — slide / sling / slip

3. Do not run near the ________. — sting / swing / swim

4. Please do not pet the ________. — snake / spoke / snail

5. Look before you cross the ________. — steps / street / stamp

6. Always ________ with a pal. — sweep / snake / swim

What other safety rules do you know?

Help your child to think of new sentences using some of the circled words.

Name ______________________________

I'd like to be in a marching band,
With a shiny gold trumpet in my hand.
I'd look my best in my hat and coat,
And I'd never, ever miss a note!

Say the name of the first picture in the row. Circle each picture in the row whose name ends with the same blend.

1.  jump 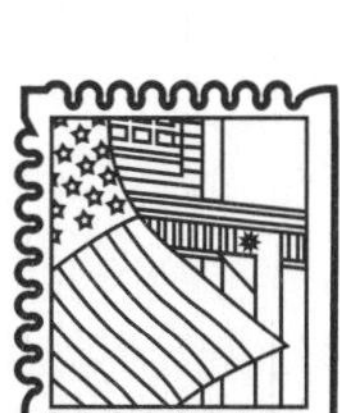  

2.  desk 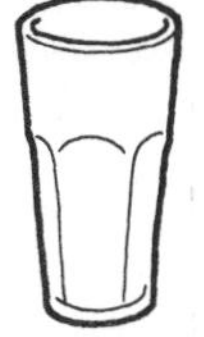   

3.  sink  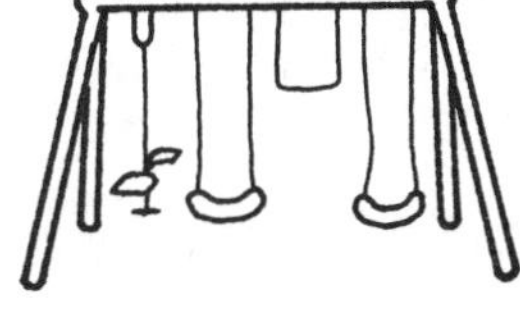  

4.  list    

5  hand   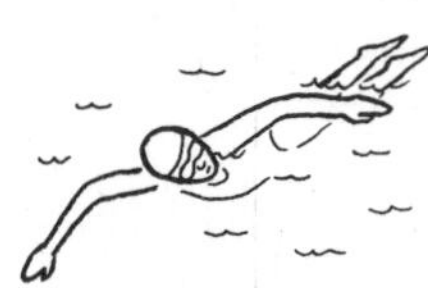 

Say the name of each picture. Print its ending blend on the line. Trace the whole word.

1. trunk
2. la
3. de
4. mi
5. li
6. wi
7. ne
8. si
9. ma
10. be
11. ju
12. ha

Ask your child to point to a picture, name a word that rhymes, and then name the letters in the final blend.

Name ______________________________

Blend the letter sounds together as you say each word. **Color** the picture it names.

1.

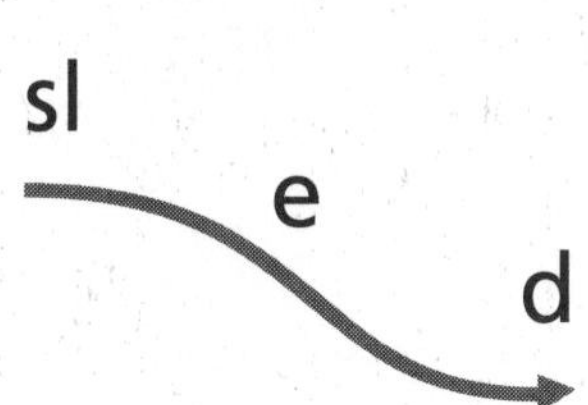

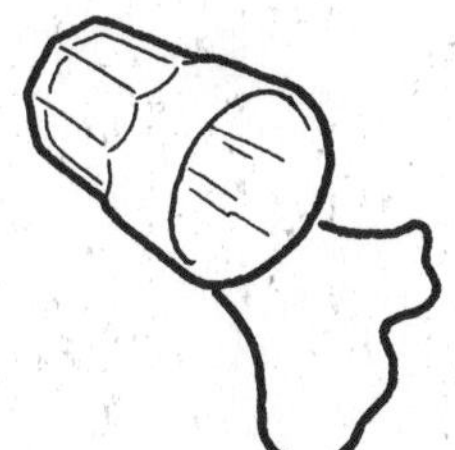

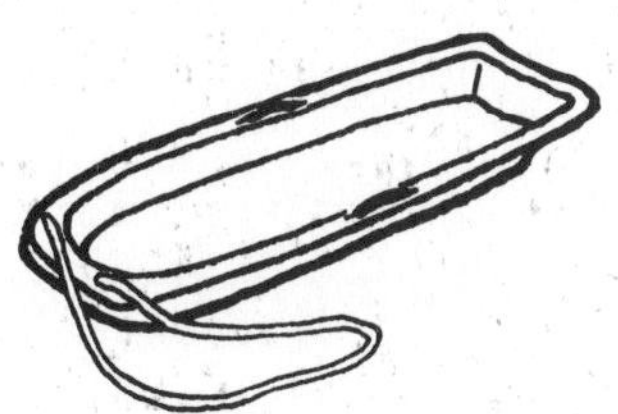

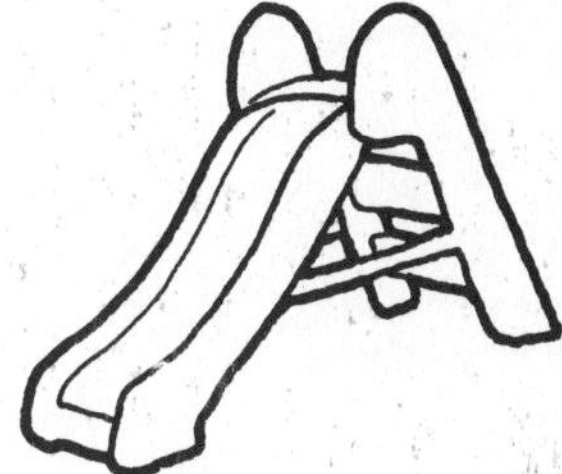

2.

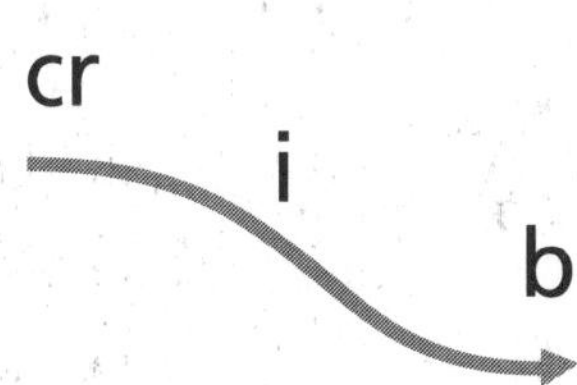

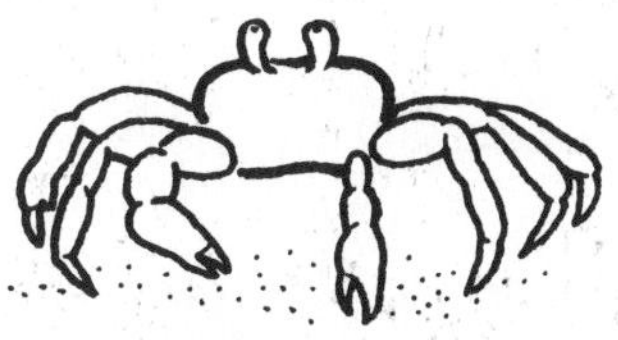

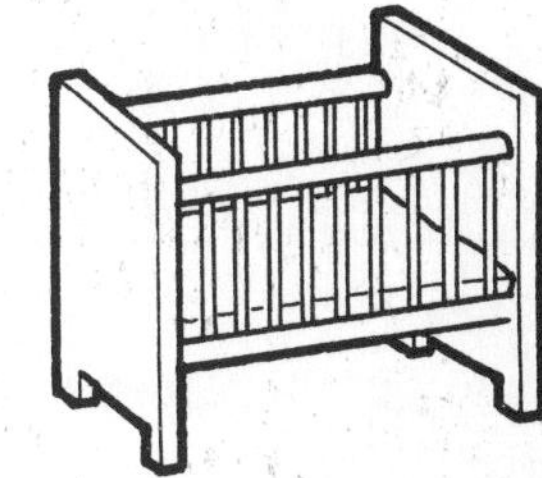

3.

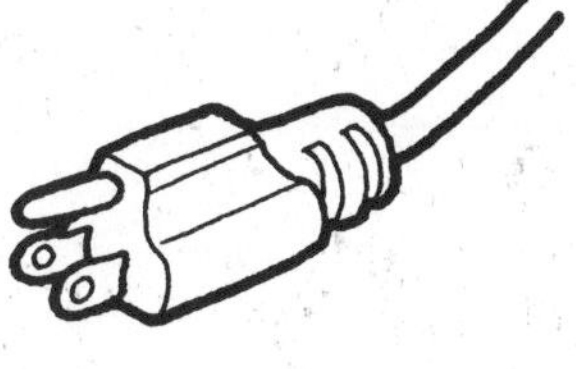

4.

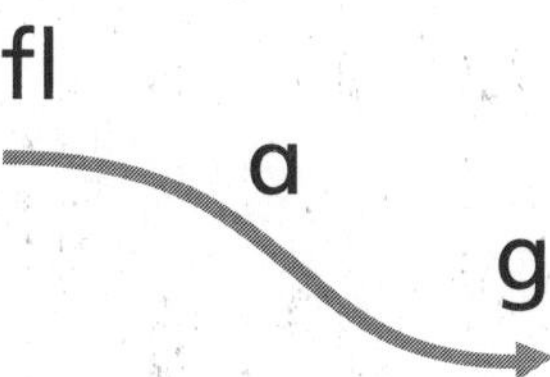

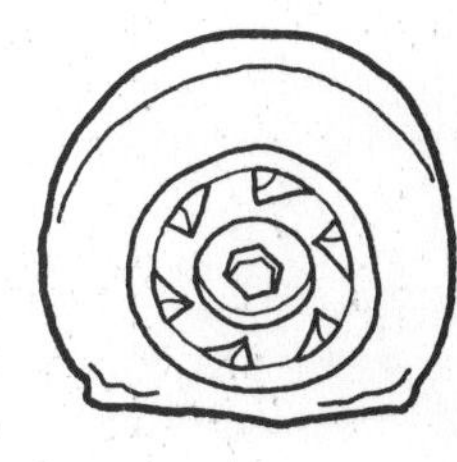

5.

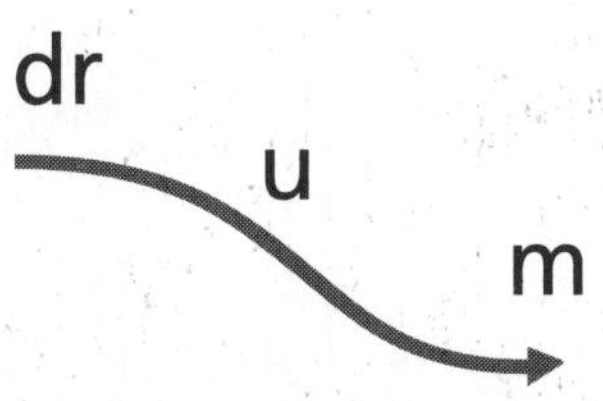

Blend the letter sounds together as you say each word. Then print the word on the line. Draw a line to the picture it names.

1. s i nk

2. l i st

3. m i lk

4. g i ft

5. j u mp

6. d e sk

Point to a word. Ask your child to name the final blend, then say a word with the same final blend.

Name ______________________

Read the story. Then, use words from the story to finish the sentences.

Fred's Bread

Fred made some bread.
He mixed flour, water,
and too much yeast.
The bread grew and grew.
Now Fred had too much bread!
He asked his friends to stop by.
They sliced the soft bread and made toast.
Then they spread jam on the toast.
They had a feast!

1. Fred made some ______________.

2. Fred asked his friends to ______________ by.

3. He and his friends had a ______________.

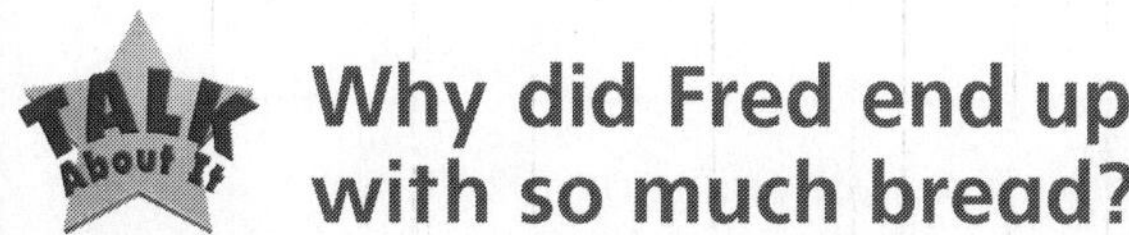

Why did Fred end up with so much bread?

Add the word part to each of the blends in the boxes. Say the word. If it is a real word, write it on the line.

tr sm br cl sl

ick

1. ____________________

2. ____________________

3. ____________________

4. ____________________

pl gr gl cl st

ay

5. ____________________

6. ____________________

7. ____________________

8. ____________________

Write a sentence using two of the words you made.

____

____

HOME

Ask your child to make up a sentence using two more of the words he or she wrote.

Name ____________________________

Won't you try my berry pie?
The crust is flaky, my, oh my.
Come on, have some.
Don't be shy.
If you won't try it, I may cry!

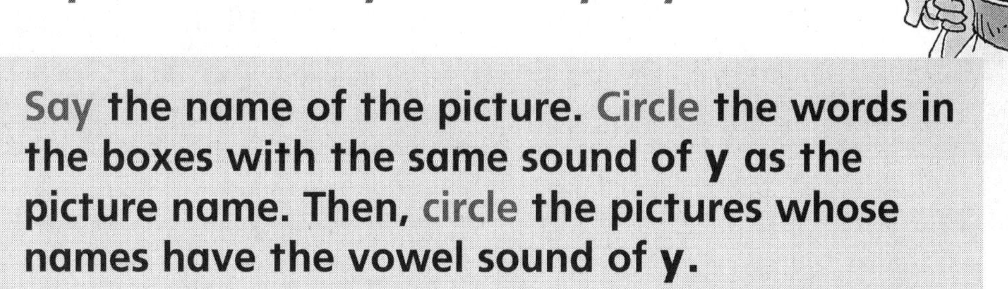

Say the name of the picture. Circle the words in the boxes with the same sound of y as the picture name. Then, circle the pictures whose names have the vowel sound of y.

1.	by	lazy	yellow	dry	yet
	my	sky	yoke	cry	yarn
2.	yes	fry	you	yard	funny
	yellow	puppy	sly	yell	windy
3. 20	fly	candy	yams	lady	penny
	pry	fairy	baby	try	pony

Say the name of each picture. Circle its name.

1. puppy buggy	2. fry fly	3. lady baby
4. funny penny	5. pony penny	6. cry try
7. spy sky	8. fifty twenty	9. sly fry

Point to each picture and help your child think of a word or name that rhymes, such as *puppy-guppy*.

Name ____________________

Say the name of each picture. Circle the word that will finish the sentence. Print it on the line.

1. Wendy can not ride a ____________________.

bony
pony
penny

2. She is too small to feed a ____________________.

puffy
poppy
puppy

3. She can not draw the ____________________.

sky
sly
spy

4. Mom will not let her eat ____________________.

sandy
candy
funny

5. I feel sad if she starts to ____________________.

my
cry
try

6. Wendy is only a ____________________.

bunny
baby
buggy

What can a baby do?

Say the name of each picture. Print the picture name on the line. In the last box, draw a picture of a word in which y is a vowel. Write the word.

1.

2.

3.

4.

5.

6.

7.

8.

9.

Ask your child to say the name of his or her picture and spell the word.

Name ______________________

Read the sentences. Use the mixed-up letters to make a word from the box. Print the word on the line to finish the sentence.

grapes	try	bread	fresh	smell

1. "The fruit looks ____________," Clare said. **s h r e f**

2. "Let us buy some ____________," said Greg. **a r p e g s**

3. "I will ____________ to find green ones." **r t y**

4. "Just ____________ the plums!" Clare said. **e l l s m**

5. "Now all we need is ____________." **e a d b r**

How do you think the plums smell?

Review consonant blends and y as a vowel: Words in context, critical thinking

Write a shopping list for your family's next trip to the store. List things to buy. Look at the words in the box for help.

bread	**drink**	**sweet**	**fruit**
plums	**grapes**	**milk**	**berry**

SHOPPING LIST

Talk with your child about what items could be added to the list.

Bake the pizza till it is crisp. Then, put it on a plate. It will taste great!

4

FOLD

Name ____________

PIZZA FEAST

Did you ever try to make a pizza? First, you make the crust.

1

Press the crust in a pan. Make it round and flat.

2

FOLD

Spread the sauce and cheese all over.

3

Name ____________________________

Say the name of each picture. Fill in the bubble beside the picture name.

1.
- ○ trip
- ○ prize
- ○ train
- ○ drain

2.
- ○ snail
- ○ snake
- ○ skate
- ○ string

3.
- ○ clock
- ○ braid
- ○ blouse
- ○ block

4.
- ○ crab
- ○ grab
- ○ club
- ○ crib

5.
- ○ flag
- ○ glass
- ○ flat
- ○ blank

6.
- ○ green
- ○ dress
- ○ drum
- ○ desk

7.
- ○ deck
- ○ drive
- ○ desk
- ○ jump

8.
- ○ clap
- ○ plant
- ○ plug
- ○ plate

9.
- ○ stamp
- ○ steps
- ○ stop
- ○ spill

10.
- ○ glue
- ○ globe
- ○ drive
- ○ glove

11.
- ○ frame
- ○ lamp
- ○ fly
- ○ frog

12.
- ○ glass
- ○ spot
- ○ spoon
- ○ smoke

Circle the word that will finish each sentence. Print it on the line.

1. ______________ the day with a good meal. Stop Start Star

2. Corn ______________ and milk are great. flags frames flakes

3. ______________ adding some fruit. Fry Try Why

4. ______________ a glass of juice. Drink Trunk Dress

5. Some ______________ is good, too. float test toast

6. Stay away from ______________ things. sweet smoke square

Read Aloud

Let it Snow!

In a blizzard, the wind blows very hard. Snow falls faster and very heavily. The temperature is close to zero. The heavy snow and blowing wind make it hard to see.

Once, a big blizzard hit Chicago. Schools and offices were closed for days. There was so much snow that some of it was sent by train to Florida. Children in Florida had never seen snow!

TALK About It

How do you find out what the weather will be each day?

Dear Family,

In this unit, "Whatever the Weather," your child will learn about contractions, words ending with **ed** and **ing,** and consonant digraphs. A consonant digraph is formed with two letters that stand for one sound. For example, the **sh** in sheep and the **th** in thermometer are digraphs. As your child becomes familiar with these concepts, you might try these activities together.

- Help your child to create a weather chart. For each day of the week, he or she can draw a picture of that day's weather. At the end of the week, ask your child to tell you what the weather was each day.
- With your child, read the article on page 269. Help him or her to identify the words with consonant digraphs and contractions and words that end in **ed** or **ing.**
- Your child might enjoy reading these books with you. Look for them in your local library.

The Snowy Day
by Ezra Jack Keats

Let's Count the Raindrops
by Fumi Kosaka

Sincerely,

____

Estimada familia:

En esta unidad, titulada "Pronósticos del tiempo" ("Whatever the Weather"), su hijo/a estudiará en inglés contracciones, palabras que terminan en **ed** y en **ing** y digramas de consonantes. Un digrama de consonantes está formado por dos letras que representan un sonido. Por ejemplo, la **sh** en sheep (oveja) y la **th** en thermometer (termómetro) son digramas. A medida que su hijo/a se vaya familiarizando con estos conceptos, pueden hacer las siguientes actividades juntos.

- Ayuden a su hijo/a a crear un mapa meteorológico. Para cada día de la semana, su hijo/a puede hacer un dibujo sobre el tiempo que hubo ese día. Al final de la semana, pídanle que les explique cuál fue el tiempo en cada día.
- Lean juntos el artículo en la página 269. Ayuden a su hijo/a a identificar las palabras con contracciones, los digramas de consonantes y las palabras que terminan en **ed** o en **ing**.
- Ustedes y su hijo/a disfrutarán leyendo estos libros juntos. Búsquenlos en su biblioteca local.

The Snowy Day de Ezra Jack Keats

Let's Count the Raindrops de Fumi Kosaka

Sinceramente,

____

Name ______________________________

It rained and poured all week.
Now it's raining again.
The puddles are growing so big!
I'm jumping and playing in them.

Say the name of each picture. Print the ending you see in the corner of the box to finish its name. Trace the whole word.

1. ed spilled	2. ed melt	3. ing eat
4. ing rain	5. ed boil	6. ing fish
7. ed row	8. ed peel	9. ing cry

Read the word below each picture. Each picture name has a base word and an ending. Trace the circle around the base word. Then, read the words beside each picture. Circle each base word.

1. jumped	asked	yelled	fixed	played
	mixed	rocked	bumped	rained
2. reading	going	telling	sailing	mixing
	asking	waiting	resting	boating
3. melted	waited	seated	heated	landed
	mailed	loaded	floated	ended
4. cooking	rowing	crying	flying	fishing
	picking	saying	eating	melting

HOME With your child, hunt for words with endings in favorite storybooks.

Name ______________________________

Circle the word that will finish the sentence. Print it on the line.

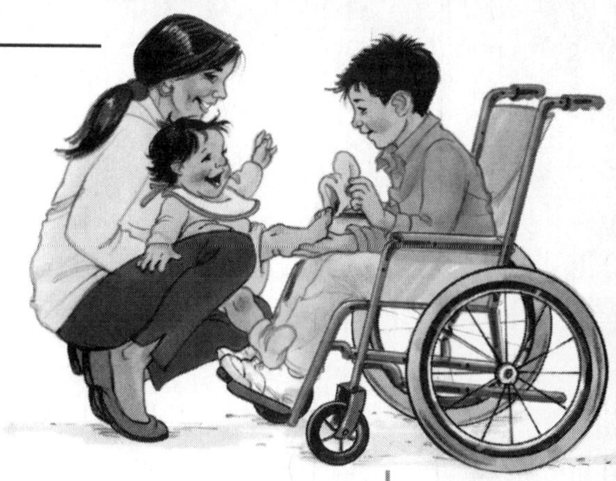

1. We were ______________ to eat.	waiting waited
2. Dad was ______________ the ham.	cooking cooked
3. Mom was ______________ for help.	asking asked
4. She and I ______________ the baby.	dressing dressed
5. Sandy ______________ the fruit.	peeling peeled
6. I ______________ the most!	helping helped

How does this family help each other?

Circle the word that will finish the sentence. Print it on the line.

1. Dad was ______ fishing.	go going
2. I ______ him to take me to Mary's home.	asking asked
3. We were ______ a ball to each other.	kicked kicking
4. Then we ______ to get wet.	started starting
5. It was ______ cats and dogs.	rain raining
6. We ______ for the rain to stop.	waiting waited
7. Then we ______ on Mary's swing set.	played playing

What does "raining cats and dogs" mean?

Using words with endings, take turns telling what you did today.

Inflectional endings -ed and -ing: High-frequency words, critical thinking

Name ___________________________________

My soft mittens are thick, not thin.
My fingers and thumbs stay warm in them.
When the thermometer says thirty-three,
Outside with my mittens is where I'll be.

Thumb begins with the sound of th. Circle each picture whose name begins with the sound of th.

1.	2.	3.	4.
5.	6.	7.	8.
9.	10.	11.	12.

Say the name of each picture. Print th or t to finish each word. Trace the whole word.

1. 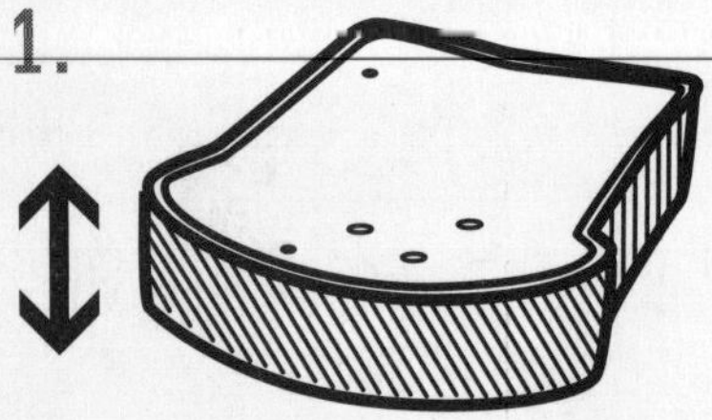 thick

2. 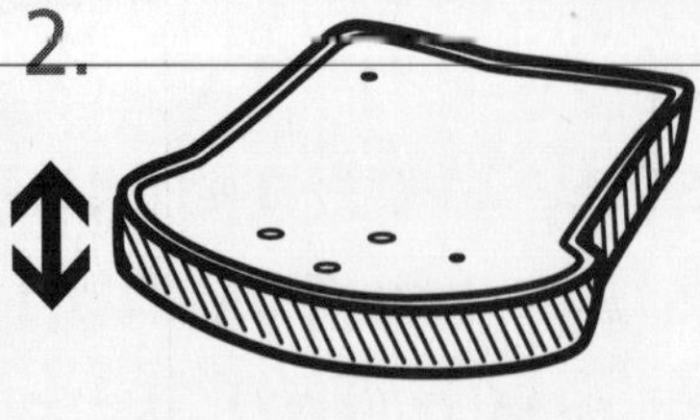 in

3. 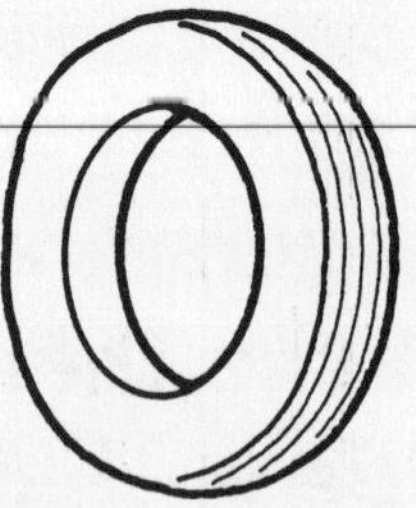 ire

4. 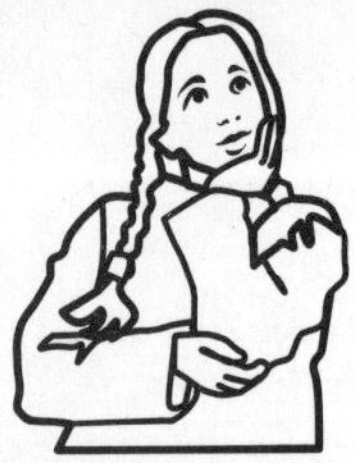 ink

5. irty

6. 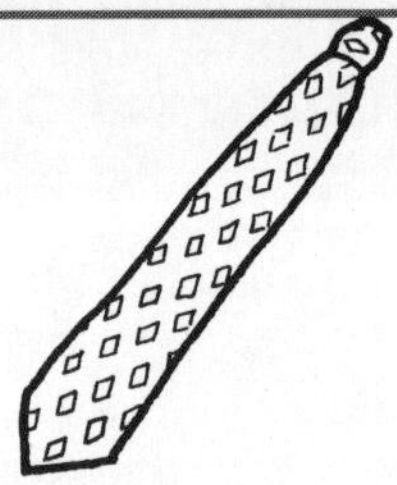 ie

7. 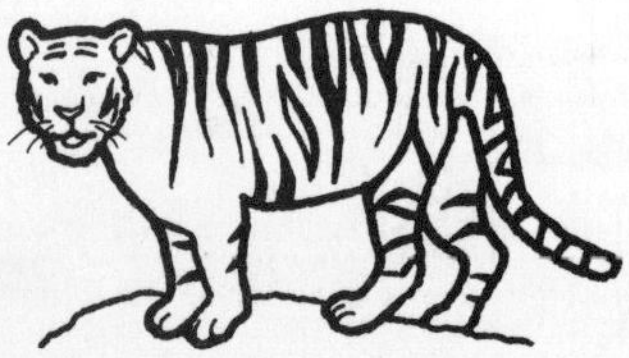 iger

8. 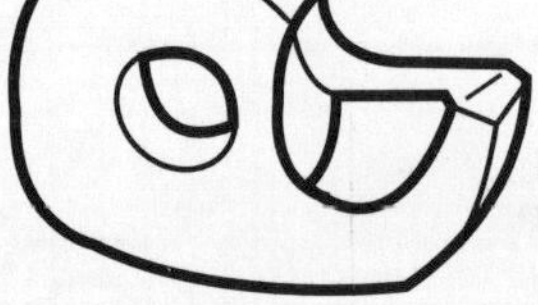 ape

9. ree

10. 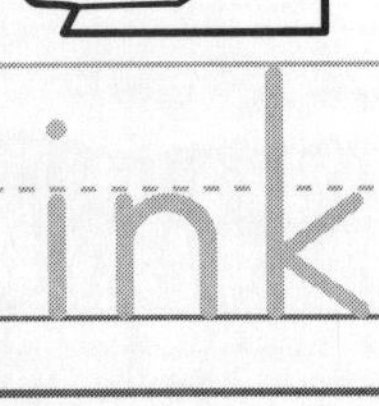 umb

11. 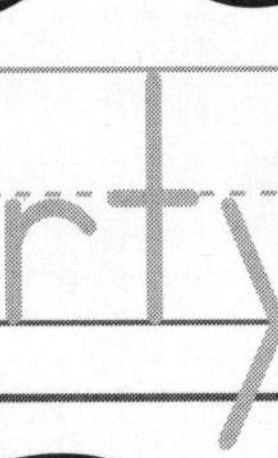 orn

12. en

Help your child to make up a sentence using words with *t* and *th*, such as *Thirty tigers had thick tails.*

Name ______________________________

The wind whines and whistles.
It whips through the tree.
It whirls around wildly,
And takes my white cap from me!

White begins with the sound of wh. Circle each picture whose name begins with the sound of wh.

1.	2.	3.	4.

5.	6.	7.	8.

9.	10.	11.	12.

Say the name of each picture.
Print wh or th to finish each word.
Trace the whole word.

1. eel	2. umb	3. ick
4. orn	5. eat	6. ink
7. ale	8. in	9. ite
10. ree	11. read	12. istle

Ask your child: *What comes after two and before four?* Take turns making up riddles for other picture names.

Name ________________________________

Shannon is in the sunlight.
What does she see?
A shiny, shimmering shadow.
She says, "You can't catch me!"

Shadow begins with the sound of sh. Circle each picture whose name begins with the sound of sh.

1. 

2. 

3. 

4. 

5. 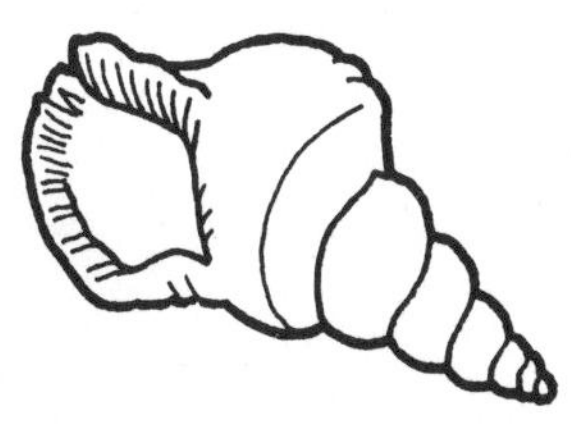

6. 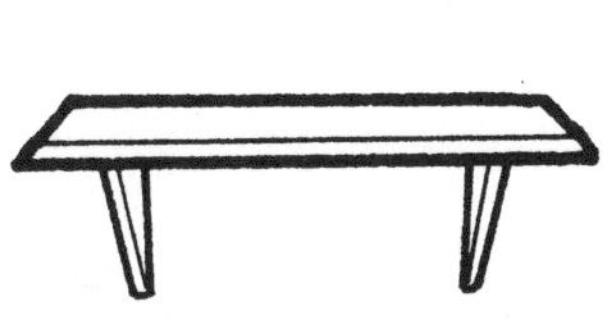

7. 

8. 

9. 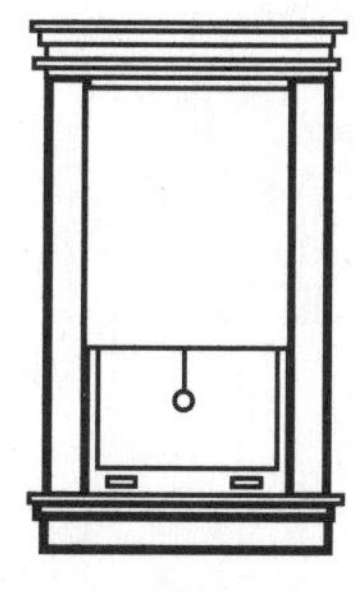

10. 

11. 

12. 

Say the name of each picture.
Print sh or s to finish each word.
Trace the whole word.

1. 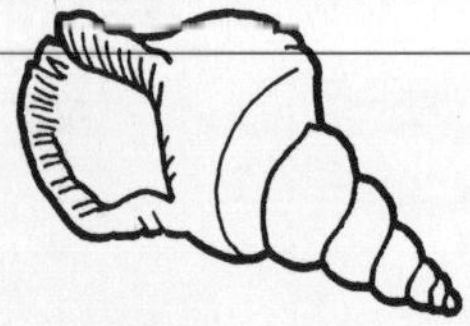 ell
2. 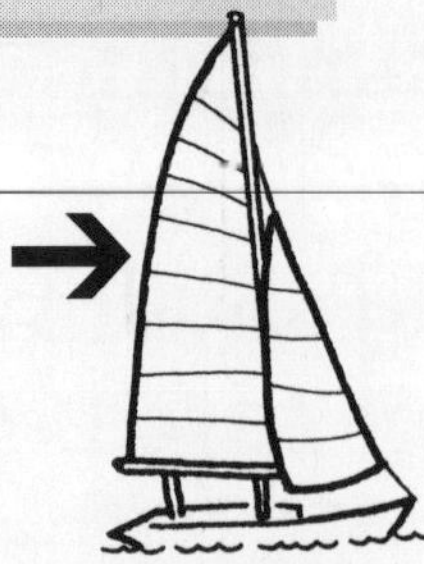 ail
3. 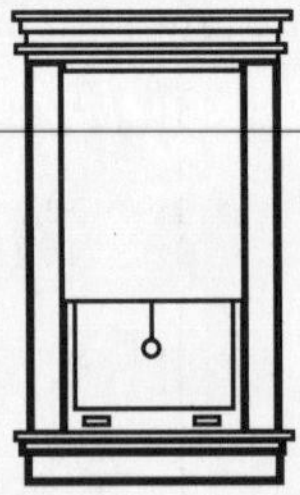 ade
4.  ix
5.  oe
6.  elf
7.  ip
8.  eep
9.  eat
10.  irt
11. 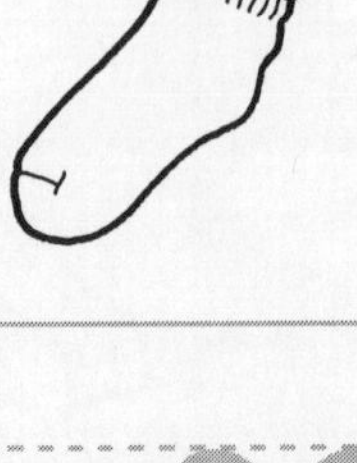 ock
12.  out

Ask your child to make up sentences using some of the words on the page.

Name ________________________________

Outside it was chilly.
Chen's pets chose to stay indoors.
Chen sat in a chair with Lily,
While Chip chased yarn on the floor.

Chair begins with the sound of ch. Circle each picture whose name begins with the sound of ch.

1. 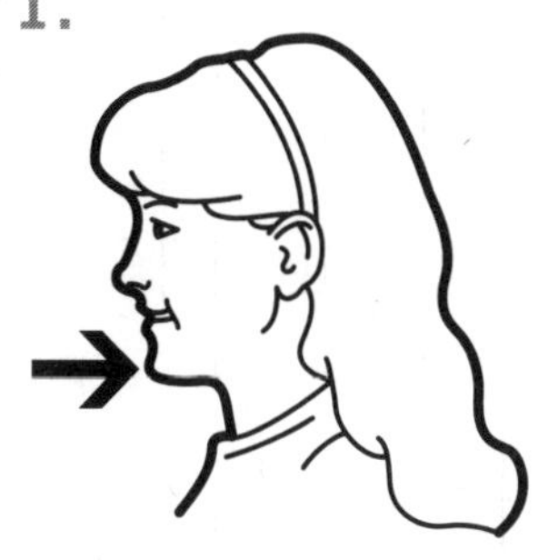

2. 

3. 

4. 

5. 

6. 

7. 

8. 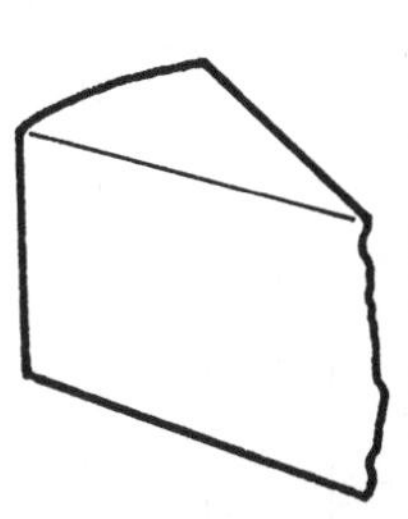

9. 

10. 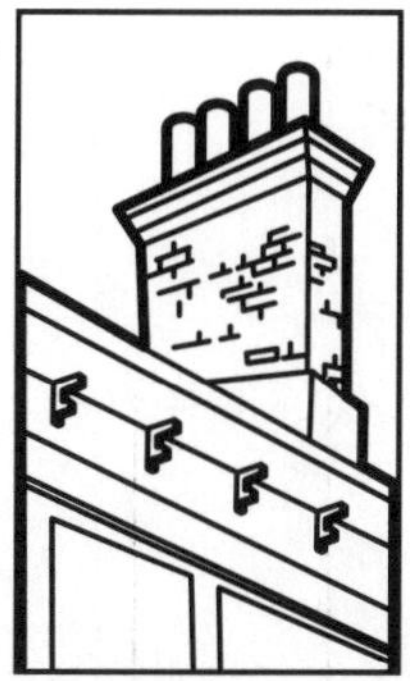

11. 

12. 

Say the name of each picture. Print ch or c to finish each word. Trace the whole word.

1. 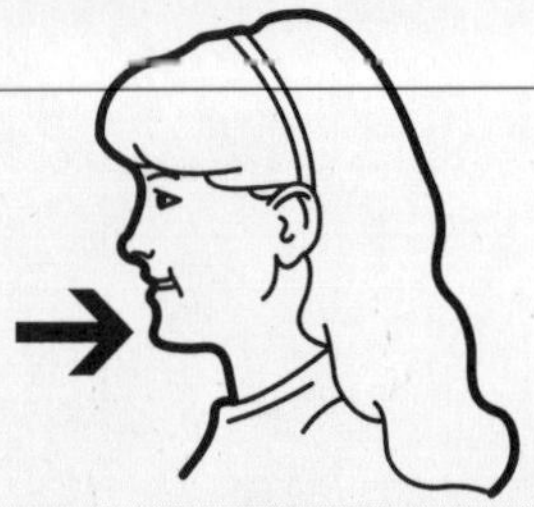 in
2.  eck
3.  oat
4. 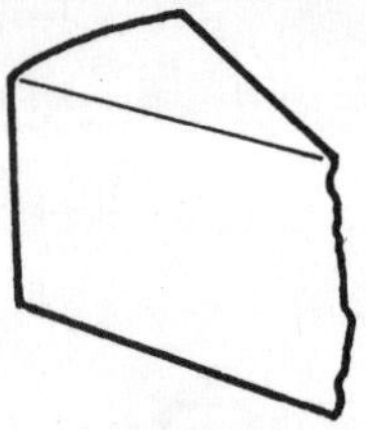 eese
5.  ube
6.  ick
7.  alk
8.  at
9. 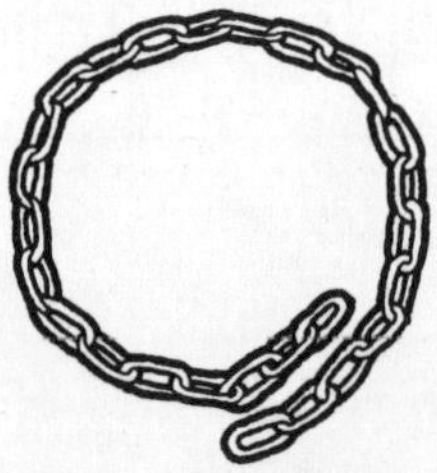 ain
10.  erry
11.  ow
12.  air

Ask your child to identify common household items whose names begin with *ch* or *c*, such as *chair* and *comb.*

Name ______________________________

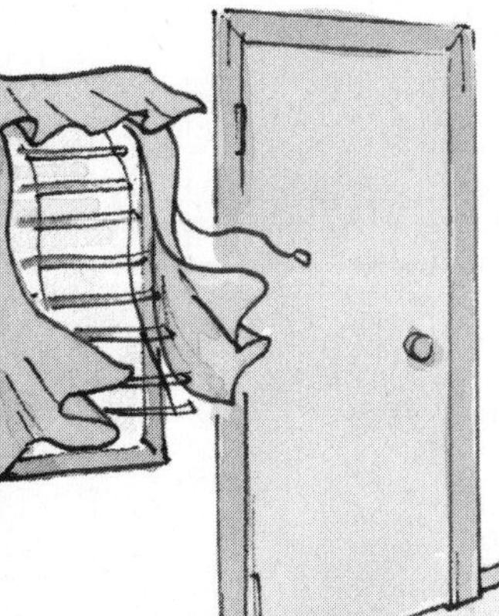

Knock, knock, knock.
Who's knocking at the door?
We know who it is—
The wind, and nothing more!

Knock begins with the letters kn. You only hear the sound of n. Say the name of each picture. Trace the whole word. Then, circle the pictures whose names begin with kn.

1.   knee

2.  think

3.  knot

4. 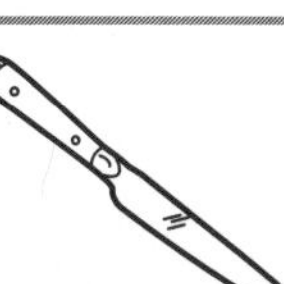 knob

5. knife

6.  whale

7. 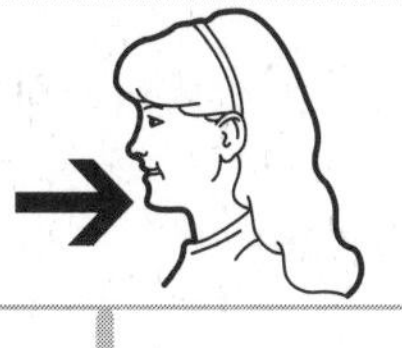 chin

8.  knock

9.  knit

Circle the sentence that tells about the picture.

1.		The tire is black and white. Chad tied a knot in the rope.
2.		Randy did not skin his knee. Kelly kneels down on the mat.
3.		Did you hear a knock at the door? Did Nick knock over the vase?
4.		I fed the bread to the chicks. I used a knife to slice the cheese.
5.		Chuck knows where his watch is. Kate turned the knob to the left.
6.		Susan knits a sweater for her sister. Jenny ties a knot with her shoe strings.
7.		The knight does not ride a horse. The knight rides a horse with spots.

HOME

Ask your child to point to and read each *kn* word.

Name ________________________________

Circle the word that will finish the sentence. Print it on the line.

1. Chuck ______________ about a sunny beach.	knows knob knock
2. We catch the bus at ______________.	thick three thorn
3. Beth puts a ______________ sheet down.	white wheat whip
4. Chuck finds ______________ in the sand.	sheets shades shells
5. I ______________ Beth a new game.	teach reach cheat
6. Then we sit and look at the ______________.	shape ships shake

What else can people do at the beach?

Read each clue. **Print** the answer to each riddle on the line. **Use** the cloud pictures if you need help.

1. My hair is called wool.
I can be white, brown, or black.

I am a __________.

2. I hatch out of an egg.
My mother is a hen.

I am a __________.

3. I live in the sea.
I am much bigger than a fish.

I am a __________.

4. I sail across the sea.
People ride in me.

I am a __________.

5. I come after two
and before four.

I am __________.

6. I am round. I help
cars and bikes go.

I am a __________.

7. I am round and red.
I am good to eat.

I am a __________.

8. I am very sharp. People
use me to cut things.

I am a __________.

Ask your child to read the riddles to you so you can guess the answers.

Name ______________________________

Blend the letter sounds together as you say each word. **Print** the word on the line. **Draw** a line to the picture it names.

1. 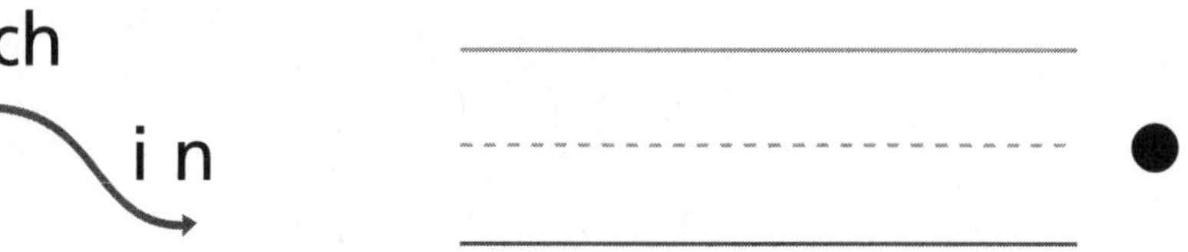
ch
i n

2. 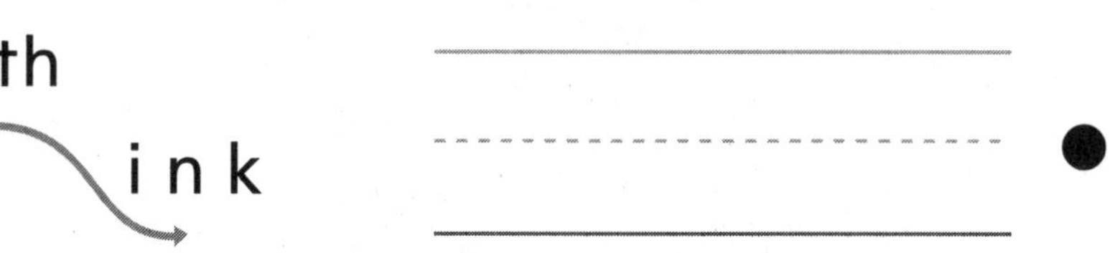
th
i n k

3. 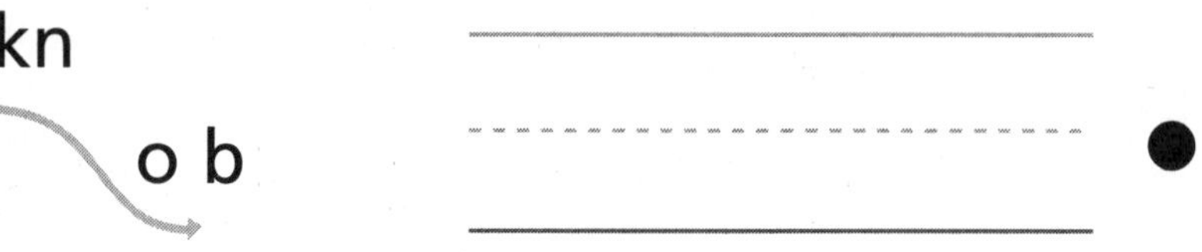
kn
o b

4. 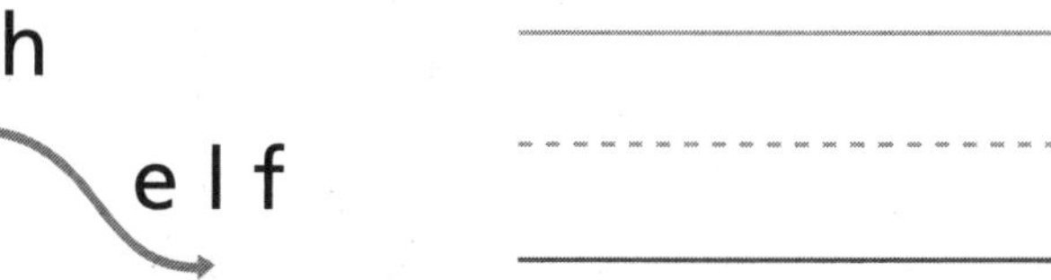
sh
e l f

5. 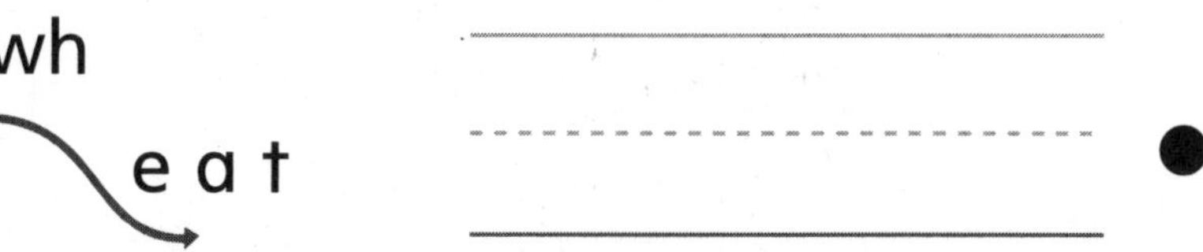
wh
e a t

6. 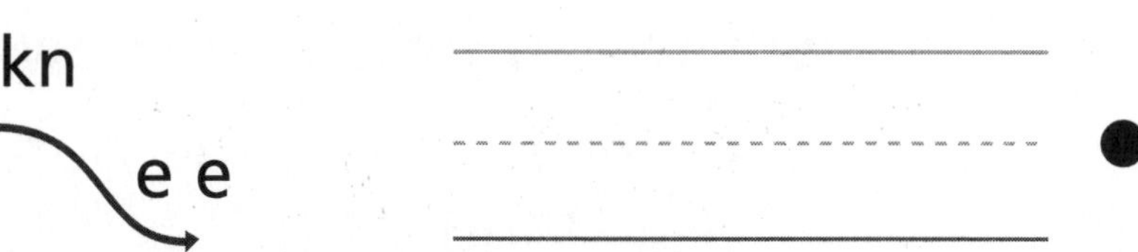
kn
e e

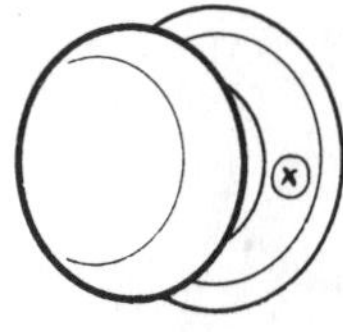

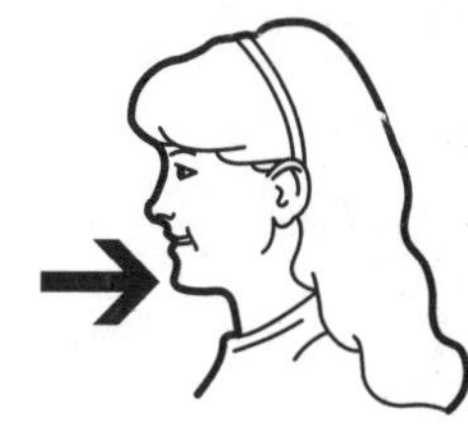

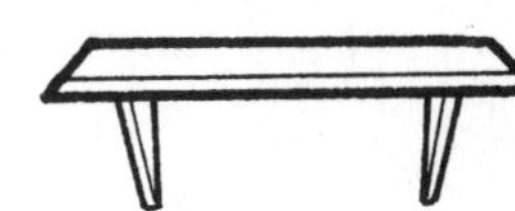

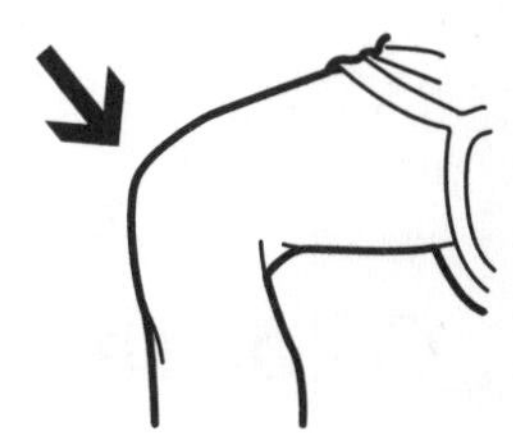

Look at the picture. Then follow the directions.

1. Color the ship black.
2. Circle the shell on the beach.
3. Write a three on the flag.
4. Color the wheel brown.
5. Color the thick rope yellow.
6. Draw a whale in the water.
7. Draw a box around each knot.
8. Color the sky blue but keep the cloud white.

With your child, make up a story to go with the picture.

Name ________________________________

Read the story. Use words in which two letters stand for one beginning sound and words with endings to finish the sentences.

Looking for Chuck

Where was Chuck?
Shari and Shane looked all over.
They knew Chuck did not like storms.
Now thunder was booming.
Lightning flashed.
Chuck was hiding.
After a while Shari sat down.
She said, "I give up."
Just then Shane said, "There's Chuck!
He's chewing his toy under your chair!"

1. ______________ was Chuck?

2. ______________ was booming.

3. Chuck was ______________ his toy.

Why was Chuck hiding?

Add the word part to each of the letter pairs in the boxes. Say the word. If it is a real word, write it on the line.

th ch kn wh sh

in

1. ______
2. ______
3. ______

th ch wh sh kn

ip

4. ______
5. ______
6. ______

Write a sentence using two of the words you made.

______

______

HOME Ask your child to think of more words that begin with *th, wh, sh, ch,* and *kn.*

These white clouds mean good weather, too. It is fun to watch them change their shapes.

4

FOLD

Name ____________

CLOUDS

Clouds come in many shapes and colors. Did you know they can tell you about the weather?

1

These clouds are showing that bad weather is near. Rain and thunder will come soon.

2

FOLD

Cirrus Clouds

These thin clouds are made of ice. They tell us that the weather will be good.

3

Name ______________________________

They'll slide down the hill.
They will go very fast.
I'll slide down, too.
I will be the last.

I will = I'll	you will = you'll	they will = they'll
he will = he'll	she will = she'll	we will = we'll
	it will = it'll	

They'll is a short way to say they will. Read each sentence. Circle the short way to write the underlined words.

1.	It will be fun to go for a ride on a sled.	You'll It'll
2.	I will get on the sled.	We'll I'll
3.	You will get on the sled with me.	You'll She'll
4.	They will all get on the sled, too.	They'll It'll
5.	Oh, no! Get off or we will fall!	he'll we'll

What are some other things to do outside when the weather is cold?

She's is a short way to say **she is.** Look at each picture. Read the sentence. Print the short way to write the underlined words. Use the words in the box to help you.

she is = she's	it is = it's	he is = he's

1. It is a nice day to play in the park.

   ______________ a nice day to play in the park.

2. He is going down the slide.

   ______________ going down the slide.

3. She is having fun in the water.

   ______________ having fun in the water.

4. He is playing on the swings.

   ______________ playing on the swings.

5. It is full of things to do!

   ______________ full of things to do!

What else can you do at the park?

Ask your child what words form the contractions *they'll*, *we'll*, and *you'll*.

Name ______________________________

I'm is a short way to say I am. Look at each picture. Read the sentence. Print the short way to write the underlined words. Use the words in the box to help you.

I am = I'm	**we are = we're**
you are = you're	**they are = they're**

1. You are going to the zoo.

   ____________ going to the zoo.

2. 

   I am going with you.

   ____________ going with you.

3. 

   We are going to see the seals.

   ____________ going to see the seals.

4. 

   They are fun, and the cubs are, too.

   ____________ fun, and the cubs are, too.

5. 

   I think we are going to love the zoo!

   I think ____________ going to love the zoo!

What other animals can you see at the zoo?

Can't is a short way to say can not. Read the sentences. Circle the short way to write the underlined words. Use the words in the box to help you.

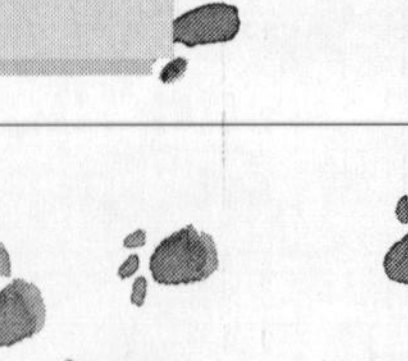

can not = can't	**does not = doesn't**
will not = won't	**is not = isn't**

1. Wags <u>is not</u> clean. He is a muddy mess!	can't doesn't isn't
2. Mom says he needs a bath. Wags just <u>will not</u> get into the tub.	won't isn't doesn't
3. Wags <u>does not</u> like baths. He runs away.	isn't can't doesn't
4. I <u>can not</u> catch him. Mom will help me.	can't doesn't won't
5. Wags <u>is not</u> muddy now. I am the one who needs a bath!	isn't can't doesn't

Who needs a bath now and why?

Using the contractions, take turns making up other sentences about Wags.

Name ______________________________

Circle the sentence that tells about the picture.

1. 	I'll eat the hot dog. I'm going to read the book.
2. 	It's in the bag. She'll sleep in the tent.
3. 	We won't go on the ride. We're on the ride.
4. 	She's going to play on the swing. They're going to like my painting.
5. 	You're going to rake the yard. We'll drive up to the lake.
6.	I can't skate very well on the ice. He doesn't like ice cream on his cake.

Fill in the bubble beside the sentence that tells about the picture.

1.
- ○ It's a dog.
- ○ It can't be a dog.
- ○ They're dogs.

2.
- ○ He's on a bike.
- ○ She's in a jet.
- ○ I'm on the bus.

3.
- ○ It won't rain today.
- ○ It'll rain all day.
- ○ I'll play in the rain.

4.

- ○ We don't like bugs.
- ○ She'll eat a hot dog.
- ○ We're eating the fruit.

5.
- ○ They'll go for a ride.
- ○ We'll go for a swim.
- ○ You're up a tree.

6.
- ○ She can't find her shoes.
- ○ He doesn't want to ride his bike.
- ○ She's trying to catch a fish.

HOME Ask your child to use contractions such as *I'll, I'm,* and *won't* to tell about himself or herself.

Name ______________________

Say and spell the words below. Print the words on the lines where they belong.

fishing	can't	melted	I'm	peeled	ship
think	knot	chin	whale	rowing	spilled

Words that have **ed** endings

1. ______ 2. ______ 3. ______

Words that take the place of two small words

4. ______ 5. ______

Words whose beginning sound is made up of two letters

6. ______ 7. ______ 8. ______

9. ______ 10. ______

Words that have **ing** endings

11. ______ 12. ______

What kind of weather do you like best? Write a description of your favorite kind of weather. Use describing words to tell about what you see, hear, or feel. The words in the box may help you.

know	I'm	playing	walking
rained	what	that	it's

HOME Ask your child to forecast tomorrow's weather.

"It isn't raining," said Trina.
"It's Dad! He's making it rain!"

4

FOLD

Name ______________________

It's Raining

Chad and Trina looked out.
"It's raining," Trina said. "We can't play out there."

1

Mom looked out with them.
"It isn't raining today," she said.

2

"I know it was raining," Chad said. Trina opened the door and looked outside.

3

CHECKUP

Name ______________________________

Say the name of each picture. **Fill in** the bubble beside the picture name.

1\.

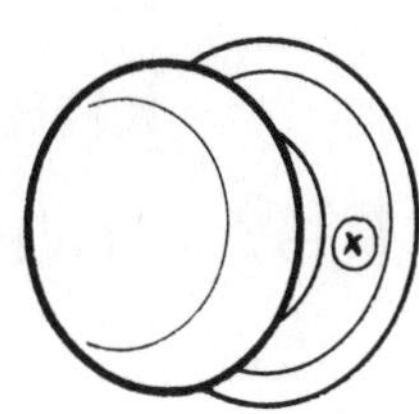

- ○ knee
- ○ knob
- ○ knife

2\.

- ○ wheel
- ○ whip
- ○ white

3\.

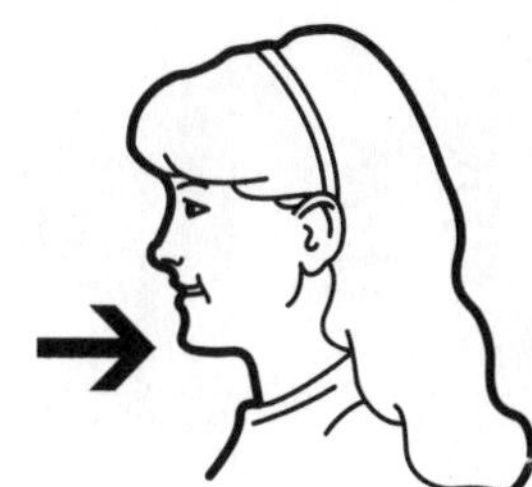

- ○ chain
- ○ thin
- ○ chin

4\.

- ○ sheep
- ○ ship
- ○ chip

5\.

- ○ thin
- ○ cherry
- ○ three

6\.

- ○ knit
- ○ knot
- ○ knock

7\.

- ○ chair
- ○ shame
- ○ chat

8\.

- ○ while
- ○ throat
- ○ whale

9\.

- ○ throne
- ○ thumb
- ○ shade

Look at the picture. Circle the word that will finish the sentence. Print it on the line.

1.	How deep do you ____________ it is?	think knew chase
2.	She's ____________ to find out.	rowing spilled trying
3.	It's up to his ____________!	knot chin whale
4.	She ____________ get it out.	isn't don't can't
5.	____________ happy that it snowed.	They're I'll It's
6.	The snow has all ____________!	peeled spilled melted